THE PSYCHOLOGY OF RELIGION

AMS PRESS
NEW YORK

THE PSYCHOLOGY
OF RELIGION

By

GEORGE ALBERT COE

Professor in the Union Theological Seminary
New York City

THE UNIVERSITY OF CHICAGO PRESS
CHICAGO, ILLINOIS

Library of Congress Cataloging in Publication Data

Coe, George Albert, 1862-1951.
   The psychology of religion.

   (Philosophy in America)
   Reprint of the ed. published by University of
Chicago Press, Chicago, in series: University of
Chicago publications in religious education, Hand-
books of ethics and religion.
   Bibliography: p.
   Includes index.
   1. Psychology, Religious.   I. Title.   II. Se-
ries: Chicago. University. Publications in
religious education: Handbooks of ethics and
religion.   III. Series.
BL53.C6   1979   200'.1'9   75-3113
ISBN 0-404-59109-4

First AMS edition published in 1979.

Reprinted from the edition of 1917, Chicago. [Trim size and text
area of the original have been slightly altered in this edition.
Original trim size: 13 × 19.5 cm; text area: 8.8 × 15.4 cm.]

MANUFACTURED
IN THE UNITED STATES OF AMERICA

TO A VERY HUMAN PERSON

To know you
is to behold the splendor of life
and its mystery

To know you
is to discover that religious faith
if it is possible
is necessary

How can I know you
and still be without religious faith?

Therefore to you
I dedicate this study of the human
naturalness of religion

PREFACE

This work is intended primarily as a handbook for beginners in the psychological analysis of religion. The foremost concern, therefore, has been to make clear the nature of the problems, the kinds of data, the methods of research, and the achieved results.

The justification for attempting such a handbook lies partly in the inherent difficulty of analyzing religious experience, and partly in conditions that grow out of the extreme youth of the psychology of religion. We are still in the beginnings—plural—of this enterprise. Of ten recent writers who have published volumes of a general character devoted largely or wholly to the subject, no three pursue the same method, or hold the same point of view as to what the religious consciousness is. I refer to Ames, Durkheim, Höffding, James, King, Leuba, Pratt, Starbuck, Stratton, and Wundt. Such disparity is not a reproach to a scientific inquiry in its first stages, but rather a sign of its vitality. But students who are approaching the subject for the first time are likely to be confused by the seeming babel, even though it be more apparent than real, or else—and this is a more common and a greater evil—to suppose that the first tongue that they happen to hear speaks the one exclusive language of science. I have therefore attempted, not only to sharpen the outlines of problems, but also to provide, particularly in the alphabetical and topical bibliographies, convenient apparatus for following up problems, and especially for setting them in a scientific perspective.

My first intention was to make this work simply a handbook. But inasmuch as even an introduction to the researches of others is bound to represent some standpoint of one's own, and inasmuch as candor is best served by making standpoints explicit, I decided to include a rather extended statement of certain inquiries and conclusions that I have found more and more interesting and, as I believe, fruitful. The upspringing of functional analysis of mental life is likely to prove immensely significant for the sciences of man, *who contemplates and judges his own functions*. But functionalism in psychology is still in its infancy—it is only now discovering its own fingers and toes. It is working with categories borrowed from biology, not clearly realizing that it has taken for its parish the whole world of values. To meet this situation I have felt it necessary, not only to assume the standpoint of functional analysis, but also to investigate it. The result is a view of religion that does not separate it at all from instinct, yet finds its peculiar function elsewhere.

I have not attempted a balanced treatment of the whole subject of the psychology of religion. Rather, I have brought into the foreground the problems that seem to be most pressing at the present moment. Here, without doubt, my own mind reveals its leanings. I have no desire to conceal them. All attention, in fact, is selective; all investigation is moved by a greater interest in something than in something else.

It is not always necessary to make one's interests explicit, but investigation of the more intimate aspects of experience that we call valuational proceeds best upon a basis of frank self-revelation. The investigator of the psychology of religion, whatever be the case with others, cannot afford to neglect the psychology of his own psychologizing.[1]

That the reader may duly weigh my tendencies, they are made explicit rather than carried along as suppressed premises in supposedly impersonal thinking—as though there could be thinking without a motived will-to-think.[2] As a further aid to critical reading of this work, I here and now set down a list of my attitudes with respect to religion and to the psychology of religion. The reader may then

[1] One writer, Professor J. H. Leuba, has set a good precedent by frankly letting his readers know something of his religious experience. Naturally, he thinks that his own experience has brought him into "the ideal condition for the student of religion" (*A Psychological Study of Religion* [New York, 1912], p. 275, and note)! On the danger of the "psychologist's fallacy" in the psychology of religion, see W. F. Cooley, "Can Science Speak the Decisive Word in Theology?" *Journal of Philosophy*, X (1913), 296-301.

[2] Such limitations are not peculiar to investigations in which, as in the present instance, the valuational aspect of consciousness is in the foreground. It is a general rule that scientific men are more certain of their generalizations than of their data. The least certain parts of psychology, for example, are revealed in current discussions of the nature of the psychical, and of the nature and method of psychology. In the same way the biologist finds himself hard pressed to say just what the difference is between a vital phenomenon and any other. Every investigator, whatever his specialty, as a matter of fact (1) selects his data, and (2) treats them from the standpoint of a particular interest. What a blessing it would be if a catalogue could be made of the principles of selection actually employed, and of the particular interests that determine analyses, in each science! But—this would plunge us into the problem of values, and into philosophy! Rather than take this plunge let us keep up the delusion that as scientific men we depersonalize ourselves into "clear, cold logic-engines"!

judge for himself the extent to which they act as prejudices.

1. The religious enterprise is to me the most important undertaking in life. Much is at stake. This importance of religion attaches to some extent also to efforts to analyze religion. For such efforts, by focusing attention on one point or another, may result in either the heightening or the lowering of appreciation for something valuable.

2. I do not appeal to any religious experience of my own as settling for me any question of psychology. Nor do I accept as authoritative the report of anyone else that such questions have been settled by his experience. Every religious experience, without exception, is to me a datum, to be examined by analytic processes that do not appear or that are undeveloped in the experience itself. Now, it is of the essence of religious dogma to assert that somebody—pope, council, prophet, inspired writer—has had a religious experience that does settle certain psychological questions concerning itself— such questions, for example, as the difference between this experience and ordinary experiences, the way in which certain ideas have got into the mind, and much more. This fact, as well as general considerations of history and of scientific method, make it impossible for me to reconcile the psychology of religion with any dogmatic authority.

3. On the other hand, the religious urgency that I have already mentioned makes me more or less cautious with regard to the content of religious tradition—particularly the Christian tradition in which I have been reared. Here I find, not a dead body awaiting dissection,

but a living being—one needing surgery, I am sure, but alive, and to live. Freedom from intellectual authority and the practice of psychologizing religious facts have rather intensified than lessened my conviction (1) that within the historical movement broadly called the Christian religion the human spirit has come to demand more of life than it has demanded elsewhere, that is, that in this religion we have the greatest of all stimuli; and (2) that this stimulus both proceeds from and points to reality. I entertain as my own, in short, the Christian faith in divine fatherhood and human brotherhood, and I work cordially within a Christian church to make this religion prevail. Quite naturally, no doubt, I assume that looking at religion from the inside helps rather than hinders analysis, and I certainly find no motive in the Christian religion for undervaluing other religions or even non-religions; the principle of brotherhood makes me expect to find something of myself in the other man's point of view. But if any reader thinks that being thus religious has warped my psychology, I request that he will do two things: (1) not rest in any general surmise or assumption, but find the specific facts that have been neglected, misrepresented, or misanalyzed, and (2) examine his own way of getting at the inside of the same facts, that is, confess his own interests as I am now confessing mine. In this way he will not only correct my one-sidedness, but also hasten the correction of his own, and science will move the faster up its zigzag trail.

4. My religious experience has been as free from mysticism as it has been from dogmatism. Indeed, the chief incitement to seek mystical experiences came to me wrapped up in dogma, and the disappointment of

my adolescence, when the promised and sought-for mystical "witness of the Spirit" did not come, caused me to turn away from both the dogmatic and the mystical approach to religion. Not far from the middle of my college days it was settled—though I could not then realize how well settled—that thenceforth I should look for the center of gravity of religion in the moral will. I do not rely upon intuitions, nor make the subconscious my refuge in the day of critical adversity. Life seems to me to be an ethical enterprise; my life problem concerns the choice of my cause, the investment of my purposes; and this, surely, implies distrust of anything that evaporates in the sunlight of my most critical self-possession.

5. From the standpoint of the moral will, the rational possibility of faith in a personal God and in life after death seems to me to be immensely important. For I conceive the ethical in social terms, and therefore for me persons are the paramount reality. If I had any merely individual self-consciousness, its continuance after death, or before death, would not be clearly worth while. Our life gets its meaning, its reality, by being social. But when once it has this meaning, how can one consent to perish or to let others perish without moral protest? If our current social thinking does not view the question of survival after death as an acute social problem, it is because we have already made an unsocial assent to the idea of a death that ends all; it is because our sociality is truncated. So with regard to God. It is socially desirable that "an ideal *socius*" should exist. If this desire is only slightly in evidence in much of our social thinking, the reason, as before, is that we have steeled

ourselves not to desire too great a social good. I, for one, am unwilling to subject myself to any *such* self-discipline. I will not curb my heart as long as its desires are truly social. My personal religion, in fact, consists, first and foremost, in the emancipation of social desire.

6. Finally, I own up to a strong aversion to dogmatism in science as well as in religion. In scientific circles, just as in religion, politics, and business, there are orthodoxies and heresies, and both orthodoxy and heresy may be dogmatic. I am inclined to think that science takes itself too seriously at times. Possibly we could become more scientific by cultivating a sense of humor! How would it do to start a "Scientific Gridiron Club" for the purpose of "roasting" our foibles? Once a year we could play the harlequin with our freshly discarded convictions and with our freshly adopted ones alike. We could see ourselves following scientific fads and running in scientific herds, being moved, like the profane, by suggestion. We could coolly gaze upon the heat and the haste with which we have endeavored to preach and to legislate for life. We could, in short, behold science as an exhibition of human nature. The psychology of religion may be expected, of course, to modifiy to some extent our religious practices and our theological notions, but it is not likely to fill with great success the rôle of prophet, or of pope, or even of business manager!

GEORGE A. COE

NEW YORK CITY
June, 1916

TABLE OF CONTENTS

PAGE

PREFACE ix

CHAPTER

I. RELIGION AS AN OBJECT OF PSYCHOLOGICAL STUDY   1

II. THE PSYCHOLOGY OF MENTAL MECHANISMS AND
THE PSYCHOLOGY OF PERSONS   14
Appendix: On the Specific Nature of Mental
Functions   32

III. THE DATA, AND HOW THEY ARE ASCERTAINED .   43

IV. PRELIMINARY ANALYSIS OF RELIGIOUS CONSCIOUS-
NESS   59

V. RACIAL BEGINNINGS IN RELIGION   76

VI. THE GENESIS OF THE IDEA OF GOD . . .   96

VII. RELIGION AND THE RELIGIONS   107

VIII. RELIGION AS GROUP CONDUCT   119

IX. RELIGION AS INDIVIDUAL CONDUCT . . .   136

X. CONVERSION   152

XI. MENTAL TRAITS OF RELIGIOUS LEADERS . .   175

XII. RELIGION AND THE SUBCONSCIOUS . . .   193

XIII. THE RELIGIOUS REVALUATION OF VALUES . .   215

XIV. RELIGION AS DISCOVERY   229

XV. RELIGION AS SOCIAL IMMEDIACY   246

XVI. MYSTICISM   263

XVII. THE FUTURE LIFE AS A PSYCHOLOGICAL PROBLEM   286

XVIII. PRAYER   302

XIX. THE RELIGIOUS NATURE OF MAN   321

ALPHABETICAL BIBLIOGRAPHY   327

TOPICAL BIBLIOGRAPHY   346

INDEX   357

CHAPTER I

RELIGION AS AN OBJECT OF PSYCHOLOGICAL STUDY

The closing years of the nineteenth century and the opening years of the twentieth mark the beginning of a definite determination to use the resources of scientific psychology in the investigation of religion. The roots of modern science reach far into the past, of course; yet a distinctly new departure was made when systematic, empirical methods were employed in order to analyze religious conversion and thus place it within the general perspective of the natural sciences.[1] Associated with the interest in conversion there quickly arose inquiry into the wider problem of mysticism.[2] Coincidently with such

[1] The earliest articles bearing on this topic are as follows: G. Stanley Hall, "The Moral and Religious Training of Children and Adolescents," *Pedagogical Seminary*, I (1891), 196 ff.; A. H. Daniels, "The New Life," *American Journal of Psychology*, VI (1893), 61 ff.; J. H. Leuba, "A Study in the Psychology of Religious Phenomena," *ibid.*, VII (1896), 309 ff.; W. H. Burnham, "The Study of Adolescence," *Pedagogical Seminary*, I (1891), 2 ff; E. G. Lancaster, "Psychology and Pedagogy of Adolescence," *Pedagogical Seminary*, V (1895), 1 ff; E. D. Starbuck, "A Study of Conversion," *American Journal of Psychology*, VIII (1897), 268 ff.; "Some Aspects of Religious Growth," *ibid.*, IX (1898), 70 ff. These articles were succeeded by the following volumes devoted largely or wholly to conversion and kindred phenomena: E. D. Starbuck, *The Psychology of Religion* (London, 1899); G. A. Coe, *The Spiritual Life* (New York, 1900); W. James, *The Varieties of Religious Experience* (London, 1902).

[2] Typical of this interest are: J. H. Leuba, "Tendances fondamentales des mystiques chrétiens," *Revue philosophique*, LIV (1902), 1–36 and 441–87; "On the Psychology of a Group of Christian Mystics," *Mind*, XIV (1905), 15–27; M. Delacroix, *Etudes d'histoire et de psychologie du mysticisme* (Paris, 1908). James's *Varieties of Religious Experience* (1902) and J. B. Pratt's *Psychology of Religious Belief* (New York, 1907) are to a considerable degree arguments for the truth of mysticism.

studies of individual life came investigations of the
earliest forms of religion.[1] Investigation of origins both
included and stimulated attempts at a critical determination of the nature of religion and its relation to
human evolution.[2] Finally, the systematization of results in general surveys of the whole field has begun.[3]
The whole constitutes a fresh chapter that belongs on
the one hand to psychology and on the other to the
science of religion.

Attempts to psychologize this or that phase of religion
are not new, of course. What is new is the use of critical,
empirical methods, and the specific results of applying
them. One could write a long history of what may be
called, in no opprobrious sense, the quasi-psychology of
religion, that is, attempts to conceive religion, or parts
of it, in terms of mental structure or of mental process,
but without a method sufficiently critical to correct
erroneous statements of fact or of law. Inner religion,
when it becomes reflective, commonly attempts to psychologize. Thus the New Testament writers, Paul in
particular, have views concerning the structure of the
mind (soul, spirit, the flesh, etc.) and the inner working

[1] For example: Irving King, *The Development of Religion* (New
York, 1910); E. Durkheim, *Les Formes élémentaires de la vie religieuse*
(Paris, 1912); W. Wundt, *Elemente der Völkerpsychologie* (Leipzig,
1913).

[2] G. M. Stratton, *Psychology of the Religious Life* (London, 1911);
J. H. Leuba, *A Psychological Study of Religion* (New York, 1912).

[3] E. S. Ames, *Psychology of Religious Experience* (Boston, 1910).
J. B. Pratt, in his article "The Psychology of Religion," *Harvard Theological Review*, I (1908), 435-54, gives an outline of the movement up
to the date of his writing.

of spiritual influences, divine and demonic.[1] Tertullian (*ca.* 155–222) defends Christianity against its detractors by declaring that "The soul is naturally Christian,"[2] and that the persecutors themselves bear unintentional witness to the things that they would stamp out.[3] He goes so far in his treatise on the soul as to attempt a psychology of the Christian soul. Augustine, Pascal, and unnumbered others found God, as they thought, by studying the soul of man.

To dissect out the quasi-psychological elements in theology would require a survey of very nearly the whole history of Christian doctrine. The natural man, creationism and traducianism, dichotomy and trichotomy, inspiration, regeneration, free will, the person of Christ—these are some of the angles from which theologians have made the mind of man, as they have believed, an object of study. Schleiermacher (1768–1834), with his insistence that religion is neither belief nor action, but feeling, gave a psychologic direction to all progressive theology. We must look for the essence of religion, he argues, in the interior of the soul itself. "Otherwise," he says, "ye will understand nothing of religion, and it will happen to you as to one who, bringing his tinder too late, hunts for the fire which the flint has drawn from the steel, and finds only a cold and meaningless particle of base metal, with which he cannot

[1] See M. S. Fletcher, *The Psychology of the New Testament* (New York: Hodder & Stoughton Co.). The title of this work seems hardly fortunate. In these days the term psychology should connote scientific method, which, of course, the New Testament writers lacked.

[2] *Apology* xvii.

[3] *Testimony of the Soul* vi.

kindle anything."[1]   Again, arguing that the reality of religion cannot be found in sacred literature, but only in the soul's experiences, he exclaims, "If you only knew how to read between the lines!"[2]

Philosophical as well as religious interests have inspired attempts at a psychological account of religion. Lucretius, quoting Petronius, declares that the basis of religion is fear: "It is fear that first made the gods." Hume opens his *Natural History of Religion* (1755) with a distinction between questions that concern the rationality of religion and those that concern its "origin in human nature." Many philosophers, indeed, have had theories of the relation of religion to human nature. Hegel, for example, regarded religion as a particular stage in the process whereby God comes to self-consciousness in man. Ludwig Feuerbach, reversing this position, held that the gods are merely projections of man's wishes, so that in religion man comes to consciousness merely of what he himself is.

Finally, the history of religion, which has made great strides during the last two generations, has commonly called psychological conceptions to its aid. What, indeed, can a history of *religion* be—as distinguished from a history of doctrines or of institutions—but an account of certain mental reactions as related to the situations in which they arise and grow?

Nevertheless, neither theology, philosophy, nor the history of religion has succeeded in producing a psychology of religion in the present sense of the term "psychology." They have turned attention to one or another phase of the enormous complex called "religion,"

[1] *Reden* (ed. of 1806), p. 33.   [2] *Ibid.*, p. 56.

and thereby they have stimulated inquiry. The history of religion has, in addition, accumulated large masses of data for the psychologist's use. Isolated views have been reached that may claim a permanent place in psychology. But a scientific psychology of religion is something more than an incident of philosophy, theology, and the history of religion. It implies, in particular, critical systematic methods for ascertaining data and for placing them within the general perspective of mental life.

The present movement for a psychology of religion is due to several new and favorable conditions. In the first place, psychology itself has just become an independent science, with many men devoting themselves exclusively to it. The first psychological laboratory, that of Wundt, was established as late as 1875. Since this date we have witnessed the upspringing of such fairly well-organized branches of the science as animal psychology, genetic and educational psychology, and abnormal psychology. Beginnings have been made, also, in social and anthropological psychology. In the second place, recent anthropological research, conducted with unprecedented thoroughness, has uncovered a vast quantity of material that bears upon the evolution of religion. Thirdly, there has occurred, chiefly in these years, a general assimilation of the historical-evolutionary principle as applied to the higher elements of culture. Notable, from the standpoint of our present interest, is the firm establishment of the historical study of the Bible, commonly called the higher criticism. Fourthly, and finally, an ancient obstacle to the scientific study of religion, the assumption of dogmatic authority, is in process of rapid dissolution in Protestant circles. Not only that; within these circles a demand has arisen, in the name of religion itself, that the nature and the mechanism of the spiritual life be laid bare. This demand grows alike from desire for the firmest control of religious processes—as in religious education—and from a conviction that for us religion must be, among other things, an original grasp upon life rather than adherence to tradition. We wish to make our religious consciousness clear as to its own meaning.[1]

The attempt to construe religion psychologically is most nearly related to general psychology, though its bearing upon theology, philosophy, and religious work is obviously direct. Indeed, the psychology of religion is properly nothing but an expanded chapter of general psychology. As we proceed, evidence will accumulate that we are dealing with something not separate in its elements from the most commonplace facts of mental life. The reasons for a separate treatment are reasons of convenience and of accommodation to existing conditions. For example: (a) The problems are so funda-

---

[1] Among practical workers in religion there is a serious misconception, however, of the whole method and significance of the psychology of religion. Clergymen, in sermons and in books, are giving the name psychology to strange mixtures of dogma and hearsay science. One writer offers us "a Christian psychology of the Christian life," which "admits sources of material as valid which general psychological science rigidly excludes." Another deduces practically a whole system of Christian doctrine—the traditional system—from a supposedly psychological analysis of Christian experience. Not a few fancy that they can draw directly from psychology new proofs of the existence of God, or of inspiration. It is significant that most writers of these types appear to be more at home in the obscurities of the subconscious than among the more clearly established facts and laws of the mind.

mental and the facts so complicated that an extensive treatment of them is inevitable. (*b*) Religious sensitivity, or prejudice, among students, and in religious circles generally, tends to deter psychologists from all discussion of religion. It is probably better to handle these difficulties in a group than to spread them out through general psychology. (*c*) Religion, though it is a commonplace fact, has nevertheless become, so to say, self-conscious. There is a partial parallel here with conditions in art and in education; in each of these three cases large masses of experience have organized themselves around a particular interest, or a particular institution, and as a consequence economy of attention is secured by a separate psychological treatment.

But can psychology penetrate to the heart of religion? Must it not forever be as much of an outsider as a man born deaf who should witness a symphony concert with his eyes only? How can one understand religion without feeling it, and how can feelings be put into words? And are not the supreme and most original religious experiences *sui generis*, extra-natural, incapable of analysis by means of ordinary methods or concepts? Let us answer these questions *seriatim*.

1. One possessed of sight but not hearing could find out many important things about symphony concerts, partly by direct observation, partly by reading what others write. In the same way the psychology of religion might be pursued with some success by one who does not "enjoy religion." Both symphonies and religious phenomena can be considered from the standpoint of processes taking place in time and space, and having parts related in definite ways to one another

and to other things. That is, there is a mechanism of religion as well as of music.

2. Nevertheless, it is true that to understand either music or religion one must have appreciation, feeling, some actual entering into an experience as distinguished from merely looking on. It is true also that feelings cannot be put into words in the sense of being transferred thereby from one person to another. But neither can anything be, in this sense, put into words. The word "gold" is not yellow; the word "wealth" makes no one rich. There is nothing, however, to prevent persons who have similar feelings from devising a terminology that shall awaken specific memories connected with these feelings. We have, as a matter of fact, a great vocabulary of appreciation in aesthetics, ethics, and religion. To understand this vocabulary one must undoubtedly have some corresponding experience of appreciation; to incorporate such a vocabulary into the sciences a common human experience is prerequisite. A psychology of aesthetics is possible because aesthetic experience, at least in its rudiments, is common to men. A psychology of the moral life is possible because moral experience is universal. A psychology of religion in the same intimate sense is possible also, provided that religious appreciations of at least a rudimentary sort are likewise common. Whether this is the fact must be decided ultimately by the progress of our study, but the diffusion of religion in both space and time justifies a preliminary affirmative hypothesis on this point. Even if, however, religion be not thus a common experience, a psychology of religion in the sense referred to under 1 above would still be practicable.

3. Are not some religious experiences in their very nature outside the scope of psychology? So all Catholics and many Protestants hold. What Catholic writers call "mystical theology" devises careful tests for distinguishing the operation of divine or demonic beings within us from the natural ongoings of the mind.[1] Benedict XIV, pope from 1740 to 1758, laid down rules,[2] which are followed today in the canonization of saints, whereby the church can become officially certain as to what is pathological and what divine in the extraordinary visitations experienced by saints and miracle-workers. A presupposition of all these tests, however, is a theory of the supernatural—a theory authoritatively imposed. The conclusion reached in any given case is not a statement of probabilities based upon observation, but rather a mixture of observation and a priori assumption.

Protestants who hold to a psychical supernatural commonly mix with the assumption of authority two other things—a theory of intuition as a source of knowledge in matters of fact—that is, in matters susceptible of regulated observation—and a habit of assuming that what is extraordinarily valuable or satisfying has laws of its own, different from those of nature at large. Scientific method is of course antithetical to all of these positions. What is more significant for our present purpose is that no *observed* separation between religious

[1] J. Görres, *Die christliche Mystik* (Regensburg, 1836–42), devotes three of his five volumes to possession and "demonic mysticism." How "mystical theology" undertakes to maintain itself in the presence of scientific psychology can be seen in A. B. Sharpe, *Mysticism: Its True Nature and Value* (London: Sands & Co.).

[2] *De servorum Dei beatificatione et canonisatione.*

and other mental processes has been pointed out;[1] the alleged separateness depends in every case upon an antecedent supernaturalistic assumption. Further, psychology has already succeeded in analyzing many of the supposedly exceptional religious experiences; they are not a scientific *terra incognita* at all.

What sorts of question, then, does psychology ask with regard to religion? An examination of publications in this field will show that two main types of problem are recognized.

First, religious experience is ordinarily a highly involved psychical complex which needs to be viewed in its elements. Conversion, which is the central topic of Starbuck's pioneer work, is such a complex. Mysticism, to which Leuba and Delacroix have given so much attention, offers a larger problem of the same kind. Stratton, noting that a remarkable crisscross of motives and beliefs appears everywhere in the sacred books of the world, has taken as his task the explanation of this seemingly self-contradictory complexity. Search for the elements of a complex appears again in studies of the genesis and growth of religion in the individual and in the race, as in those of King, Pratt, Durkheim, and Wundt.

Secondly, religion has a peculiar relation to the valuational phase of experience. In pre-eminent degree religion, even more than philosophy, is a wrestling with destiny. It will wring a consciously adequate life out of the hard conditions of existence. With this value aspect of religious experience in mind we unearth new

[1] This will appear more and more clearly as our analysis of religious experiences proceeds.

facts, and we face a new aspect of all the facts. What is it, Professor James asks, that the devotee fixes his heart upon, and what are the results of his spiritual exercises—results in the current everyday terms of value? Höffding judges that the fundamental axiom of religion is "the conservation of values."[1] King and Ames are chiefly interested in discovering the functions that religion represents in the life of man as a whole, and how these functions originate and grow. Concerning any religious phenomenon—say a sacrifice, a dance, or solitary mystic contemplation—we must ask, not merely what sort of god or what theory of the universe is here involved, and not merely what sensations, emotions, and so on make up the complex, but also what the devotee is after, whether he gets what he is after, and how this particular good is related to other goods in the total self-realizing life of man. This phase of religious life is objectively present not less truly than the parts into which we resolve mental complexes.

The distinction between these two types of investigation involves problems that will occupy much space in succeeding chapters. At this point, however, it will be well to understand clearly that resolving a mental complex into its elements does not answer all legitimate questions concerning the nature of an experience. Let us imagine ourselves called upon, for example, to give a complete psychological account of a mother fondling her baby. We see right away that we have before us a complex, the mothering process, which must be analyzed into its part processes. Here are touch and sight sensations, ideational activities, emotions, and

---

[1] H. Höffding, *Philosophy of Religion* (London, 1906), p. 10.

instincts, all connected with corresponding neural processes in nerve endings, transmission tracts, and brain
centers.   Thus we resolve the complex.   Each part of
the machinery is discriminated from other parts, and we
behold all working together.   This is the mothering
complex.   But something remains still; it is mother-love,
of which thus far we have said not a word.   In our
analysis of the mothering complex the baby is simply a
stimulus of touch and sight, an excitant of nerve endings,
a part of a mechanism.   But within mother-love, that is,
within the actuality of the experience, what is a baby?
What is the baby, that is to say, to the mother, and
what is the mother to herself, now that a child of her
very own has come?

Heaven's first darling, twin-born with the morning light, you
have floated down the stream of the world's life, and at last you
have stranded on my heart.

As I gaze on your face, mystery overwhelms me; you who
belong to all have become mine.

For fear of losing you I hold you tight to my breast.   What
magic has snared the world's treasure in these slender arms
of mine?[1]

We must, indeed, analyze mind process just as we do
the movements of the planets, treating the mind as a
mechanism; and neither human affection nor religion
has any claim to exemption from this taking to pieces.
But these personal realizations demand that they also
be understood.   There is something in poetry that is
not metrics, something in music that is not vibrations,
something in our social and ethical experience that is
not a complex of states of consciousness.   Never shall

[1] Tagore, "The Beginning," from *The Crescent Moon.*

we understand this something by merely reanalyzing the mechanism. As well might we explain a line of poetry by merely marking the quantity of its syllables. We must go forward to a psychology of values, functions, self-realizations.

A certain distrust of psychology that now and then appears among religionists is not altogether groundless. For there is "something more" to conversion and other religious experiences than the sum of the part processes that have mostly occupied the attention of psychologists. Ordinarily, however, religious critics of the psychology of religion fall into a scientific pitfall. They assume that the "something more" is just another part process co-ordinate with those already recognized by psychology, whereas the missing thing is not another wheel in a machine, or another event in a series, but the individual wholeness of self-realization. Wiser than these objectors are those who say, "Whatever the process or mechanism of conversion or of prayer, the man changes for the better, he has more real life than he had before."[1]

[1] I purposely refrain from giving a formal definition of religion at the outset of this study, partly because definitions convey so little information as to facts; partly because the history of definitions of religion makes it almost certain that any fresh attempt at definition would unnecessarily complicate these introductory chapters; partly because, in this subject at least, a definition, if it is to have vitality, must be an achievement—it cannot be "given" by one to another. The observant reader will notice, however, that my whole discussion of method and point of view in the psychology of religion (chaps. i and ii) gradually unfolds a definite conception of the nature of religious experience.

CHAPTER II

THE PSYCHOLOGY OF MENTAL MECHANISMS AND THE PSYCHOLOGY OF PERSONS

The methods and the points of view of each science have to be worked out within the science itself; they may not be prescribed in advance. Whoever thinks of scientific method as a ready-made sieve that needs only to be shaken vigorously in order to separate the factors in any and every kind of experience that may be poured into it misconstrues the whole history of scientific research. To be thoroughly empirical implies that we look ever for that which cannot be expressed in the old categories.[1] The history of each science reveals not only an increasing body of recorded facts, but also growth in the fundamental conceptions that define the science and its methods. It is not to the disparagement but to the credit of psychology to say that in its short history it has brought forth, alongside of innumerable researches in limited areas, a set of remarkable problems concerning itself. What is "the psychical" which psychology will investigate? What are the objective marks of the presence or absence of the psychical? Can it be meas-

[1] Psychology is the greatest sufferer, but not the only one, from the tendency to erect a point of view or a method into a dogma. Consider the following not uncommon assumptions: (1) that one who masters the methods in a particular branch of scientific investigation becomes thereby a *scientific man;* (2) that the irreducible ultimates in physics must suffice for the analysis of living beings; (3) that the really fundamental factors in mind are those which biology takes account of; and in general (4) that the different is not really different!

ured? How is it related to the physical? What part
does the psychical play in vital processes?

All these questions are in debate today. Some of
them have the utmost interest for the psychology of
religion because they involve, in a fundamental way,
the contrast that was reached in the last chapter between
mental mechanism and personal self-realization. This
distinction emerges when we attempt to answer the
question, What is the psychical? The commonest
answer is that by the psychical (for which consciousness
is the more usual term) we mean such facts as sensations,
feelings, and impulses to action, and that these are known
primarily by introspection. Psychology accordingly has
commonly understood itself to be the science of "states
of consciousness *as such*," that is, without regard to
their relation to any metaphysical soul or ego. This
point of view has justified itself by the fruit it has borne,
which is nothing less than the winning of a place for
psychology among the empirical sciences. To the objection that there can be no "psychology without a soul,"
the effective reply has been successful psychologizing
without saying anything about the soul! It is not at
all surprising that students, and even professional
psychologists, come to think of mental life as compounded of simple elements, after the analogy of chemistry, or as a mechanism of which sensations, feelings,
and the like are the ultimate units.

Is this, however, "the" psychological point of view
or "a" psychological point of view? A convenient
pathway toward an answer is to examine an instance of
the assumed psychological elements or facts, say a
sensation. It must be so amenable to observation that

you and I can talk about it as a particular object ascertainably present. It is easy to discuss sensations of touch, taste, and so on in general, just as we used to talk about atoms; but what is required is that we point out and identify a particular sensation as actually occurring. Paradoxical as it seems at first, we may have to conclude that sensations as well as atoms are not facts of experience but constructs from experience. For, first, when you offer me an objectively observed case, it turns out to be your sensation. Now, your sensation is a fact for me, not by virtue of my own direct observation, but by virtue of a process of construction from other data. Moreover, in what sense can you say that even you observe this sensation? Not to mention other difficulties of introspection, see what happens when you attempt to count your sensations for a few seconds. You discover that either you are counting objects rather than sensations, or else putting arbitrary bounds to each sensation. No atoms of mental life appear to you at all, but rather a continuous flow which has various aspects, of which the sensational is one. Your sensations are constructs for you as they are also for me. We can now understand, in part, why Professor James, at the conclusion of his brilliant analysis of "states of consciousness as such," declares that, after all, "states of consciousness themselves are not verifiable facts."[1]

When we reach this insight, three courses are open to us: First, we may go on as before analyzing states of consciousness as such, but we must then recognize that the material in which we work (sensations, feelings, etc.) is not mental life in its concreteness, but rather certain

[1] *Psychology* (Briefer Course), p. 467.

abstracted aspects of this life. It is by this abstracting, aided by analogies derived from the structure of the brain and nervous system, that psychology has drawn its pictures of complicated mental mechanisms—the mechanism of sense-perception, of memory, of emotion, and so on.

In spite of the abstractness of such psychology, and in spite of the objection that will be noted in the next paragraph, there is no likelihood that we shall ever dispense with this method of approach to mental life. These aspects of our experience are actual aspects, and these mechanisms, though they are the psychologist's mental constructs out of elements that are themselves constructs, have uses both theoretical and practical that correspond to the parallel constructs of physics and chemistry. If, however, anyone speaking in the name of psychology should suggest that mental mechanism is all there is to mental life, he would be convincing only to those whose analysis stops short of the primary empirical data.

The status of "states of consciousness" is in fact openly challenged in the name of psychology itself. The behaviorist movement, which represents the second of the three possible courses, says substantially this: Let us observe and experiment upon the movements of our own bodies and of animal bodies, making the least possible reference to accompanying consciousness. By noting outer acts we shall arrive at the most secure generalizations concerning the very life that traditional psychology has attempted to construe by treating it as a subjective phenomenon. Behaviorism in its extreme form declares that the assumption of consciousness has never helped in the solution of any problem.[1]

Undoubtedly this movement arises out of a real need, and its influence upon psychology is almost certain to be wholesome. It is well that we are thus challenged to exhibit the actual data with which psychology works, and to see how much can be learned from bodily movements and physiological changes as such. But, while behaviorism is likely to be a permanent point of view, particularly in the study of animals, it is not likely to crowd consciousness out of psychology. How far—to take a prominent problem of behaviorism—can analysis of the learning process go without taking account of satisfactions and annoyances?[2] And, in general, has not some behavior *meaning?* From one point of view conversation, for example, is just behavior, that is, a set of co-ordinated movements of lips, tongue, vocal cords, diaphragm and intercostal muscles, facial muscles, eyes, hands, etc. Analysis of these movements will very likely help us to understand what happens when two men converse. But to ignore everything in conversation except such movements is to leave out the function of it, which is the interchange of meanings between persons. *For his purposes* the behaviorist may avoid discussing this function, but he should at least realize that thereby he *chooses one among several points of view.* Behaviorism, in short, represents simply a new division of labor within the field of psychology.

[1] J. B. Watson, "Psychology as the Behaviorist Views It," *Psychological Review*, XX (1913), 158-77.

[2] E. L. Thorndike, one of the leading behaviorists, though he consistently endeavors to express our reactions as far as possible in terms of muscular and neural activity, makes much of "satisfyingness" as a factor in the formation of new connections.

Both of these types of psychological interest, then—the "states of consciousness" type and the behaviorist type—necessitate a third type. The concrete experience out of which we abstract "states of consciousness" is the experience of being a personal self. Each sensation, feeling, or other "element" of structural psychology is simply a particular discriminable aspect of a self-realizing life. Sensations and feelings are not known to have any other kind of existence, and what other kind of existence they could conceivably have has never been explained.[1] Now, since self-realizations are not less actual than sensations, but more so, and since much of our behavior is communication of self-realized meanings, we must have an empirical science of self-realizations, or, in short, of selves. This is psychology *par excellence,* because its data are the most concrete and the most distinctive.[2]

Several recent developments show how inevitable it is that sooner or later we should advance from a

[1] When we desire to represent the consciousness of lower animals, we invariably image to ourselves some fragment of our own self-realizing life. We are helped by our memories of dreams, and of the vague states between waking and sleeping. Our own memory gaps also help us to conceive lower degrees of organization than our own. Further, the instinctive and other automatic factors in our own life make it clear that adaptive response could be abundant even if there were little consciousness in the animal making the response. We have no experience, however, that enables us to construe mere atoms of a consciousness that is not in any degree an organized, self-realizing consciousness. Behaviorism avoids the difficulty here involved by thinking of animals *as if* they had no sensations, or pleasures and pains.

[2] Since 1900 Professor Calkins has contended that since states of consciousness are "facts-for-selves," psychology must be a science of selves as well as of states. See her article, "Psychology as Science of Selves," *Philosophical Review,* IX (1900), 490–501. How such psychology differs from the old "psychology with a [metaphysical] soul" will appear as we proceed.

psychology of states to a psychology of individual persons or selves.

1. Various branches of the science are obliged to take as their unit the self-realizing individual life. Abnormal psychology, for example, would be practically meaningless if it contemplated states of consciousness *as such* instead of individuals who vary from an assumed norm of self-realization. Similarly, child psychology is required to get the child's point of view, that is, to view experience from the standpoint of child selves. Folk psychology is in a parallel situation. Social psychology, too, turns attention to the self-realized relations of individual to individual.

2. Many influences—philosophical, theological, psychological—are focusing attention upon values as an aspect of experience. A "value" is anything experienced or thought of as satisfying, or the contrary. Here we are in the sphere of interests, preference, individual attitude, self-realization.

3. The attempt to relate psychology to biology has caused us to think of mental process as a part of active adjustment to the conditions of life. Here mental process comes to be thought of as mental function, which is mental action directed toward advantage, the furtherance of life—in particular, life that realizes its own improved state.

The standpoint of "function" emerges, in fact, in each of these fresh psychological growths. Here a functional psychology, or a psychology that recognizes the functional standpoint, is being created. Here belong the problems of the second type that appeared in our first chapter. Religious experiences have a mechanism, to be sure, but they are occupied *about* ends or values—what Tagore calls "the *realization* of life."[1] This is increasingly the case as we move upward in the scale of religions. At the summit of culture the character of each religion consists in its working conception of life's values, and the religious status of the individual is judged by his scrutiny, choice, and pursuit of ends. Accordingly, the psychology of religion may be expected to be predominantly functional. Therefore the idea of mental function needs to be carefully examined at the outset. We shall see that it is far less simple than one might suppose.[2]

What do we mean by "function"? As we use the term here it applies to living beings only. It signifies the part that any organ or process has in maintaining, reproducing, or improving the life of an individual or of the group to which an individual belongs. The function of teeth, for example, is to tear, cut, crush, and grind food, *so that* the digestive juices may reach all parts of it, *so that* it may be assimilated and built into living cells, *so that* the individual or group life may go on in strength.

[1] Rabindranath Tagore, *Sādhanā: The Realization of Life* (New York, 1913).

[2] The chief critical discussion of the relation of functional to structural psychology is J. R. Angell's "The Relations of Structural and Functional Psychology to Philosophy," one of the *Decennial Publications of the University of Chicago*, 1903, printed also in *Philosophical Review*, XII (1903), 243–71. The article has abundant footnote references. See also G. H. Mead, "The Definition of the Psychical," *Decennial Publications of the University of Chicago*, 1903. The first work on general psychology to be written systematically from the functional point of view was, I believe, J. R. Angell's *Psychology*, the first edition of which appeared in 1904. The clearest, most systematic discussion of the functional standpoint in the psychology of religion is chap. ii of E. S. Ames, *The Psychology of Religious Experience* (Boston, 1910).

Function implies that an organ or process is *for* something—the point of view is teleological.

But a functional or teleological point of view may mean any one of three discriminable things:

First, functions may be methodological devices. The categories "means" and "end" do not in this case imply that the object under investigation employs means *for the sake* of attaining ends, but only that this is a convenient method whereby the investigator may organize a multitude of facts into unity. Here function is approximately the relation of part to whole, the relation expressed by the word "for" being kept in the background. This is substantially the standpoint of biology. Biological descriptions, it is true, attribute ends to living beings. Thus, there is a "struggle for" existence. Animals "seek" food, and they "seek" their mates. Certain organs reach out "for" food, others protect "against" enemies. Concerning the human appendix vermiformis we ask what it is, or ever was, "good for." Probably this objective reference of "means and end" is unavoidable. Nevertheless, for very good reasons biology generally refuses to develop the notion, and even labors to restrict the teleological reference as much as possible.[1]

Secondly, psychology, however, has to recognize ends as objective facts. For *mind as we know it best may be described as preferring something as distinguished from something else, seeking the preferred thing, and experiencing success or failure.* Otherwise expressed, *the processes with which the psychologist has to do tend to define their own functions or ends, as merely biological processes*

[1] The present debate over vitalism illustrates the fact that the biological point of view is *a point of view.*

do not. Functions are no longer merely devices of the investigator's mind; they are objective data for investigation.

Thirdly, it is possible to suppose that all nature is guided toward some single good or system of goods. In this case one and the same mental process might be functional in three senses: (*a*) its biological function might be, say, prolongation of life, the "value of life" being here merely a methodological device of the biologist; (*b*) its psychological function also might be prolongation of life, but here the "value of life" is objectively realized, and what constitutes "a valuable life" is judged by the living being himself; (*c*) its cosmic function likewise might be prolongation of life, but here the individual life has super-individual significance, possibly significance that it is unaware of. Emerson says that Michelangelo, when he designed St. Peter's at Rome, "builded better than he knew":

> These temples grew as grows the grass;
> Art might obey, but not surpass.
> The passive Master lent his hand
> To the vast soul that o'er him planned;
> And the same power that reared the shrine
> Bestrode the tribes that knelt within.[1]

Teleology or function in this third sense is traditionally an object for theological or philosophical rather than scientific investigation.

Let us now come a little closer to the notion of a functional psychology. We have seen that a function is to be defined by reference to the advantage or value toward which the process in question moves, and that

[1] *The Problem.*

mental process defines its own ends. It follows that psychology does not discover for us the functions of mind, but rather records the steps in mind's self-discovery of its own functions. It follows, further, that some of our surest knowledge of mental functions is had by telling one another about our desires and our satisfactions.

The bluntness of these statements will be justified if it leads us to face the implications and the difficulties of the functional standpoint. A first difficulty may be stated as follows: How is the notion of function to be applied to processes of too low an order to define their own aims—the instincts, for example? Here psychology is tempted, not only to use biological conceptions, but to rest in them. Human life is then thought of in terms that can be applied indiscriminately to men and the lower animals; life is said to consist fundamentally in feeding and procreating.

But there is a complementary way to get at the functions of the instincts. For the instinctive is not a stage of life that is lived through and left behind; it is a coefficient, not only of rudimentary mind, but also of the highest self-consciousness. Here fresh values appear that could not have been guessed before. Take as an example the mothering instinct that has been alluded to. Starting in the animal series as an unreflective impulse, it becomes in the human race maternal *affection*, which helps to give ethical character to the family, and finally deepens and expands into one of the great factors in our whole ethical life.[1] Affection between the sexes illustrates the same principle. Biology views it as simply

[1] Cf. W. McDougall, *Social Psychology* (Boston, 1909), pp. 66-81.

a part of the reproductive process. But lovers value each other as persons. The idealizations of affection are not merely subtle glorifications of sexual acts or of reproductive results. "In thine eyes, my darling," said a dying man to his wife, "have I beheld the Eternal." More than this: affection between one and one becomes an important factor in solidifying the monogamic family and the whole ethical order of which it is a part. Here instinct is taken up into a larger scheme of things than appeared at earlier stages of life, and a different scheme. An instinct that we have in common with the brutes attains a function in which brutes have no share. Accordingly, mental evolution is no mere extension of biological functions, but also the emergence of fresh functions.[1]

Another difficulty meets us when we try to think through the notion of mental function as adjustment. Adjustment *of* what *to* what? The temptation, as before, is to oversimplify by taking "adjustment" in the biological sense of physical organisms securing survival in a given physical environment. Mind then appears as a favorable variation in the sense of a new means whereby such an organism survives in such an environment. That mind does promote the survival of some individuals is clear enough; but is this an adequate description of mental function as adjustment? Let us

[1] The claim of Dewey that a thing is fully explained as soon as its genesis is described is true on condition that "genesis" is made sufficiently broad to cover the whole evolution of function. But if "genesis" refers merely to the earliest functions, and if genetic explanation consists in classifying the later-developed functions under the earlier ones, then we have the kind of oversimplification that reveals similarities but conceals differences.

consider first the notion of environment from the stand-point of the mind itself.

Does mental adjustment consist in accommodating ourselves to an environment already given? Limiting attention for a moment to physical nature, we may say unhesitatingly that the business of mind is far less adjustment of ourselves to environment than adjust-ment of environment to ourselves.[1] Consider how mind is already bound up in what we call the external world. How rarely are we alone with non-human nature! We fly from the city to the country in order to be with nature, but our eyes meet fields and fences, roads and houses. We seek the forest, but we follow a trail made by man; and if perchance we visit an untrod wilderness, still we reach it, and penetrate it, and care for ourselves in it, by means of instruments that are the work of men's hands and minds. Wilderness experiences, besides, are rare. Nearly all our so-called physical environ-ment is made up of such things as houses and high-ways, shops and factories, tools, coins, books, polluted rivers, smoke—in all of which man meets man, not merely things. This is, indeed, the chief aspect of our encounter with the physical. A house is what men live in, a knife is what men cut with—incarnate pur-poses. And such, for the most part, things remain. Only by abstract afterthought do they become merely physical.

[1] It is one of the paradoxes of our departmentalized science that at the very moment when biology came to look upon mind as a favorable variation, the ability of mind to modify nature was denied by psychology. Apparently we are nearly done with such *kenotic* psychology. See, e.g., C. H. Judd, "Evolution and Consciousness," *Psychological Review*, XVII 1910), 77–97.

Nor is even this the whole story. Nearly all our reactions to these things are molded upon customs or pre-existing man ways. From washing one's face in the morning to donning one's pajamas at night one does chiefly the things that are socially prescribed. This conformity of the individual to his group is a theme of satirist and of social psychologist alike. So shortsighted is the notion that the function of mind is simply adjustment to the physical environment.

But the notion of social adjustment also has its own kind of evasiveness. Social psychology shows that "myself" and "other-self" are not first given, and then adjusted, but that the two arise in consciousness as reciprocal aspects of one and the same experience.[1] Therefore, in the adjustment that takes place between you and me, neither of us is a merely given environmental fact; neither is simply accommodated to the other, but both of us are in process of becoming persons, even in the act of social adjustment. Accordingly, that to which we adjust ourselves in our social functions has to be defined as an ideal toward which we co-operatively move. Stated thus generally, the principle may seem to be obscure, but see how simple it is in concrete cases. When I start a fire in my fireplace in order that my friend and I may enjoy an evening together, I do not adjust myself to the wood or to the fireplace—I adjust them to my friend and myself; nor does either of us merely accommodate himself to the other. Conversation is far different from this. It is, in fact, a method whereby we two

[1] This, which is now a commonplace, was brought to general recognition in this country largely by J. M. Baldwin's *Social and Ethical Interpretations* (New York, 1897).

mutually modify ourselves so as to be adjusted to a common ideal.

This partially answers our other question, What is it that secures adjustment through mental functioning? Psychology is cautious here. It wishes especially to avoid the unworkable notion of the soul as a thing-in-itself, apart from particular experiences. By fixing attention upon states of consciousness as such psychology was able for a time to postpone consideration of what it is that secures adjustment in the functions called mental. But the problem is forced upon us by the necessity of recognizing a difference between the concept "process" and the concept "function." Mental function implies such things as need, want, desire, purpose, ideal; and these lead away from states, thought of as merely compounded, toward the notion of self-realizing personality. The shyness of psychology toward any such notion as personality is not without justification, it is true. The only way to secure freedom from dogmatic and speculative entanglements has been to ignore certain troublesome problems. But surely we cannot absorb "process" into "function" and still retain process as mere change *per se*. Nor are we helped by speaking, as many are doing, of mental processes as functions of "the organism." Such terminology merely conceals or evades the problem. To substitute for "organism" the term "psycho-physical organism" or "mind-body"[1] locates the problem, to be sure, but it does not face it. "Function" means that something in the end is better off. *What* is better off, and what is it *to be* better off?

[1] Ames, *op. cit.*, p. 20.

If, on the other hand, we attempt to construe function from the standpoint of particular responses to particular stimuli,[1] we encounter some peculiar difficulties. In the first place, is our datum "stimulus and response" or "situation and response"? In many cases, at least, the objects that stimulate us get their specific stimulating quality from the interest of the moment. A loaded table is not the same thing to a starving man that it is to a sated one, nor is sudden immersion in water the same thing to an experienced swimmer that it is to one who has not learned to swim. If we attempt to get below such situations to *mere* stimuli, we think of each item thereof as stimulus *of* a particular sensation. Now, inasmuch as sensations are not concretely existing things but only aspects of a total experience, a stimulus of a sensation is itself only an aspect of a total situation. Our responses are made to situations rather than to stimuli. Further, since responses are functions, they have a predetermined tendency. There is no such thing as response in general, or strictly random responses. For example, learning by "trial and error," in animals and in man, involves as one primary factor the learner's "set" *toward* something.[2] A mental reaction, then, at whatever level we take mind, is a response *toward* something as well as *to* something, and this "toward" reveals the nature of the reactor.

What, then, are we who are the termini of adjustment functions? By way of answer one is tempted to say,

[1] Cf. Irving King, *The Development of Religion* (New York, 1910), p. 11.

[2] E. L. Thorndike, *Psychology of Learning* (New York, 1913), pp. 13, 22, 26.

Why not ask the neighbors! We are mutually defining our wants and forming our purposes, and this is what defines *us*. A person is any reactor that approves or disapproves its own reactions, or that realizes consequences as successes or failures of its own. In the functions best known to us persons are adjusting themselves to the ideals or standards of personal-social life that they set before themselves, and to this end they are *using*—not adjusting themselves to—whatever they regard as subpersonal.

The supposed obscurity of the notion of personal selves is not native to this concept—the obscurity has been imported into it by attempting to construe the more clear (our socially communicable desires and purposes) in terms of the less clear (animal life that lacks means of communication). *Human functions are just what they seem to be from a fully achieved human point of view.*[1] Functional psychology, accordingly, should be, first and foremost, a psychology of personal self-realizations. The functional psychology of religion must be this above all things else.[2]

[1] To think of human functions as merely *complex cases of subhuman function*, as King seems to do (*op. cit.*, p. 39), endangers the functional point of view altogether. This may be seen in the tendency of this passage of King's to construe mental life in terms of combinations within a mechanically controlled system.

[2] Ames, who attempts to construe the functions of religion from a quasi-biological point of view, exhibits two quite natural consequences: (1) His notion of function, in spite of the general clarity of his exposition, contains a fundamental obscurity. "Adjustment" is his basal category, but just what is adjusted, and to what, does not distinctly appear. "The organism," it is said, "adjusts itself to its environment," but the adjustment "occurs *through* the psycho-physical organism" as though this were mere instrument. Yet the adjustment in question is an adjust-

It remains to state in summary fashion what would constitute such a psychology of persons. (1) Its distinctive material would be society in the strict sense of this term, that is, persons communicating their desires and purposes to one another, and thereby co-operating with or opposing one another. (2) The focus of attention would be *mental* functions, that is, action conscious (or becoming conscious) of its own direction and approving (or disapproving) it. (3) The method would be genetic, that is, the material would be so analyzed and arranged as to exhibit the coming to conscious purpose of both the individual and the race. (4) Mental content, accordingly, would be treated from the standpoint of the use made of it in the interpretation of life's meaning, and mental mechanism from the standpoint of the purposed control of life. (5) The characteristic special problems would concern the experience of values: as, (a) What objects do men value? (b) What is it in each class of objects that makes them valuable? (c) How are the different classes of value related to one another? (d) In what parts of our total experience is each class of value realized? (e) In what order and by what method do valuations evolve?

ment "in" the psycho-physical organism. See pp. 15, 18. These phrases indicate the inadequacy of the merely biological point of view, but they do not establish a clearly different one. (2) His expositions of religious experience are most objective when he deals with the lower forms of religion, in which instinctive action is most prominent, and most subjective when he reaches the highest religion, in which self-realizations take more distinctively personal forms. By "subjective" here I mean particularly a disposition to *reinterpret* the values of the developed personal will. Perhaps the clearest example is Ames's treatment of the functions of the idea of God.

APPENDIX

ON THE SPECIFIC NATURE OF MENTAL FUNCTIONS

From the preceding discussion it must be obvious that any adequate functional analysis of religion depends upon the notion of "function" that is employed. What, then, is the specific nature of mental functions? How distinguish them from others— say, physiological functions? This question is so fundamental, and it has been investigated so little, that I venture to reprint, with slight modifications, an article on the subject that has already been published in the *Psychological Review* (XXII [1915], 87–98), under the title "A Proposed Classification of Mental Functions":

Whenever anything is declared to be a function of mind, we should be able to discover both the general sense in which the term "function" is used, and also the setting of the particular function in question within a functional whole. This is as much as to say that classification of mental functions should have a place in functional psychology that will correspond to the position now occupied in structural psychology by lists of mental elements and modes of combination. Up to the present time such a systematic background has been lacking. As a consequence, the undefined fringe of meaning in discussions of functions leaves still too much room for misunderstanding one another, or even one's self. Further, the lack of classification implies that we are not yet ready to begin describing functions in terms of functional laws. Such is the unsatisfactory situation out of which the following discussion attempts to take a single step.

The approaches thus far made toward a classification of mental functions fall into the following classes:

1. Affirmations of the purposive character of mind, without any list of specific functions.[1]

2. The oft-made assertion that the fundamental functions of all life, mind included, are nutrition and reproduction. At a

[1] E.g., J. E. Creighton, "The Standpoint and Method of Psychology," *Philosophical Review*, March, 1914; H. Münsterberg, *Psychology, General and Applied*, 1914, and R. M. Ogden, *Introduction to General Psychology*, 1914.

later point I shall ask what, as a matter of fact, mind does with these two vital processes. At once, however, I would point out that some of the so-called "irradiations" from primitive hunger and love—for example, science—have characters of their own which it requires some violence to call either nutritive or reproductive.

3. To each item in a structural classification of mind Angell has added the question, What is its function? There results what might be called an engineer's drawing of mind as an adjusting mechanism. It goes far toward supplying the functional classification that I am seeking, and as a consequence I shall borrow rather freely from it. That it needs supplementing, however, should be clear from these two considerations: first, Angell's list of functions is not based upon similarities and differences among the functions themselves; he merely finds and describes a function for each element of structure; secondly, his genetic method keeps his eyes fixed upon the earliest mental reaction, the *terminus a quo*, whereas our problem—the direction of mental movement—requires us to consider also the most developed reaction as a *terminus ad quem*. I find no fault with Angell for not answering questions that he does not raise, but functional psychology must surely incorporate into itself a fuller description of the interests of developed mind. After we have named early utilities, and even after we have made such generalizations as that mind extends the control and organization of movements, something in the nature of function still remains over. To illustrate: If you should ask what are the functions of a dividing engine, I might answer by showing how each wheel and lever contributes to the accurate control of movement, and I might generalize by saying that this instrument as a whole has the function of so adjusting our motions as to enable us to make extremely minute divisions of a surface. This would be a functional description, no doubt, yet beyond it lies the destination of the whole, namely, certain sciences in the interest of which the dividing engine exists at all. Just so, the proposition that mind increases the extent and the fineness of our adjustments needs to be supplemented by inquiry into the terminal meaning of the whole.

4. A fourth approach to a functional classification proceeds as follows: Mental functions are correlative with interests;

interests have their roots in instinctive satisfactions; therefore an inventory of instincts would be *ipso facto* a list of the functions of mind. Let us, then, look to our original nature, that is, to our unlearned tendencies to react in specific ways, or to take satisfaction in predetermined kinds of mental occupation. The program is attractive, and we shall see that it yields results that have an important bearing upon our problem, though not quite the results that are commonly expected. For, first, the "original" nature of man means the part of his nature that is disclosed antecedently to all culture, that is, before the mind has performed some of its most characteristic acts.[1] Secondly, the broad mental areas traditionally called instincts are disappearing from the psychologic map, and in their stead there is appearing a vast, indefinite number of narrow adjustment acts. For example, Thorndike says that "reaching is not a single instinct, but includes at least three somewhat different responses to three very different situations."[2] Thus, the farther back we go in our mental history the greater the difficulty of functional classification, unless we constantly look forward as well as backward. On the other hand, the very minuteness and rigor of Thorndike's analysis reveal certain general, forward-looking tendencies. Thus, there is a tendency to be or to become conscious;[3] there is an original "love of sensory life for its own sake";[4] there is spontaneous preference for experiences in which there is mental control;[5] finally, there is a native capacity for learning.[6] In short, there are "original tendencies of the original tendencies . . . . original tendencies not *to* this or that particular sensitivity, bond or power of response, but *of* sensitivities, connections and responses, in general."[7] Here, I take it, is where interests, in the proper sense of the term, come in. If we are to define our mental functions by our interests, we must consider, not merely tendencies to this or that sensitivity, but also and particularly our tendencies to organize or do some-

---

[1] E. L. Thorndike, *The Original Nature of Man* (1913), pp. 198 f.; also *Education* (1912), chap. v.

[2] *Original Nature*, p. 50.

[3] *Ibid.*, p. 170 f.

[4] *Ibid.*, p. 141.

[5] *Ibid.*, pp. 141 f.

[6] *Ibid.*, p. 171.

[7] *Ibid.*, p. 170.

thing with our sensitivities. Some results of Thorndike's analysis of such tendencies I shall take over into my own classification.

5. Some of the conditions for a general classification of mental functions are fulfilled in recent discussions of value.[1] Here function is treated as function; it is not confused with elements of structure, nor is a given function identified with its earliest, crudest form. Sense of direction *from* something *to* something is here. Urban's list of values, in particular, conveys a sense of the general direction of the movement of mind. What is still needed is something like a combination of Angell, Thorndike, and Urban. The reason why lists of values need supplementing is twofold: first, they do not comprehend mind as a whole, for example, its biological aspects; secondly, several types of value, as will presently appear, are not simple functions, but functional complexes.

These converging lines in recent psychology may be summarily described as follows: (*a*) All mental process whatsoever is purposive, and it should be analyzed from this as well as from the structural standpoint—that is, mental functions must be determined. (*b*) The human mind is functionally as well as structurally continuous with the animal mind, so that a classification of functions must include the biological point of view. (*c*) The *termini* of mind, by which functions are defined, include conscious interests, or self-defining ends. (*d*) Several specific functions of both the biological type and the conscious-interest type have been defined here and there in scattered places.

What remains to be done is to systematize these results; to discover and, if possible, to fill remaining gaps, and to show the relation of the resulting functional concepts to older, more current psychological categories. The whole must, of course, be description, not evaluation. The work of functional psychology is not to tell us what we ought to prefer, but to determine, as a matter of observable fact, what mind does actually go toward and "for." Two main divisions, each with several subdivisions, are implied in what has already been said.

A. *Biological functions.*—To occupy the biological standpoint—which is simply a point of view used temporarily for

[1] The chief classifications of value are summarized by J. S. Moore, "The System of Values," *Journal of Philosophy*, VII (1910), 282–91.

certain purposes, and not necessarily more true or fundamental than other points of view—is to think of living beings without reference to any approvals or preferences, any "better and worse." The biological functions of mind consist in quantitatively determinable increases in range of response to environment. Thus:

1. Increase in the spatial range of objects responded to.

2. Increase in the temporal range of objects responded to.

3. Increase in the range of magnitudes to which response is made.

4. Increase in the range of qualities responded to.

5. Increase in the range of environmental co-ordinations to which co-ordinated responses are made.

This list will remain the same whether we approach the facts from the behaviorist standpoint or from that of traditional psychology. I call these functions mental for two reasons: because they characterize mind in its most conscious as well as its less conscious stages, and because these directions of movement, though they are established before we reflect upon them, become, after reflection, conscious purposes.

The relation of this analysis to the popular categories, nutrition and reproduction, requires a word of explanation. To begin with nutrition, what has mind, as a matter of fact, to do with it? (a) Mind connotes changes in the feeding reaction that fall under one or more of the above-listed functions. But the law here is a general one; it applies likewise to protection from weather, from accidents, and from enemies, and it applies also to social organization, science, and art. As far as range of response is concerned, then, we need no special nutrition category. (b) Mind connotes success in a competitive struggle over a limited supply of food. Increase of mind makes a difference here, but in what? Can the difference be expressed in terms of nutrition? No; for nutritive functions would go on at least as well if no competition occurred, or if the mentally inferior animal had happened to get the food instead of the mentally superior one. The difference made by mind is that some new object or quality is responded to, whereupon the more differentiated response may be perpetuated by inheritance or by training. Here the function appears to be not nutrition but the production of a more specialized individual.

(c) It is at least as correct to say that mind moves away from as toward nutrition. For, correlative with the growth of mind is restriction of feeding to specialized kinds of food, and consequent increase in the mechanical cost of getting it. The ocean brings food to an oyster; a cat must hunt for its living. Everywhere the discriminative appetite is the expensive one. (d) If we scrutinize cases in which feeding appears to be the end of conscious effort, we find, almost if not quite invariably, that the very act of consciously seeking food gives to nutrition the place of means to some experience beyond itself. The labor movement illustrates this principle on a large scale. Even if the central stimulus of this movement could be identified as hunger (which is doubtful), the conscious end of the struggle is home life, leisure, culture, the education of children, free participation in the determination of one's destiny. (e) But it may be said that mind has stabilized the food supply and produced a more even distribution of it. Civilization will soon reach a point at which famines can no longer occur. What, it may be asked, is the meaning of the present movement for agricultural instruction, and indeed for vocational training in its whole extent, if not just this, that men want enough to eat? Here, indeed, is excellent material for answering the question as to what mind is about when it seeks food. The crucial question for us is whether the direction of the mind's movement here can be defined as from hunger to repletion. Of course, food is an object of conscious desire. So is getting to Albany on time an object of desire on the part of one who is traveling from New York to Buffalo by way of the New York Central. The road to our social ends certainly takes the food-supply route. But, as in the case of the labor movement, social food-seeking that begins instinctively awakens, sooner or later, a consciousness of the social values broadly called cultural, and these it is that define the specifically mental destination or function.

Turning now to the question whether reproduction should be accounted a mental function, we find the course of evolution not at all ambiguous. Reproduction is most prolific in the lowest ranges of life. Mental development is clearly correlated with decrease in the birth-rate. How many factors are involved in this decrease I will not attempt to say, but certainly mind is one of them. Herbert Spencer realized this fact,[1] though he did not bring out the full significance of it. John Fiske's two essays on human infancy[2] carry us much farther. Mind individualizes the various living beings that are involved, first the offspring and then the parents. The obvious mental function is not reproduction of existing types, but the production of certain new, more specialized types. Mind does not stimulate reproduction any more than it stimulates hunger; it does not increase fertility any more than it increases assimilation. But just as mind specializes foods and increases the cost of feeding, so it individualizes living beings and increases the cost of each individual. The whole may be viewed as on the one hand an increase of inhibitions, and on the other hand a focalizing of dispersed attention. In short, the biological functions of mind can be altogether expressed as increase in the range of objects and qualities responded to, and in range of co-ordination of responses.

B. *Preferential functions.*—Our discussion of nutrition and reproduction has already brought us face to face with conscious preferences, that is, mind defining its own direction. We may take for granted, I suppose, that satisfactions are, in general, a sign of unimpeded mental action, and that we can tell one another about our satisfactions. One may, indeed, be mistaken as to what one likes, that is, as to what it is in a complex that makes it likable, but such mistakes can be discovered and corrected, chiefly by further communication. The functions of our second main division, then, are always qualitative (implying a 'better and worse"), and they are scientifically known through communication by means of language. Thus it is that many preferences have already been successfully studied, such as color preferences, the likes and dislikes of children with respect to pictures and with respect to future occupations, merit in handwriting, merit in English composition, merit as a psychologist, the comic, persuasiveness, even moral excellence.[3] Such experimental studies have the effect,

[1] *Principles of Biology*, Part VI, especially chaps. xii and xiii.

[2] Reprinted under the title, *The Meaning of Infancy*, in the "Riverside Educational Monograph" series (Boston, 1909).

[3] H. L. Hollingworth gives a list of "order of merit" researches in "Experimental Studies in Judgment," *Archives of Psychology* (New York, 1913), pp. 118 f.

not merely of discovering preferences, but also of adding precision to preferences already recorded in the world's literature. Would that a Hollingworth might have been present throughout human evolution to record the growth of human preferences. As the case stands, we must combine experiment upon present preferences with the less precise study of life as reflected in literature, art, and institutions.

Where shall we look for a basis for the systematic subdivision of preferential functions? Suppose we compare early types of reaction with late ones, say Thorndike's picture of original nature with value analyses, which represent developed interests. Let us begin with the fact that there is satisfaction in merely being conscious. To be conscious, then, we may count as the first preferential function. Note, next, that satisfaction attaches to mere movement of attention from one object to another, as in "love of sensory life for its own sake." May we not say that a second preferential function of mind is to multiply its objects? A third appears in the preference for experiences that include control of objects. A fourth is closely related thereto, namely, the arrangement of objects in systems—it is a function of mind to unify its objects. This is seen all up and down the scale from the spontaneous perception of spatial figures in the starry sky to the ordering of an argument.

These four preferential functions appear to be fundamental, that is, not further analyzable. If we turn, in the next place, to the usual value categories to see whether we may not find further unanalyzable functions, we come upon the interesting, not to say strange, fact that ethical, noetic, religious, and even economic values presuppose a function that they do not name. Each of these types of value depends upon the existence of a society of intercommunicating individuals, yet it seems not to have occurred to anyone to include a social category—simply and specifically social—in discussions of either functions or values. Should not the fifth preferential function in our list, then, be the function of being social, of having something in common with another mind, in short, of communicating? The justification, not to say necessity, for recognizing a simply social function of mind exists, not alone in the social presupposition of several recognized values, but also in a long series of genetic studies which, from one angle after another, have revealed the fundamentally social nature of consciousness.[1]

There remains for consideration our aesthetic experience. Doubtless it involves functions already named, particularly the functions of unification and communication. But it seems to contain also an attitude somewhat different from those already named, the attitude of contemplation—the taking of satisfaction in objects merely *as there*, without regard to anything further that may happen to or with them. Hence I add contemplation to the list.

The preferential functions, then, are these:

1. To be conscious.
2. To multiply objects of consciousness.
3. To control objects, one's self included.
4. To unify objects, one's self included.
5. To communicate, that is, have in common.
6. To contemplate.

Some omissions from this list require explanation. Play is omitted because it involves a complex of 1 and 2, generally 3, also sometimes all six, and because it is fully exhausted therein. Truth is omitted because, as far as it is not an abstraction from actual intellectual functioning, I hold it to be analyzable without remainder into functions already named, especially 4 and 5.[2] No ethical function appears because the three objectives that it includes—control, unification, socialization—already have appropriate recognition in the list.[3] As to economic value, it seems to be exhausted in the notion of control within a social medium.

[1] It is true that these are commonly studies of content rather than of function, and that "I" and "thou" appear therein as "idea of I" and "idea of thou." For the purposes of merely structural analysis this is doubtless sufficient. That is, structural analysis as such has no place at all for the experience of communication. On the other hand, communication will loom large in any adequate general analysis of mental functions.

[2] Cf. A. W. Moore, "Truth Value," *Journal of Philosophy*, V (1908), 429–36.

[3] Cf. J. H. Tufts, "Ethical Value," *ibid.*, 517–22.

Finally, religion is without a place in the list because it offers no particular value of its own. Religion is not co-ordinate with other interests, but is rather a movement of reinforcement, unification, and revaluation of values as a whole, particularly in social terms.[1]

It will be asked, no doubt, whether the functions of mind can be named without any direct reference to instinctive desires. In addition to what has already been said concerning nutrition and reproduction—that they are, so to say, constants that find a supply at every level of mentality—it may now be added, as a general truth, that mental activity exercised upon the objects of instinctive desire does not satisfy the desire in its initial form, but modifies the desire itself. For example, what has at first only a derived interest as means to something else may acquire an interest of its own, and become an end. This is surely the way that science has come into being, and very likely art also. The evolution of parental and of conjugal relations offers abundant examples of the truth that the distinctive work of mind with our desires is to differentiate and recreate them. Our list of mental functions, accordingly, does not specify particular instincts, but only the primary ways in which mind works among them.

A question may arise, also, as to whether higher desires or ideal values ought not to appear in the list. Is not the most distinctive achievement of mind in the realm of desires, it may be said, the mastery of certain ones in the interest of others? I agree that "the desires of the self-conscious" must be recognized as having a character of their own,[2] and that a list of mental functions must do justice to them. "The valuation of persons as persons constitutes a relatively independent type, one which presupposes a differentiation of object and attitude."[3] The list as it stands, however, will be found to do justice to this differentiation. Here are self-control, self-unification, self-socialization, with the implication that all this applies to any and every self, both actualized selves and ideal selves.

[1] G. A. Coe, "Religious Value," *ibid.*, 253–56.

[2] A. O. Lovejoy, "The Desires of the Self-Conscious," *ibid.*, IV (1907), 29–39.

[3] W. M. Urban, *Valuation, Its Nature and Laws*, (London, 1909), p. 282; see also p. 269.

Finally, inasmuch as no pleasurable sense quality of objects is mentioned in the list, but only "objects, one's self included," doubt may arise as to whether the functions here named are not merely formal and contentless. Functions would indeed be merely formal if they were so defined as to imply indifference to the specific qualities of things. "Pure intellect" is certainly a mere abstraction, never a function. In a list of "preferential functions," however, satisfactions are everywhere presupposed, not ignored. Granted both agreeable and disagreeable objects as data, our question is what mind does with such data. Psychology is, of course, free from the old hedonistic fallacy that the only thing we can do with satisfactions is to seek for them, and that the only thing we can do with dissatisfactions is to avoid them. What we try to do in the presence of such data is to control and organize them, sifting out an item here, deliberately enlarging an item there, *all in the interest of being, so to say, at home with one's self and with one's fellows. In short, the preferential functions here named represent persons as mutually attaining freedom in the world as it is. Such persons are as concrete as anything can conceivably be.*

CHAPTER III

THE DATA, AND HOW THEY ARE ASCERTAINED

What does one do when one is religious? This is the first question that the functional psychology of religion has to ask. "What one does" means first of all external acts that another can observe, such as the religious dance of a savage, the going to church of one of us, or the founding of a hospital by a religious society. If we could construct a complete catalogue of the religious acts of men, women, and children at all stages of culture, it would be most illuminating.

But it would be illuminating chiefly because we should read into it appropriate meanings. Into one act we should read hunger, or anxiety regarding the food supply; into another, fear of demons; into still another, hope of an ideal society. In order that these "readings in" may be true and not arbitrary, we need to note, in addition to religious acts, any further expression of men's meaning in these acts. We must imaginatively get inside the experiences that we would understand. This is not always easy. Suppose, for instance, that we observe some savages moving about rhythmically to the accompaniment of drums; we call this a dance, and at once we are in danger of giving it a meaning too closely analogous to that of our own dances. Again, if we discover that this dance is like a buffalo hunt or a battle, we may call it a dramatic representation, and then falsely imagine that it has close relations to our own dramatic interests. It is essential, then, that we should know what men tell about their religion as well as what they do. The telling is partly speech, partly pictorial or symbolic art.

What a particular man or a particular group mentions as the meaning of an act must be compared, of course, with what other men and groups say about the same or similar acts. Earlier utterances are to be compared with later ones, so that, if possible, meanings may be seen to develop according to some law. We who psychologize are not required to accept as the value or meaning of religion what religion asserts of itself at any one stage, high or low, but we analyze these different self-realizations in order to see in what direction they are going as a whole.

The present movement for a psychology of religion attempted at the outset to get at its data in a most direct way, namely, by going to living men and women with questions concerning their experiences. Starbuck's *Psychology of Religion* is based, for the most part, upon returns from question circulars—also called questionnaires. An active discussion of the question-list method has followed.[1] Among its limitations may be noted:

1. *Unintentional selection of data.*—(*a*) The distribution of the question lists can be known to cover the sources of possible data evenly and adequately only now and then. (*b*) Responses are usually made by some only of those who receive the circulars. Since the non-responding attitude may well be connected with some fact of religious life, those who respond cannot be assumed to rep-

[1] See Topical Bibliography under the head, "Methods in the Psychology of Religion."

resent the whole. (c) When several questions are asked, it is common for respondents to answer only a part. (d) Rarely, if ever, may we assume that a respondent gives all the important data concerning that which he describes. He selects what seem to him the things most important or appropriate. (e) The questions commonly present a set of categories into which the answers are expected to fall. Persons whose experiences happen to be hit off by these categories have a special incentive for responding, while persons who find no category that seems to fit them have incentive for not responding. Thus, the returns tend to become weighted in the direction of the investigator's own presuppositions.

2. *Answers suggested by the questions.*—A great part of our intellectual process is not thinking in any strict sense, but drifting with the idea that happens to be presented. See how much yonder cloud resembles a castle. Of course it does! So the answer to a question concerning one's inner life is likely to be bent to the question itself. The terminology of the question may determine the terminology of the answer, regardless of appropriateness. The respondent may naturally and properly adapt himself to the mood of the questioner. The form of the question may recall certain things and put others out of mind. In short, the attention of the respondent is likely to be passively controlled, so that the question partly creates its own answer.[1]

3. *Inaccurate observation, especially when introspection is required.*—The distortions that occur in most persons' observations, and especially in our notions

[1] An extensive investigation of this process among school children is reported by A. Binet, *La Suggestibilité* (Paris, 1900).

about ourselves, are notorious. It is vain to expect question circulars to elicit psychological items all ready to be catalogued, summed up, and generalized.[1]

4. *Inaccuracy of memory.*—Memory tends to drop out some items and to reconstruct others. The question-circular method has no means of checking up such errors.

5. *Inaccurate or inadequate description.*—Description as well as observation requires training. In matters of religion many persons seem incapable of freeing themselves from the stock phrases to which they have listened in churches and Sunday schools. Other persons simply lack vocabulary, and therefore use inappropriate terms. Finally, a standard of accuracy and precision is generally lacking.

6. *Necessity of interpreting returns.*—A few census-like returns, such as date, age, place, and the like, can safely be counted and offered as statistics of the persons who make the returns. But even here caution is necessary because of liability to memory errors, and because the thing dated, such as "conversion," may not be the same in all the returns. Beyond this nearly everything has to be interpreted by the investigator. For example, traditional or biblical language can often mean several different things. "Doubts" may mean either an intellectual attitude or an emotion of insecurity. "Sense of sin" has correspondingly different uses. "Conversion," when it is not used in the New Testament sense of a

[1] Various clergymen have sent out question lists concerning such subjects as "why men do not go to church." The obvious superficiality of the ordinary results is just what should be expected. Attempting to make observations by proxy may bring in interesting returns, however, because the questions themselves elicit fresh reactions.

voluntary turning about, means anything from shaking hands with a revivalist, as a sign of religious desire, to the profoundest reversal of emotions and of likes and dislikes. And not only must terms be interpreted by the investigator, but whole situations must be reconstructed by him from given fragments. He must allow for the respondent's probable ignorance of certain factors; for bias produced by training; for the influence of conditions probably present but not proved to be so; for individual peculiarities gathered by the investigator from the tone of the whole response. Such interpretation may be skilfully done, and it may be as worthy of confidence as similar interpretations made by historians, but it requires the greatest caution and balance, and in the end its results, like history, lack exactness.[1]

On the other hand, it would be hasty to assume that question circulars are scientifically useless. A large part of the data in several scientific fields is, in fact, gathered by question lists called report blanks. Further, there is no absolute separation between questions asked of a subject in a laboratory and questions asked of subjects under other conditions. The main difference is in the degree of our knowledge of the stimuli actually present. In either case we accept more or less of the subject's observation of himself. It should be remembered also that the question circular need not, and should not, be

---

[1] Starbuck has used his returns with caution and in an objective spirit. He has avoided the worst pitfalls into which question-list researches have fallen. Yet his numerical tabulation of emotions, motives, and the like shows nothing more than general drifts present in unknown proportions.

isolated from other instruments of research. Now and then details can be run down by personal interviews or experiment.[1]

Question-circular returns are effective in establishing at least three types of generalization: (1) External situations in which some broadly recognized psychical event takes place. Such facts as age, date, and social environment can often be ascertained with approximate accuracy. Largely through this method one great generalization of this type has been established, namely, that there is a causal connection between religious conversion of the emotional type and the physiological change during adolescence. (2) The existence of contrasting types within a specified field. This certainly is a valuable psychological service. In the matter of prayer, for example, and in general in the individual realization of God in a high form of religion like the Christian, there are striking differences of type. Self-assertion characterizes one individual, self-abnegation another. Some persons have a mystical-emotional realization of God, while others find him through abundant, free activity. Further, this method is important because it definitely establishes the existence of contrary reactions in groups, such as religious denominations, that may seem to be homogeneous. (3) The existence of a tendency or drift within a group may be ascertained, even though the extent or depth of the drift may remain unknown. Thus, a question that I once asked concerning the nature of their call to the ministry elicited from a significant number of ministers in a denomination that cultivates emotional realizations the surprising fact that their call

[1] See Coe, *Spiritual Life*, chap. iii.

contained little of this element, but much of prosaic, common-sense procedure.[1]

Data for the psychology of religion are gathered, in the second place, by scrutiny of literary or other records of religious life.[2] Here fall biographies and autobiographies; scattered passages in general literature; sacred literatures, which include (often in mixture) history and biography, myth, hymn, prayer, ritual, and theological or metaphysical thought structures;[3] finally, inscriptions, pictures, statues, temple architecture, and the like.[4] Such sources for what men tell about their religion have one advantage over the question list, namely, that the investigator certainly does not influence the original records. They have been produced in the ordinary course of life or of religion, and often the absence of psychologizing makes them psychologically

[1] To judge the feasibility of a given question-circular enterprise, the following questions will be found useful: (1) How much of it concerns matters in which non-expert testimony is likely to be adequate? (2) Does it formulate answers, or does it merely suggest situations, leaving the respondent to formulate his response? (3) Does it offer alternative answers or classes into which the respondent is to fit himself? If so, are the alternatives exhaustive and mutually exclusive? (4) Is the language such that the respondent will get the points intended by the questioner? (5) What is the point of the whole list? If trustworthy responses were made in adequate number, how would our knowledge be advanced? Is this knowledge accessible in any more direct or trustworthy fashion?

[2] James's *The Varieties of Religious Experience* is based largely upon autobiographic records. Another specimen is Royce's study of Bunyan in *Studies in Good and Evil*. A more extensive research based on this method is Delacroix's *Etudes d'histoire et de psychologie du mysticisme.*

[3] Many writers have dipped into the records of the ethnic faiths, but Stratton in his *Psychology of the Religious Life* bases thereon nearly the whole of a psychological theory of religion.

[4] An example is Harrison's *Themis* (Cambridge, 1912).

the more valuable. Nevertheless, there are difficulties
that must not be ignored.

1. The biographical and autobiographical material
that is available is triply selected. First, the individuals
portrayed are selected by biographers and autobiogra-
phers upon principles that, even where they can be
ascertained, have little relation to the psychologist's
interest. Secondly, the material that is recorded in each
case is also selected from a larger mass, and again from
motives that produce no psychological classification.
Thirdly, the psychologist selects the writings that he
will analyze. James has been criticized, for example,
for selecting too large a proportion of extreme and even
morbid cases. In short, this material is valuable chiefly
because, like question-list returns, it establishes the
existence, in unknown proportions, of certain types of
religious experience.[1]

2. Sacred literatures offer the extraordinary advantage of being religiously motived, so that they present
to us, as it were, religion itself at some stage of its
ongoing. Nevertheless, even here we find comparatively
little that is naïvely religious. Men make a written
record, for the most part, because they have become
reflective and therefore selectors. Much is motived by
desire to explain, reconcile, or systematize, as in myth and
theology. Some of the records are made in the interest of
a cause, an idea, or a party, and consequently the writer
maintains silence concerning shady aspects of his own
religion, but gives prominence to such aspects of his

[1] A. R. Burr, in *Religious Confessions and Confessants*, is so unconscious of these difficulties as to suppose that a "definitive" collection of
data on religious experience could be made from autobiographic confessions.

opponent's religion. Ritual formulae, in turn, commonly give words to be said rather than things to be done, whereas these latter are essential to most rites. Prayers and hymns, on the other hand, sometimes let us see far into the religious mind, but even 'here the meaning is likely to depend upon historical conditions that are not specified. Indeed, sacred literatures as a whole arise and grow as parts of a historical movement which they only partly reflect. Different historical and literary strata, for example, are often present in an Old Testament story. As a consequence of all this, we can rarely make sure of our psychological data by merely reading a piece of sacred literature. "Blessed are ye poor," says Jesus according to Luke; "Blessed are the poor in spirit," according to Matthew. What, then, was Jesus' actual point of view? It is scarcely necessary to add that many of these difficulties attach themselves to the study of inscriptions and of religious art.

In the third place, data are found by anthropological research, chiefly among the lowest peoples, but in part also among the less sophisticated ways of culture-races. The amount of material now in print that bears upon the religion of savages may properly be called immense. Much of it has the peculiar value for psychology that it enables us to get near to the beginnings of religion. In the matter of origins, definitely ascertained facts are now taking the place of speculation or of inferences drawn from our own highly developed processes. We are on the way toward knowledge of the evolution of religion that will be comparable to our knowledge of the evolution of man's physical organism. That the road is not a straight and broad one, however, may be gathered, not only from the conflicts and rapid changes of theory in this field, but also from the following considerations:

1. Almost every fact of the savage's mentality has to be interpreted. He can directly tell us about it far less than can be directly told by question-list respondents concerning their inner life. Further, the interpreter is generally not the fact-gatherer. The psychologist is obliged to make the best he can of data gathered by other persons who may not have had in mind his own questions, interests, or points of view.

2. Here, as in other evolutionary studies, a Janus-faced difficulty is almost unavoidable. At our end of the evolution stand highly complex processes and a set of preferences, ideals, or valuations that we call higher as distinguished from lower. At the other end of the scale we seek for minimal complexity, and for lower, instinctive preferences, both process and preferences being such as to connect man with the animal series. Evolution implies that we are to think these extremes as somehow one; the complex must be seen to come out of the simple, the high values out of the low. Consequently we tend to overlook contrasts. We do it, on the one hand, by oversimplifying our own culture, or by forced classification of the higher with the lower; or, on the other hand, by attributing too much to particular phenomena of the savage mind. By combining the two—oversimplification on the one hand and overloading on the other—almost every item of savage religion has been made to carry the religious universe on its back. The gods are ghosts of dead men; the gods are nature-powers that smite the attention; the gods are imagina-

tive projections of some social unity. The psychical root of religion is fear; the root is the experience of sex; the root is the economic interest of some group. Totemism, magic, sacrifice, myth—each has loomed overwhelmingly. The movement from myth to theology, from spell to prayer, from the festivals of fertility-gods to Easter, from mystery-initiations to baptism, from totemistic eating of the god to the eucharist, from taboo to Sunday and other sanctities, from the instinctive sense of tribal solidarity to the ideal of a kingdom of God, from spooks to hope of heaven—this movement, this mass of evolutionary ties between us and our ancestors easily creates an impression that our religion is a vestigial phenomenon, a remainder from savage crudity, whereas religion has evolved away from as well as out of savagery. The nature of this evolution will be gone into at some length in chap. xiii. Meanwhile, we may well remind ourselves that analysis establishes differences as well as similarities, and that the differences between two things are neither wiped out nor explained by placing them in the same evolutionary series. Finally, we have no right to assume that origins are in the past alone. Evolution may be original at every step, and may be going on with originality in our own experience. We ourselves may conceivably live within the sources; they may even be pouring themselves forth with greater freedom than in the case of early man. For these reasons one may hesitate to follow Wundt in his conviction that an anthropological-genetic account of religion is *the* psychology of religion.

In the fourth place, data may be ascertained by experimental methods. An indirect experimental contribution is made, of course, by laboratory studies of part processes that enter into religious reactions, such as suggestion, emotion, and belief-formation. Theoretically, integral religious experiences, with sincere and complete letting go, might be evoked under laboratory control. But the difficulties are obvious. The whole laboratory spirit of aloofness from all interests except analysis stands in the way. A case is on record of an experiment in which the subjects read or listened to religious sentiments under controlled conditions, and then wrote introspective records of the results. The upshot of the experiment concerns rather the psychology of language and of edifying discourse in general than analysis of religious experience.[1] A very different procedure appears in another report—a study of the elements of certain services of common worship. By employing the order-of-merit method, which has already been referred to in the Appendix to chap. ii, it was found possible to determine the relative values of these elements for a group of fifty persons.[2] The order-of-merit method consists fundamentally in this: The same set of items is placed by each one of a large number of persons in the order, "first," "second," "third," etc., on the basis simply of more and less without regard to how much. Thus, colors or pictures may be arranged in an order of preference, or stories may be arranged on the more specific basis of "more or less humorous." By

[1] W. Stählin, "Experimentelle Untersuchung über Sprachpsychologie und Religionspsychologie," *Archiv für Religionspsychologie*, I (1914), 117–94.

[2] See a summarized report of a paper read by Mark A. May before the New York Branch of the American Psychological Association in *Journal of Philosophy*, XII (1915), 691.

combining these judgments, and by the use of certain statistical methods of analysis, it is possible to construct a scale of merit for the items concerned, and even to establish some definite quantitative relations. There appears to be no reason why this method may not be used to determine value relations in religion for far larger groups than the one here studied.

There is a place, also, for the field use, as distinguished from the laboratory use, of experimental methods. In the religious education of children, in the conduct of worship, in the whole plan and organization of a religious society, particular factors can often be identified, sometimes changed at will. Many a rough-and-ready experiment in religion has been made in the interest of religion, and various modes of control have thus evolved in religious communions. There is nothing to prevent the deliberate, scientifically controlled refining of such experiments.[1]

A final caution must be uttered against taking the notion of method too narrowly. If one should ask, for example, how Höffding ascertained the data of the third division of his *Philosophy of Religion*, an answer could hardly be given offhand. He makes little use of anthropology, or of sacred literatures, or of religious biographies, or of question-list returns; yet his analysis of the religious experience is among the most noteworthy. The reason is that, though he adduces few new data, he sees far into common facts. Now, this far-sight of his is not an accident; it is rather the ripe fruit of

[1] A beginning has been made, for example, in the ascertainment of the reactions of children to common worship. See H. Hartshorne, *Worship in the Sunday School* (New York, 1913).

long experience with psychological facts and problems. We may say, then, that in addition to the digging out of fresh material, research may take the direction of fresh analysis of material that is commonplace.

APPENDIX

GERMAN VIEWS OF THE "AMERIKANISCHE RELIGIONSPSYCHOLOGIE"

Two American productions in this field, Starbuck's *Psychology of Religion* and James's *The Varieties of Religious Experience*, have been translated into German, both under the influence of interests that center in theology. Around these works an interesting discussion has arisen that concerns the task and the method of the psychology of religion. Faber, *Das Wesen der Religionspsychologie*, gives abundant references to books and articles on the subject, besides contributing an extended essay of his own. Various German theologians saw in the two works just referred to methods that seemed to open up vast possibilities of increase in scientific knowledge of religion. In addition, they found support for theological or transcendental presuppositions in this branch of psychology, and some of them attempted to fuse psychology and what may be called metaphysical theology. On the other hand, there have come, partly from theologians also, sharp criticisms of the methods of the two American writers just named, and strenuous opposition to theologized psychology. In his *Probleme*, Part IV, Wundt regards James's book as not psychology but an extract from a pragmatic philosophy of religion.

In this German discussion the phrase "the American psychology of religion" has sprung up. It is used, as far as I have discovered, in a very narrow way, and I regard it as misleading. It is used narrowly because it takes works published from 1899 to 1902 as sufficiently typical. It is misleading because, first, it ignores the fact that the methodological faults in these earlier works were promptly pointed out in this country and have not been repeated, and, secondly, it ignores the great distance in methods and results between the two authors already named and Ames, King, Stratton, and Leuba. I shall go into no critique of the special methods of these writers, but instead I refer the reader to review articles listed in the Alphabetical Author List under their respective names.

One general word, however, should be said. American writings on the psychology of religion have, as a whole, a common characteristic with respect to method. In one form or another, with few exceptions, they assume that psychological analysis applies to function as well as to structure. They conceive their task as analysis of a certain phase of the struggle to live. They ask how this struggle gives rise to religion, and what religion contributes to the struggle. Here is an attempt at a dynamic view. It tends to make the psychology of religion talk about life in concrete terms like those of ordinary conversation. If, as a consequence, Starbuck uses religious terms where we should like to have him use those of psychology, and if James offers the testimony of individuals as a finality where we think further analysis is possible, these are not essentials of method, but instances of failure to use it adequately. The notion of function in the valuational sense is still a new one in scientific psychology, and it is in process of development. I have already expressed a conviction, not only that it is an inevitable point of view (among others), but also that it cannot reach its own full development as a psychological concept without presupposing the personal selves that are implied in conversation and in friendship. This is not equivalent to admitting a transcendental principle into empirical science. It is at most an extension of empirical inquiry with respect to human desire and motive, and to what men mean by their will-acts.

Wundt's magnificent contribution to the psychology of early mythological and religious ideas comes to us associated with certain positive conceptions of method and point of view. The final source of religion for him, as for most American writers, is man's appreciation of what helps and hinders in the struggle to live. The psychical spring of the whole mythological complex is no Why? or How? but some immediate relation to man's weal and woe. But, the circle of mythological notions having once been formed by the common mind, we have therein, it appears, the whole psychological explanation of religion. At least Wundt is sure that the psychology of religion must be genetic, and that genetic psychology is the psychology of early man. Thus, if I correctly apprehend Wundt's position, man's first-developed functions are somehow more explanatory than his later ones, and a group mind can be a source of religion in a sense in which an individual mind cannot. It is not clear to me why, upon Wundt's own principles, this must be so. There seems to be no ground whatever for the assumption that early steps in an evolution are explanatory in a sense in which later steps are not. Nor do I see any evidence for, but a great deal of evidence against, the notion that the struggle to live merely repeats itself upon the same plane. In other words, while Wundt adopts a functional point of view for the first crude impulses that express themselves in mythology, and there arrests his use of functional method, there is need that the method should be applied through the entire evolution of religion, and to the experiences of individuals as well as to the thought forms of early groups.

CHAPTER IV

PRELIMINARY ANALYSIS OF RELIGIOUS CONSCIOUSNESS

What, then, should we understand by religion? The fate of definitions of religion does not invite to the making of new ones. If by definition is meant the formulation of an inclusive major premise from which to deduce the particular qualities of a class, then, in our case, there is no motive for defining. Psychology does not demonstrate what must be, but only opens our eyes to see what is. What we need at the outset is not so much an inclusive idea as a fruitful point of view. Any point of view is fruitful to the extent that it stimulates us to see and to seek facts, evermore facts.[1]

Without more ado, let it be said that experience can teach some definite lessons as to the relative value of several points of view. Relatively unfruitful, first of all, is the defining of religion by reference to a certain content of belief, as: "Religion is belief in God," or "belief in God, and the acts that follow therefrom." The reasons for this unfruitfulness are briefly these: (1) The fluid character of the content of religious belief. Personal and impersonal gods, good and evil gods, spirits of many sorts, heroes and demigods, bulls, snakes, earth, sun, *mana* (simply a diffused power that does the

[1] This seeing and seeking includes, as a matter of course, the organizing of facts into systems. One who does not classify and relate misses the facts themselves.

great things), "nature"—which of these marks off religion? Somewhere each is believed in, somewhere each is involved in men's religious acts. (2) The existence of a religion (Buddhism) the theology of which refuses to assert the existence of gods or of spirits. It is not correct to say that Buddhism is a religion without god-beliefs, for the mass of Buddhists have gods a-plenty. But the thinkers of this faith, from Gautama onward, are consciously free from such belief. (3) The incorrectness of the intellectualist psychology that has assumed that religious ideas are self-sustaining logical entities. These ideas are sustained by something that makes them interesting or important—by impulses and emotional attitudes. Religion is not a product of intellectual leisure, but of the grind of existence—a grind that ever seeks to transform itself into freedom and joy. We shall have scant appreciation of beliefs themselves until we ask what makes them germinate and grow.

Relatively unfruitful, likewise, are definitions of religion that reduce it to feeling. They move downward, it is true, from beliefs toward impulses. For this reason Schleiermacher's famous formula, "Religion is a feeling of absolute dependence," has been immensely vivifying to a theology whose traditions had been intellectualistic. Nevertheless, a general conviction has been reached that religion cannot be reduced to a single phase of mental life—the entire mind is involved. Not only so, but the religious feelings themselves demand to be understood by reference to the situations in which they arise and the part they play in the total adjustment process.

Seeing that religion concerns the whole man, some theologians would define it substantially as follows:

Religion is the total reaction of the mind to what it conceives as superior powers upon which its good depends. This formula deserves careful analysis. The idea of ends, values, adjustment, is at last admitted to the definition. Nevertheless, no desire, no function, no good, is specified so as to be identifiable. Religious reactions are to be discriminated from others by "what the mind conceives as superior powers." Now, this is simply an improved way of saying that a certain content of belief is the differentia. If anyone doubts that this is a fair interpretation, let him ask whether or not "superior" is here used in a general or a specific sense. Does it apply, for instance, to a superior army on which the good of an inferior one depends? Clearly, a particular kind of superiority has been singled out but not defined, and belief in beings of this kind is made the criterion of religion. Therefore the difficulties of all intellectualist types of definition are present here also. And a still further difficulty is present. The concept of *religiously* superior powers must have been achieved by a process of some kind. Must not this process have been a religious one? Men think because they have a motive for thinking, because some interest spurs them on. It is because a religious interest is already present that men achieve the notion of religiously "superior powers."[1] The point of view will be more fruitful, then, if we include this interest.

---

[1] Wundt, after arguing with power that affective states are the moving spring of the myth, and that early man is interested above all things in the means for carrying on the struggle to live (*Mythus und Religion*, 2. Aufl., I, 62), nevertheless maintains that religion, "in the only true sense of the word," is born with the rise of the god-idea (*Elemente der Völkerpsychologie*, p. 369).

There is no occasion for quarrels over formal definitions. The most that a formal definition can do, in any
case, is not to convey knowledge, but to assist in the
organization of knowledge. Each of a dozen definitions
of religion might conceivably be justified on such ground.
Our present problem, accordingly, is not to say what all
men ought to mean when they use the term "religion,"
but rather to indicate the direction of attention or the
organizing idea that is at present most useful in the
psychology of religion. The present work represents a
conviction that a dynamic or functional point of view
is the one that is actually yielding the most fruit.[1]
Accordingly, our immediate aim is to give a preliminary
description of religious consciousness in terms of value.
What this requires can be made clear by a word of com-
ment upon two recent, carefully constructed definitions,
both of which employ the concept of value, but find
the differentia of religion elsewhere. W. K. Wright
says that religion is "the endeavor to secure the conservation of socially recognized values through specific
actions that are believed to evoke some agency different
from the ordinary ego of the individual, or from other

[1] Even Royce, whose interest is more philosophical than psychological, explains his conception of religion thus: "The idea that man
needs salvation depends, in fact, upon two simpler ideas whereof the
main idea is constituted. The first is the idea that there is some end
or aim of human life which is more important than all other aims, so
that, by comparison with this aim, all else is secondary and subsidiary,
and perhaps relatively unimportant, or even vain and empty. The
other idea is this: That man as he now is, or as he naturally is, is in
great danger of so missing this highest aim as to render his whole life a
senseless failure by virtue of thus coming short of his true goal."—*The
Sources of Religious Insight* (New York, 1912), p. 12. For a recent
example of attempts to define religion by a single phase of it, see W. D.
Wallis, "Fear in Religion," *Journal of Religious Psychology*, V, 257–304.

merely human beings, and that imply a feeling of dependence upon this agency."[1] Here the values involved in religious consciousness are limited to those that are already socially recognized. What, then, shall we call the experience in which a prophet, dissenting from socially recognized values, makes appeal to what he regards as a higher standard? *Reconstruction of life's ends* is in this case central in a movement that no one would hesitate to call religious. A second characteristic of Wright's definition is that the differentia of religion is found in the means whereby certain ends are sought, not in the ends themselves. With this Leuba is in agreement. "It is not the needs which are distinctive of religion, but the method whereby they are gratified,"[2] he says. The method that he has in mind reminds one of certain theological definitions that have already had our consideration. "Religion," says Leuba, "is that part of human experience in which man feels himself in relation with powers of psychic nature, usually personal powers, and makes use of them."[3] Here the divine beings of religion appear as mere means to ends, the ends being completely determined, it appears, without reference to the gods. Both in what it says and in what it assumes this definition requires scrutiny. We are within the horizon of functional psychology; let us see just where.

[1] "A Psychological Definition of Religion," *American Journal of Theology*, XVI (1912), 385–409.

[2] *A Psychological Study of Religion*, p. 8.

[3] *Ibid.*, p. 52. To get the full significance of this statement of Leuba's, the whole of Part I should be read. In an Appendix he has arranged an array of definitions, intellectualistic, affectivistic, and voluntaristic.

In the first place, to say that A is used as a means to B assumes that a valuation has occurred; certain things have been judged to be important. In the definition now before us, where and by whom has this valuation been made? The category of means and end can be used in either of two ways—the reference may be to a valuation already made by others, or to a valuation now offered by the author of the definition. In the one case we have a descriptive definition, in the other a normative one. That Leuba's definition is normative rather than descriptive may be asserted, not only on the ground of his general view that the psychology of religion is normative for both religious belief and religious practice, but also on the specific ground that, historically considered, religion has not, either uniformly or as a whole, given to its gods the alleged position of mere means subordinate to certain ends. Descriptively taken, ends are just what, from the reactor's own point of view, is felt and judged to be most important. Now, in the religious consciousness of mankind in general, so far are the gods from uniformly taking a secondary place that they appear, not seldom, as supreme judges and correctors of men's purposes, and even of the desires of the heart. In the progressive religions, particularly, we behold men adjusting their *ends* to what they conceive to be the divine will or the divine nature. Nay, the god himself becomes in various cases an end consciously sought—the devotee desires to help his god, or the god is enjoyed and loved in the same objective way in which one member of a family relates himself to another.[1]　No

---

[1] "The gods stood as much in need of their worshipers as the worshipers in need of them."—J. G. Frazer, *Magic Art and Evolution of Kings*, I (London, 1911), 31.

doubt the mind of man constructs the idea of gods in accordance with the general laws of ideation; no doubt the will of the god is an idealization of man's human social experience, but herein men feel that they face ends, finalities, not mere means. If my own conviction should be that, *in reality*, divine beings do not exist, and that what men regard as their own ends are not *really* controlling in human conduct, and that the only *good* of all these god-ideas and all these self-devotions is to promote ends fully definable without reference to the divine—if this were my conviction, it would be *my valuation* of religion, and not a descriptive definition of religious consciousness or of religious function.[1]

We already see that religious consciousness often involves, sometimes supremely is, a consciousness of ends or values. This fact suggests a possible point of view for the study of religion as a whole. Possibly the chief thing in religion, considered functionally, is the progressive discovery and reorganization of values. Possibly the central function of religion concerns ends rather than means. Without doubt "chief" and "central" as here used imply valuation, or an interest of a particular kind. Let us change our phraseology, then, and say that possibly it will be *interesting* to see how and how far the phenomena commonly called "religious"

---

[1] Leuba's procedure has an extraordinary likeness to that of traditional theology. Both argue as if definitions were mental reproductions of *realia* instead of being merely useful points of view for the organization of facts. Both, therefore, define religious experience from the standpoint of a present valuation of it, rather than from the standpoint of the experience itself. Both, as a consequence, attempt to control religion by means of a definition.

can be organized among themselves and related to other phenomena from the voluntarily assumed standpoint of value.

Leuba's definition presupposes that men have needs, and apparently that these needs are a constant, while the means used to supply them are variable. Viewed from the evolving standpoints of the evolving human mind, however, needs evolve, values are discovered, and man comes thus gradually to *himself* and not merely to fresh means for static ends. Examples of this evolution of values that we have already drawn from the parental and the sexual instinct may now be used as the starting-point for a more general study of human desires. A little reflection will justify five propositions which, taken together, may serve to introduce the method of approach in which the present work is interested.

First, human desire is not extinguished when its immediate satisfaction is attained. This is plain enough in the case of our higher values. Knowledge, once attained, does not dampen but inflames the desire for knowledge. The acquisition of money rarely fails to restimulate and intensify the processes of acquisition. Even in our directly instinctive desires a parallel over-flow occurs. Our so-called "bestial" excesses are hardly bestial, for the way of a beast is to satisfy his appetite and then stop, whereas the way of a man is to extend his appetite. And appetite, as we have seen, does not always move upon a single level statically fixed, but rather grows refined, and sometimes becomes the servitor of ideal ends. Note, for example, how a single term, "love," is used for all grades of reaction, from merely instinctive sex attraction to the most deliberate self-devotion in which the original biological connotation has completely disappeared.

Secondly, human desires undergo a process of organization toward the unity of the individual. The way of human desiring is to *take account of wants*. Thereby we objectify our desires, compare them, and arrange them in scales more or less refined. Thereby we attain to character in the sense not merely of being different each from every other, but also of being functionally more than any desire or any set of desires.

Thirdly, human desires come thus to include a desire to have desires. The desires of the lower animals become organized after a fashion. Rats and mice learn not to touch the tempting morsel that the trap displays. A frog that is making for shore stops—"freezes"—if a bass approaches. Here is a kind of regulation of desire. Men as well as other species are molded in this stern manner. But men mold themselves. They form desires, not merely to have this or that object, but also to be this or that kind of man.[1] Here lies the deeper meaning of education. It is socially organized desire that certain desires rather than others should control human life.[2]

Fourthly, human desires undergo a process of organization toward social as well as individual unity. Education considered as socially organized desire is only one instance. That the individual is not a mere

[1] For a clear exposition of this fact see A. O. Lovejoy, "The Desires of the Self-Conscious," *Journal of Philosophy*, IV (1907), 29–39.

[2] Thorndike thus defines the aims of education: "To make men want the right things and to make them better able so to control the forces of nature and themselves that they can satisfy these wants. We have to make use of nature, to co-operate with each other, and to improve ourselves."—*Education* (New York, 1912), p. 11.

individual, but that individuality itself has a social reference, is now a commonplace of genetic psychology.

Fifthly, human desire, growing by what it feeds on,
refining itself, judging itself, organizing itself, becomes
also desire for the conservation of the human desire-
and-satisfaction type of experience.   Education, for
example, has already come to involve enormous expendi-
ture for ends that are to be realized only gradually after
the death of those who pay the cost.   National consciousness in general endows the future with present
value.   We shall not fully understand the passion of the
patriot until we see within the economic causation of
national conduct a desire that economic values shall be
assured to future generations, and, within loyalty to a
people's culture or institutions, the identification of
present interests with history yet to be made.   The
larger thought, too, of a world-destiny, or even of cosmic
meaning, involves a present desire that desire-and-
satisfaction as we know it may never end.   Thus we
desire to endow our values with the added value of
time-defiance.

What name have we for this whole desire-within-
desire, this whole revaluation of values that both makes
us individuals and organizes us into society?   In each
phase of life a part of the process appears.   We revalue
the seeing of the eye and the hearing of the ear, and
aesthetic values emerge, art is born.   We reflect upon
what we want when man meets man, and moral values
emerge as a control even of the instincts out of which
they arise.   So, also, out of relatively thoughtless thinking there springs a search for norms of thought and for a
self-evidencing or rational standpoint.   Here, then, are

three points at which desire has organized itself by reference to ideal values—aesthetic values, ethical values, and noetic values. That this is a characteristic human process probably no one will deny. But, if so, we should expect to find at least beginnings of the revaluation of life as a whole. We should look for historical foci at which men's sense of the value of life becomes something like a whole reaction.[1] That is, the law of revaluation should sooner or later reveal itself as a desired ideal, as a willed reaction creating instruments for itself and having a history.

It is no new thing to say that what men call religion is, at its focal points, a reaction, solemn or joyous, in which the individual or the group concentrates attention upon something so important that it is, for the consciousness of the moment, life itself. Early religion reflects the felt crises of early life, as hunger and war, and particularly these crises as organizing points for the life of a group. National religion, again, represents the nationally felt interests, such as a race conflict, a political struggle, an economic anxiety, a social self-criticism. And a parallel use of the term religion is common among us. Wherever men intensely identify themselves with something as their very life, there you will almost certainly find "religion" the descriptive term. At first sight one might wonder why there should be such dogged clinging to a term. Why does one encounter a "religion" of beauty, a "religion" of science, a "religion" of duty, a "religion" of social enthusiasm, each of which has

---

[1] As Leuba says, what religion aims at is life in its greatest possible fulness. This ideal fulness, however, is not exactly a sum of particular satisfactions.

shaken off the forms of all historical religions? Is not this a sign that all values press for organization into wholeness of life, and that this is just what religion has been about from the beginning?[1]

Any reaction may then be considered as religious to the extent that it seeks "life" in the sense of completion, unification, and conservation of values—any values whatever. Religion does not introduce any new value; it is an operation upon or within all our appreciations. If we are to speak of religious value at all, we should think of it as the value of values, that is, the value of life organizing and completing itself, or seeking a destiny, as against the discrete values of impulsive or unreflective existence.[2] The "new life" that is so prominent at different levels of religion gets its material from the life that now is. Tribal initiations introduce the youth to a "new life" that is new to him as an individual, but not to the tribe. Similarly, Christian regeneration simply enthrones such domestic qualities as love. Heaven is a projection of joys known on earth, and hell merely focuses earthly woes. Even communion with God is an extension of love and friendship as they are experienced among men.[3]

[1] Economic values—"his money is his god"—and even direct sense satisfactions—"whose god is their belly"—are not excluded from the general proposition that values tend toward organization as "life." Here again the already existing use of religious terminology is psychologically significant.

[2] It would be scarcely an exaggeration to say that any kind of strong excitement is sure to appear somewhere as religion. There is a grain of psychological truth in the assertion of some romanticists that any utterly absorbing passion is *per se* sacred.

[3] In the Zend-Avesta, Zarathustra asks Ahura Mazda, "O Maker of the material world, thou Holy One! which is the first place where

Two recent definitions of religion approximate this point of view. Höffding's "axiom of religion," namely, "the conservation of value," has attained a celebrity that is deserved, for it is, if I mistake not, the first instance of a definition of religion constructed wholly from the conception of values. Yet "conservation" is only one phase of the desire-within-desire upon which we have now fixed our attention. The overflow that is religion is not merely more of the same, but also an immanent criticism whereby what would otherwise be merely a serial order of desires and satisfactions is organized into the unity of personal and social lives, so that they, and they only, in the end, have value.

Strictly functional, also, is the definition of Ames: "Religion is the consciousness of the highest social values."[1] Here values are the differentia of religion, not (as with Wright and Leuba) merely the genus.

the earth feels most happy?" When this question is answered, Zara-thustra asks, "Which is the second place where the earth feels most happy?" and so on to the fifth. Ahura Mazda answers that the places where the earth feels most happy are: (1) the spot on which one of the faithful steps when he offers sacrifice to the lord of the wide pastures; (2) the place whereon one of the faithful erects a house with a priest within, with cattle, a wife, children, and good herds within, and where all the blessings of life thrive; (3) where one of the faithful cultivates most corn, grass, and fruit; where he waters the ground that is dry, or dries the ground that is too wet; (4) where there is the most increase of flocks and herds; (5) where flocks and herds yield most dung. See *Sacred Books of the East*, IV (Oxford, 1880), 22–24.

This is an early description of religious values. They are here arranged in a hierarchical order—the god (cultus or religious value), the family (social-ethical value), the occupation (economic value). Further, ethical value is made to include the economic, and religious value to include the ethical (note the position of the sacrifice and of the priest).

[1] *Psychology of Religious Experience*, Preface.

Further, values are not taken discretely, but they are conceived as in process of organization. Exactly why religion is here limited to social values, and specifically to the highest of such values, however, is not quite clear. Is not a man religious who is desperately seeking to save his own soul, or when he enjoys purely private ecstasy of communion? Or, to state the matter in another way, is not such an experience functionally continuous with experiences in which salvation is conceived socially? Further, how does Ames differentiate religious consciousness from social consciousness as such? If "highest" be given a specific content (so that we could say, for example, that a man is not religious until he accepts this or that social standard), the definition is obviously too narrow; but if "highest" refers, not to a specific set of standards, but to a law of social valuation in accordance with which men criticize and reconstruct their standards, then Ames's point of view is to this extent (but not further) identical with the one here suggested. As a matter of fact, in the body of Ames's book, "highest social values" appear again and again to deliquesce into the social as such.

To propose, as I have done, that we think of religion as an immanent movement within our valuations, a movement that does not terminate in any single set of thought contents, or in any set of particular values, may easily seem to make religion elusive if not vague. But the difficulty is with the thing itself, not with the proposed point of view. That religion is in fact the most puzzlingly elusive phase of experience is fairly deducible from the history of thought about religion. And we can convince ourselves of the fact likewise by direct inspection of current phenomena. How, for example, would one describe the attitude expressed in the following poem?

WAITING

Serene, I fold my hands and wait,
  Nor care for wind, or tide, or sea;
I rave no more 'gainst Time or Fate,
  For lo! my own shall come to me.

I stay my haste, I make delays,
  For what avails this eager pace?
I stand amid the eternal ways,
  And what is mine shall know my face.

Asleep, awake, by night or day,
  The friends I seek are seeking me;
No wind can drive my bark astray,
  Nor change the tide of destiny.

What matter if I stand alone?
  I wait with joy the coming years;
My heart shall reap where it hath sown,
  And garner up its fruit of tears.

The waters know their own, and draw
  The brook that springs in yonder heights;
So flows the good with equal law
  Unto the soul of pure delights.

The stars come nightly to the sky;
  The tidal wave unto the sea;
Nor time, nor space, nor deep, nor high,
  Can keep my own away from me.
          —John Burroughs, in *The Light of Day*
                    (Boston, 1900).

That the attitude here is religious seems obvious; but just what is the attitude, and what is the relation of it to knowledge on the one hand and to the complex of one's

specific purposes and activities on the other? Whatever
we call it, we have here within one's particular valuations an immanent critique which is also a movement
toward completeness, unity, and permanence of the value
experience as a whole.[1]

If the question be asked wherein, then, religious value
is distinct from ethical value, the answer is that it is
not distinct from ethical or any other value. When
ethical value attempts its own ideal completion in union
with all other values similarly ideal and complete, what
we have is religion in the sense in which the term is here
used. The sphere of religion, as of ethics, is individual-
social life. In this life religion refers to the same persons,
the same purposes, the same conditioning facts, as ethics.
In most ethical thinking, however, a difference is recognized. For ethics commonly limits its attention to cer-

[1] The present European war furnishes excellent illustrations of the
intensification and unification of the valuational phase of consciousness.
One single interest tends strongly to overshadow and even swallow up
all others in each of the warring groups. Each individual mind becomes
organized, and all the individuals of a nation become thoroughly focused
at a single point. There is now only one thing that counts, *and it must
be*—this is the spirit. And behold, it is conscious of itself as religious!
From Germany, from France, from England, from Canada, comes news
of extraordinary ethical elevation and religious tone. The French flock
to their neglected churches. There are revival outbursts in the trenches,
and the soldiers either have visions or else are ready to believe that
others have had them. Ministers are confident that a new era for faith
is dawning.

Let us attempt an analysis of this movement of the mass mind.
In the first place, this is not a response to new evidence (in the logical
sense) for the old religion. The new convincingness of "things unseen"
lies altogether in the emotion-producing qualities of the new situation.
In the second place, the recognized religiousness of the emotions produced in each of the national situations obviously depends upon *intensification* and *unification* of desire and action, and not upon the particular

tain values only, whereas religion is interested in all values, in the whole meaning of life. Even within the sphere of social values this distinction between a narrower and a wider horizon is commonly made; for ethics, as ordinarily understood, limits itself to the visible life of men, while religion goes on to raise the question of extending social relationships to the dead and to divine beings. But we must not imagine that naming a horse is the same as putting a bit into his mouth. If, becoming restive under the phrase "mere ethics," one insists upon making ethical ideals a norm for the whole of experience, what happens is the very effort at completion, unification, and conservation of values to which the name religion is here given.

qualities of the things desired. The German consciousness and the English consciousness are religious in exactly the same sense. Each is certain that God is on its side, and that the enemy is moved by base motives. On each side there are such ethical phenomena as sense of obligation, postponement of self-regard, submission to discipline, self-sacrifice, and the glow of a good conscience. Each side is sustained and calmed in the horrible welter by trust in the God of might and of justice. In the third place (I anticipate principles that will be discussed in later chapters), the idea of God is here in process of derivation from the form and the interests of the social organization. A newspaper writer has remarked with entire justice that monotheism is inappropriate and inconvenient for nations that are fighting for nationalism. It will be found, I think, that only to the extent that people are able to criticize the acts and purposes of their own nation from the standpoint of world-welfare is there any vital monotheism at all. That is, just as the intensity of faith reflects the intensity and unification of values, so the breadth of faith reflects the breadth of social outlook and self-criticism. On the other hand, it is not improbable that the idea of one only God, which is already held in a somewhat wavering fashion, will assist in organizing a world-society.

CHAPTER V

RACIAL BEGINNINGS IN RELIGION

Not only is it difficult to find out just what the lower races do in the way of religion, and why they do it; it is difficult for us who are not anthropologists to understand the findings of anthropology. In the present chapter we must make an effort to reverse many of our customary notions of how men act, and think, and feel. Thus:

1. If you ask me in what sense I am religious, you throw me back upon myself as an individual. I say, "Whatever life may mean to others, to me it means so and so." If, now, we imagine that such personal realizations are the first things in religion, and that the earliest religious group or community is an aggregate of such individuals, we reverse the facts. The religious individual is a late and high development out of the religious group.[1] How a group as such can be religious we can see, however, by recalling our own experiences as members of crowds— a college class, a political meeting, or an audience at a concert. Under such conditions it is perfectly natural for us to feel and act and even think in ways that are impossible to us in private.

[1] Not until the national-religious consciousness of Israel had been battered down by other nations did the notion of a direct personal relation to Jahwe take firm root. Ezekiel, chap. 28, transfers the notion of guilt and innocence from nation or family lineage to the individual.

2. The early group was not a merely impulsive mass, like a mob.[1] It had definite, complicated, and rigidly enforced ways called customs. Custom is "the way we do." It is orally transmitted from one generation to another, largely in initiation ceremonies that induct adolescent boys into the life of mature men. Custom is enforced upon any possibly recalcitrant individual, not only by social scorns and disabilities, but also by terrible fears of unseen beings. Now, early religion is a body of customs, a group possession, in which the individual shares "of course" rather than by personal conviction. He raises no questions, he sees no need of an inner life.

3. The interests of the group are narrow, and they include only a minimum of what we mean among ourselves by "intellectual interest." The things that occupy early man are food-getting, marriage, birth, sickness, death, initiation, war, protection from beasts and from the weather. These are the interests that underlie the beginnings of religious as well as other customs. Causal inferences as such, wonder at nature, and effort to think consistently are far less in evidence.

[1] Strictly "primitive man" is a more or less speculative entity. Even if we take as primitive the Congo pygmies and similar types (W. Wundt, *Elemente der Völkerpsychologie* [Leipzig, 1913], pp. 12–22), it does not follow that their ways will yield the greatest possible illumination as to the beginnings of religion. Not until the evolution has proceeded an appreciable distance are the data present for defining the problem of origins. The study of beginnings is a study of something that has begun. In the present chapter "early group" implies a stage of culture in which religion is, so to say, just articulate—it utters itself in ways sufficiently stable and sufficiently institutional to enable us, looking both backward and forward, to discern the direction of the mental movement.

Such intellectual life as exists is, indeed, closely connected with religious rites and ceremonies, but it consists for the most part of crude picture-thinking, which is the direct, unreflective product of emotions primarily connected with the interests already named.

4. Life is not departmentalized as with us. Religion, morality, and law are as yet an undivided mass. Totemism, for example, is at once a form of tribal organization with various laws, consequently a body of prescriptions for individual conduct, and finally a kind of religion.

5. The whole is to be thought of as instinct action passing up through group consciousness (custom) toward personal experience and reflection. Basal to all that men do is instinct action; it does not express an antecedent idea, but under the stimulus of accompanying pleasures and pains it gives rise to discrimination and so to ideas as patterns for future conduct. Action is definitely adjusted before ideas become definite. Further, the first programs of action are those in which the instinctive impulses of an individual are restrained and organized, not by his own reflection, but by the direct pressure of the group upon him. No doubt the variant individual, the relatively great man, has always influenced others to a special degree, but in earliest society he and they are alike caught up in the common movement of the group.

We are now ready to note the phenomena of early tribal life to which we may ascribe religious significance. Let us begin with what is most external and obvious, reserving for the next chapter a further word as to the inner significance of the whole.

1. The tribe or clan has a formal ritual or certain ceremonies connected with the food supply, and intended to help in securing it. Typical of such ceremonies are mimetic "dances" representing the animal or plant from which food is obtained. Often an animal mask is worn, or a skin, or antlers. Various objects connected, or supposed to be connected, with the source of food are employed, as meal, water, snakes (e.g., the Moki snake dance), or the whole or a part of a food animal. The ceremony is likely to include a feast in which the food animal is devoured. The obvious inutility of such acts tempts us to think of them as "mere ceremonies" or as merely dramatic performances. This temptation is strengthened when we discover that the performers are commonly unable to give a coherent reason for what they do. To a considerable extent the original reason has been forgotten. Nevertheless, sufficient traces of ancient meanings remain in the mythical tales connected with the ceremonies, and particularly in the acts performed, the instruments used, the time of the year, etc., to enable us to judge with certainty that these food ceremonies were originally intended as participation in the actual work of food-getting—rain-making, for example. The type of thinking here involved will presently be described under the head of "Magic."

2. There are ceremonies, largely mimetic, connected with war, as the "ghost dance" of certain American Indians. These ceremonies are originally an attempted manipulation of the forces upon which victory is supposed to depend.

3. Adolescent boys are initiated into the tribal secrets and customs, and sometimes girls are introduced

to adulthood, with elaborate and solemn rites. In the case of the girls the reference is to prospective marriage. With the boys the reference is to such functions as the chase, war, and the men's secret society, with its traditionary lore and its methods of governing the tribe. The initiation rites are sometimes prolonged and intricate. Commonly the boy is subjected to tests, which really constitute training, of his courage and of his ability to endure pain. Inspirations in the form of dreams or visions are sometimes sought and obtained.

4. There are rites connected with marriage, birth, and broadly with sex. Sex consciousness is, in fact, prominent in religion even up to some of its highly developed forms. The spring festival referred at once to the rebirth of vegetation, the yeaning of animals (note the prominence of the bull, the ram, etc.), and to human reproduction (hence phallic symbols, and even sexual license).

5. A certain member of the group, the medicine man or shaman (equivalent terms), has particularly close relation to all these affairs. He is a specialist in things religious, the predecessor of priesthoods. He goes into trances, has visions, is a soothsayer, foretells events, detects criminals, prepares charms and amulets, expels the demons from sick bodies, uses suggestion and hypnosis upon both himself and others. He is largely a trickster, but a half-believing one, nevertheless, because of the elements in his practice, chiefly suggestion and self-hypnosis, that he does not control by trickery.

Coming, now, to closer quarters with these phenomena, we note that at one point or another they represent both the social organization and current ideas as to how the important values of life are secured.

1. *Totemism.*—Each clan is designated by the name of some object, usually an animal, sometimes a plant. One clan is the Eagles, another the Kangaroos, and so on. The Eagles are blood-relatives of all eagles by virtue of descent from a common ancestral eagle about whom imaginative tales (myths) gather. An Eagle will not ordinarily kill an eagle. Even if the totem animal is good for food, his life is sacred, except that it may be taken (but with apologies) in emergencies, and except, also, that he is eaten at ceremonial feasts of the clan. Now, this eating of a totem animal is not mere eating as we think it; rather, the savage believes that he thus absorbs something of the strength, or courage, or cunning of the species. Nay, more; not only is the totem animal, as we have seen, a sacred animal, but by partaking of it one arrives at the very source of power and is united with it. The feast is a sacrament.

2. *Mana.*—The totem animal has its power or cunning, and it is sacred because it has *mana* (which has various names among different tribes, as *orenda, wakonda,* etc.). Men eat the totem animal in order to obtain *mana.* A large endowment of *mana* is what gives the medicine man his skill. The successful hunter or warrior succeeds because he has *mana;* the unsuccessful one lacks it. The spirits all have it. This is what *mana* is. It is, so to say, the source of what is important. It is not defined to thought as either personal or impersonal, for the distinction between personal and impersonal has not yet begun to be clear. Yet the idea of *mana* has been hastily interpreted as "high gods of low peoples" and even as an aboriginal monotheism.

3. *Taboo.*—We have seen that the totem animal must not be killed like other animals, or subjected to ordinary uses; he is taboo. A person who violates this taboo becomes himself taboo; he, in turn, must not be touched until ceremonies (such as lustrations) for removing the taint have been performed. From the totem animal taboo develops outward in various directions. Articles connected with the sacred meal or with the tribal initiation; the spot where the solemn ceremony of initiation is performed; the time of its performance; the name of the totem; the person of the chief and his property—all these have been taboo in one place or another. The priestly code of the Old Testament, with its minute prescriptions concerning the "clean" and the "unclean," and concerning the "holy" things that must not be touched, together with the avoidance of the use of the name Jahwe, illustrates taboo in a highly developed form. "Clean" and "holy" have here a sense far different from our ordinary usage. To early thought both the powerfully good and the mysteriously evil are taboo. The dead body of a man is held in especial horror—it is taboo. A woman is taboo at childbirth. These prohibitions and many like them are enforced by fear. Whoever violates one of them delivers himself over thereby to evil powers that may work him all manner of harm. The idea here is not infection in our medical sense, but rather a putting of one's self under the influence of hostile powers not clearly defined.

4. *Magic.*—Among low types of savages magic is omnipresent. To see what it is, let us examine some instances. For example, women are found wearing in their hair combs upon which are inscribed symbolic

marks for keeping away the diseases that the wearer fears. A hunter, similarly, scratches upon his weapon some mark, such as an animal figure, to insure success. To produce a shower, water is sprinkled or a gourd rattle is sounded. To injure an enemy, one makes an image of him and pricks or burns it, or one obtains some of his hair or finger-nail parings and treats them in a similar manner. Three ideas are here commonly assumed: that a part separated from the whole (as nail parings, or even one's name) still influences the whole (sympathetic magic); that imitating anything, which is possibly thought of as manipulating an actual part of it, tends to bring the action itself to pass (imitative magic); and that spirits (demons in the broad sense, not merely evil beings) can be induced or compelled to work for men to produce either good or evil. That we are here within the atmosphere of *mana* also is clear from the fact that the medicine man, who is such by virtue of his peculiar possession of *mana*, is chief magician.

5. *Spiritism.*—We have just seen that magic is largely a commerce with spirits. But we must now notice that "sympathetic" and "imitative" magic existed before the notion of spirits had become definite. Animism, in the sense of belief in a soul separable from the body and therefore able to survive bodily death, was achieved only through considerable reflection, which may have required a long period of time. Probably the first interpretation of death did not regard it as ending what we have come to call life, but only as modifying it. The dead man was the same sort of object that he was before, but with circumscribed powers. Even when the body decayed, something of the man hovered around

the spot. Indeed, to prevent so feared a being from wandering about, the body was sometimes fastened in its place, a stake being driven through it into the ground, or a pile of stones being laid upon it. But various experiences—men seen in dreams and hallucinations, for example—led to the notion that a man has a "second" that can wander abroad. At death, of course, it takes its final departure from the body, and thenceforth leads the life of a spirit or demon in the full sense of the word. When this belief has been reached, magic becomes to a considerable extent spiritism in practical operation, that is, the influencing of events by first influencing or controlling spirits that have power over events. Magical processes mediate both good (so-called white magic) and evil (black magic). Commonly, however, magic comes under the ban, or at least disapproval, of society as something dark and dangerous. It becomes a secret practice, employable by individuals, in contrast with the ceremony of the tribal or established religion. When one people conquers another, the gods of the conquered are likely to live on as the arch-spirits of magic. Mediaeval witchcraft, which was transplanted to the American colonies, had its roots in the pagan religions that Christianity supplanted. This particular magic became a "diabolical" counterpart of Christianity. There was a supreme evil divinity, with angelic subordinates and with sacraments and festivals; and there was supposed to be an obedient society of men, its members signed and sealed, to correspond with the church.

6. *The myth.*—Broadly considered, the myth is simply the thought aspect of any well-established practice of the sort now outlined. Mythology is picture-thinking, a

mass of stories, of which we have a living specimen in our own Santa Claus tales. These stories are authorless, being the common product, as they are the common possession, of the group; howbeit, quicker minds must have contributed more than slower minds to the structure. Myths are at first believed, just as children believe in Santa Claus. In some cases the retelling of the myth is a part of a solemn ceremony, and then the tale itself is supposed to have potency with respect to the beings that it tells about. What occasions give rise to myths, and what determines their content? So much of mythology concerns the sun and the other celestial bodies that one recent theory would have it that mythology as a whole is man's early interpretation of the prominent or striking phenomena of the sky. Again, it has been thought that, finding himself using certain names and titles having original reference to animals, he invented tales to fit the names. It is as if we should explain the fact that a certain white man is called Mr. Black by imagining a black ancestor who transformed his skin to white. Finally, it is held that the myth is the intellectual expression of the ceremony, often an attempt to account for it. Whereas the ceremony was once regarded by some students as a dramatic representation of an antecedent myth, a later view is that, finding themselves performing a customary rite, men gave a quasi-rational color to their acts by gradually elaborating a myth or a set of myths.

The matter is complicated, but all in all the last is the general direction in which we find the richest results. The decisive facts, it appears, are these: (*a*) Comparison of the content of many a people's myths with the content of its ceremonies makes clear that the two are most intimately related. (b) But the ceremony originated in an attempt to repeat some supposedly effective part of an early utility act, such as hunting, fishing, or planting and reaping. (c) With early men, as with us, habitual social activities that have a strong emotional accompaniment tend to become a ritual which survives its first occasion, and persists even after its original significance is forgotten. Under such conditions imagination and reflection produce reasons for the act. Afterthoughts which suppose themselves to be forethoughts are common at all stages of culture. For example, the ordinary notions as to why human beings wear clothes are almost parallel to mythology. A still better example is the reason for the Sabbath given in one of the creation stories—we rest on the seventh day because God did so when he created the world. Here the custom, already existing, gives rise to a fanciful causal account of it. (d) But the myth is not held down to its original function or occasion—it grows with growing interests and with growing insights. For example, the Greek spring festival, originally intended to promote fertility, gathers a considerable part of its thought content about the snake, which is supposed to fertilize the earth. But the snake does not end here; it lives on in wider reaches of thought as a phallic object, as sacred to Asklepios the healer, and in close relation even to Hermes and Zeus.[1] Here solar mythology appears thoroughly fused with fertility mythology, which, in turn, springs out of festivals in which men originally believed that they were practically assisting the processes of reproduction and growth.

[1] Harrison, *Themis*, chap. viii.

(*e*) Finally, with increasing culture, the myth yields up its supposed literal truth, and becomes a foundation for drama, poetry, and a reasoned theology.

7. *Fetishism.*—A fetish is an inanimate object, known to be such, but supposed to be the abode, for the time being at least, of a spirit, or at least of some sort of superior potency that makes it of special value to its possessor. Doubtless the earliest fetishes were simply natural objects of such unusual form as to awaken astonishment, or so related to one's pleasure and pain as to awaken unusual emotion. Later, appropriate objects are *made into* fetishes by the medicine man or "witch doctor"—that is, he selects or compounds the object and causes a spirit or potency to enter it. The possessor is likely to carry it upon his person to insure good luck. If it does not work, it may receive a scolding or a beating, and ultimately it may be thrown away and a new fetish procured. This description applies particularly to Africa.[1] Fetishism is perhaps not so much a stage in the general development of religion as a fungous or degenerate growth. It is magic in its lowest form, which involves also spiritism in its lowest form. It is arbitrary, individualistic, often anti-social.

We are at last ready to attempt a functional characterization of early religion. Our fundamental questions are, What types of value-consciousness prevailed? and What measures were taken to complete, unify, and conserve the values that were recognized? As to the recognized values, we shall come near to the whole truth if we think in each case of a small group of men (horde, clan, tribe) struggling to maintain and perpetuate

[1] R. H. Nassau, *Fetishism in West Africa* (New York, 1904).

itself as a group, and therefore absorbed in co-operative food-getting, in co-operative protection from beasts, weather, and human enemies, and in the strict regulation of a few social relations (as marriage), all of which is thought of as dependent in part upon a mysterious, diffused power (*mana*) and in part upon more specific beings of demonic, yet human, type. The measures taken, over and above what we count as industry (hunting, herding, agriculture), are the ceremonies and festivals already described. Through these ceremonies tribal man looks for abundant food, success against enemies of all kinds, and maintenance of the social order. To complete their values, men here seek *plenty;* to conserve them, men seek to produce a *stable social order* that shall be continuously in favorable touch with the powers upon which food and other goods depend; to unify values, the measure is again a social one, namely, the production in the individual of willing, or rather automatic, *subordination of desires to social standards* (customs), *which in turn the group shares with a larger social or quasi-social order* (the totem species, *mana*, spirits of ancestors). Belief in *mana* is one important root of the distinct god-belief that later appears. The totemic common meal will give place to sacrifice and a merely symbolic eating of the god. The ceremony will become worship. The social order that supports the ceremony will broaden into nation, church, humanity. The social ideal will grow refined and humane, and its scope will enlarge even to the thought of a spiritual-moral world-order, either existing or to be achieved. Finally, the social focusing of life's values, here forced by custom, will ultimately emancipate the individual from custom and lead him into inner freedom that more than fulfils the law.

Such, in very brief, is early religion, and such is our own spiritual lineage. We see: (1) that religion is present among early men because the functions of religion with respect to values are performed, rather than because any particular type of ideation or of belief prevails; (2) that early religion comprehends every interest that is felt to be important; (3) that it springs directly out of instinctive behavior, such as food-getting, marrying, fighting; (4) that religion grows in a peculiar way out of the social instincts that underlie custom and group organization; (5) that, as far as origins are concerned, religion is continuous with magic and spiritism, though it often tends, as we shall see, to grow apart from them; (6) finally, that, though animal gods or quasi-gods preceded gods in human form, nevertheless anthropomorphism is fundamental to the whole.

Concerning magic and anthropomorphism a word or two more must be said. As to the relation of magic to religion, three positions have been held. Frazer at one time was of the opinion (subsequently modified) that religion arose because magic, which preceded it, did not work.[1] Leuba contends at great length that magic and religion are separate in origin and in inner principle; the mark of magic being *control* of hidden powers; that of religion *persuasion* of psychic beings.[2] King holds that, though religion and magic have a common root, magic is or tends to be an individual, non-social, and often anti-social use of the same sort of powers that religion

[1] J. G. Frazer, *The Golden Bough.*

[2] *A Psychological Study of Religion*, Part II.

employs.[1] The following facts seem to be of decisive importance for this whole problem: (*a*) Religious ceremonies in which prayer is used to persuade a god are historically continuous with ceremonies in which effects are supposed to be wrought otherwise than by psychic process, for example, by eating the totem animal. On the other hand, in developed religions gods are sometimes controlled rather than persuaded.[2] Further, magic seeks much the same values as religion, such as health, protection from enemies, and success of various sorts, and the religious and the magical methods of seeking these values have such common root ideas as influencing the whole through a part of it (as getting influence over a god by using his name), and securing something by imitating it (mimetic dance, dramatic rehearsal of the adventures of the god, symbolical sacrament). Finally, *mana* (the taproot of god-belief) and also spirits are used by the medicine man, who is the precursor of priesthoods at the same time that he is head magician. All this looks toward a fundamental unity of origin and inner principle. (*b*) Numberless ways that we can observe among ourselves bring the magical and the religious into the closest relation. A child declared that a prayer by a certain minister was of no avail because he prayed with his eyes open. Christians who refuse to pray except in the name of Jesus display an attitude that is obviously a survival of the magical use of names. Mothers are

---

[1] *Development of Religion*, chap. vii.

[2] J. H. Breasted, *Development of Religion and Thought in Ancient Egypt* (New York, 1912), shows that for a long period Egyptian religion was largely a body of devices for getting power over the gods (see p. x and Lecture VIII).

anxious about their babies until the rite of baptism has been administered. Multitudes wear amulets upon a cord around the neck, referring the protective effect to some saint. By a word priests change bread and wine into flesh and blood. It requires no stretching of either term to call these things either religion or magic. (c) On the other hand, however, we see religion, or at least official religion, separating itself from magic and condemning it. "Thou shalt not suffer a witch to live." Traffic with the gods of a conquered people is by the conquerors condemned as diabolical magic. Magic, further, can be and is practiced in secret, and by individuals, whereas the religious ceremony is above all things a group act for group ends.

The conclusion toward which these facts point is that, though magic and religion have a common origin and are historically and psychologically continuous with each other, there is a genuine and profound difference. Religion organizes life's values and seeks them socially; magic fixes upon any particular value and seeks it individually or at least independently of the larger social order. Because it lacks the social quality of religion, magic magnifies wonders, and glories in supposed events and connections that lack moral significance. Thus it is that magic so commonly seeks out supposed secret laws of nature in order to control events, whereas religion, all in all, brings worshipers into submission to beings of a social sort.

Let us notice, finally, the anthropomorphic character of the whole movement. Certain external facts are plain. Before men believed in gods having the human figure, the totemic animal ancestor was a quasi-divinity. Not only so, but the totem animal is intimately associated with early gods that have the human form. The human god transforms himself into the animal; or is part animal, part man; or is accompanied by the animal; or bears the figure of the animal on his clothing—in short, the human god evolves from the animal. Therefore, it is said, theriomorphism precedes anthropomorphism. But a distinction must be made between two senses of the term form (-*morphism*), between the physiological sense and the psychological. The order *therio-* to *anthropo-* is primarily physiological. Back of it is the psychological fact that the qualities of men, *as men then conceived these qualities*, were attributed to the totem animal, especially the totemic ancestor. To suppose that primitive man formed his notions of animals by a strictly objective procedure like that of our naturalists at their best is to invert the actual way of the mind. No, the bear is a brother or an ancestor because of the manlike thought and motive that the Indian thinks into him. Anthropomorphism, in the psychological sense, inheres in religion as such from the beginning.

APPENDIX

THE RELATION OF THE SEXUAL INSTINCT TO RELIGION

Various writers have held that the psychical origin and the permanent psychical support of religion are to be found in the sexual life. The facts that give rise to this theory are as follows: (1) the wide distribution of gods of procreation, of phallic symbols, and of sexual acts as a part of religious ceremonial; (2) the discovery of a sexual factor in mental disorders that take the form of religious excitement, depression, or delusion; (3) the existence of various sects that connect spiritual yearning or perfection directly with sex, either in the way of indulgence or in the way of suppression; the phenomena range from license on the one hand to the sanctification of virginity on the other, with polygamy and various other sorts of control between; (4) the imagery of courtship and marriage that figures so largely in mystical literature, together with evidence that sexual sensations and desire, in certain individuals, are a factor in mystical ecstasy; (5) the close connection between conversion experiences and adolescence; (6) the emphasis upon "love" in the Christian religion.

These facts indicate some sort of psychical connection between sex and religion. But to determine what this connection is we must have a more scientific method than that which seeks to explain religion by picking out some one widespread phenomenon that happens to attract one's attention. By this loose method a pretty strong case could be made for the proposition that fear is the psychical origin and support of religion, or that economic interest is *the* controlling one. The problem, too, needs to be sharpened. On the one hand, there must be such an inventory of original human nature as will put us on the lookout for all the elements in the great complex called religion. On the other hand, pains must be taken not to oversimplify, particularly as regards early religion. Further, we must face the question, How are instincts as a whole related to the desires that are usually regarded as higher?

Postponing to later chapters the discussion of various phases of this problem, I shall at this point briefly indicate the conclusions toward which recent studies of original nature, of primitive religion, and of individual religious experience in higher religions seem to be tending with respect to the general relation of the sexual instinct to religion: (1) The earliest religion known to us is not an individual experience (as might be the case if sexual instinct were the sole source) but a group enterprise. (2) The instinctive basis of social grouping is complex, sex being only one factor. (3) The interests of the earliest religious groups known to us include those of sex, but other interests, such as the economic, are always prominent. (4) Throughout the history of religion this complexity prevails. The act of making war, or of administering justice, or of protesting against the oppression of the poor, or of repentance for any kind of wrongdoing, or of aspiring toward any ideal good, may have a religious aspect *directly*—that is, because of its own felt importance. (5) Phallic symbolism, which is widespread, appears commonly in connection with rites that have to do with the fertility of the earth, that is, with the food supply. This is true, for example, of the serpent, and of whatever phallic symbols the "high places" of the Old Testament bore. The sex interest, that is to say, does not necessarily dominate religion even here. (6) Where sex interest does succeed in dominating religion, as in the worship of Astarte, it is opposed and finally defeated by religion, not by irreligion. (7) Some of the emotional "reverberations" of sex, as in adolescence, have a pervasive influence which religion shares along with the social, the aesthetic, and the intellectual life. But in religion, as in social organization, art, and science, this is only one factor of a complex. (8) In some notable instances religion takes a social-ethical ideal as its cause. The Christian principle of "love" is an example. Here it is *parental* instinct that comes most clearly to expression. It has, in fact, the controlling place, for the love that is required between men is that of brothers, the sons of a common father.

The interesting suggestion has been made that primitive man's first notion of spirit possession and of transcendent mystery may have arisen directly from the intensity of feeling and of emotion in sexual intercourse, together with the involuntary character of sex excitement. Hence it is inferred that the first objects of worship were the sexual organs, and that the first gods were simply imaginative representations of sex experience.[1] The origin of religion in the race must doubtless be sought in some sort or sorts of excitement that jogged primitive man out of his habitual modes of conduct. There is plenty of evidence that sex excitement has a place here, but this evidence is paralleled point for point by evidence of the presence of other sorts of intense excitement also. The capacity of sexual excitement to awaken new modes of conduct or of thought, moreover, was limited by the fact that, sexual promiscuity or at least very early sexual union being allowed, desire was promptly satisfied, and the strains that fixate attention

[1] See Theodore Schroeder, "Erotogenese der Religion," *Zeitschrift für Religionspsychologie*, I (1908), 445–55.

for a considerable period were lacking. That is, the sexual life tended to have the character of habit and commonplaceness. On the other hand, the uncertainty of the food supply and the vicissitudes of war and of disease created situations most favorable to the sort of repeated fixation of attention out of which a new mode of conduct and of thought emerges. Hence the great prominence in early religion of ceremonies connected with the food supply and with the maintenance of group solidarity. For a discussion of religion in adolescence, see the chapter on "Conversion."

CHAPTER VI

THE GENESIS OF THE IDEA OF GOD

The term "god" connotes qualities not clearly present in either spirits or *mana*. The spirits with which early man had dealings were often vague, shifty, lacking in the qualities that command respect. One might say that they were objectifications of men's unorganized impulses. *Mana*, especially as contained in the totem ancestor, is more stable and awe-inspiring. Yet it lacks clear individuality. The gods, on the other hand, are manlike, have individuality or character, and are relatively exalted. Men establish relations with them by prayer and by various relatively permanent social arrangements, such as vows and covenants. We have now to ask how it is that, starting without any god-idea at all, men got themselves gods.

Because of our traditions, many of us tend, whenever "the idea of God" is mentioned, to think of it as an explanatory or philosophical concept. Consequently, when inquiry is made as to its origin, we are prone to ask from what facts early men might have reasonably inferred the presence of divine beings. But it is certain that the genesis of the idea is not to be found in the controlled thinking that we call philosophy. The idea reaches back to, and is continuous with, *mana* and the spirits, which, in turn, are continuous with still more inchoate conceptions. Our search will not stop short of the crude impressionism in which thinking started.

Our problem is twofold: first, to find out what ideas of a more elementary sort were used in building the god-idea, and, secondly, to determine the functions involved, the desires that found satisfaction in or through it.

Five elements commonly appear in the early mythological representations of the gods: (1) the form or the ways of some species of animal; (2) the form and the ways of man; (3) the ways of spirits, as hyper-rapid movement, making one's self invisible, taking possession of a man or an animal;[1] (4) some phenomenon or process of nature; (5) *mana*. In a sense each of these five may be regarded as an origin of the god-idea, but no one of them is *the* origin. Nor is there a single, exclusive line of descent. Individual men may have been deified, but euhemerism is clearly in error in supposing that all worship is worship of the dead. Even the hero-gods of Greece, it appears, are not reminiscences of great civilizers or deliverers, but of early fertility festivals.[2] Again, divine beings arise out of spiritism, and no doubt the notion of disembodied spirits has played a part in all developed god-ideas. According to Wundt, the god-idea proper arises through fusion of two antecedent ideas, demon and hero. Yet nature-powers, too, have had a part in the entire development. The fruitful earth, the fructifying rain, the progression of the seasons, the sun and the moon, the sea, the mountains—elements like

[1] This fact throws light upon the question whether magic and religion have separate origins. *The gods themselves are to a large extent magicians.* By a word, or by the use of some talisman, they impose their arbitrary will upon nature.

[2] Harrison, *Themis*, particularly p. 215.

these commonly appear in early god-ideas. And, in all and through all, there runs the idea of *mana*, the "it" that separates the very important from the commonplace.

In spite of the tendency of religion toward conservatism, these elements have been mobile. A people's conception of its god grows and changes with the changing experience of the people. Gods, like men, can take on new interests and occupations, or move from one realm to another. They are influenced by the company they keep, as is evident from changes that follow fresh intercourse between two religions. They can even coalesce with one another.[1]

In the sense of taking a thing to pieces, we have here, in brief, the genesis of the god-idea. But we still need to inquire what controls these combinations and recombinations. Why are they made at all? *What are men about* in the whole process, and why do they single out just these elements and form just these combinations? The answer is difficult, chiefly because it requires on our part desophisticated imagination. How would we ourselves spontaneously act, or tend to act, in the simple situations of early man? Let us see how we do act when, being taken off our guard, we fail to use the accumulated wisdom of the race. A man who unexpectedly pounds his thumb with a hammer gets angry with it. One who stubs his toe kicks the offending obstacle. If a knotty stick of wood "refuses" to split, we "get our dander up"

[1] These processes are excellently illustrated in the religion of Egypt, and in the part that it contributed to the religious syncretism of the Roman Empire. See J. H. Breasted, *Development of Religion and Thought in Ancient Egypt* (New York, 1912).

and "go for it" with savage blows. In our unsophisticated moments we "contend" with storms; at the height of such a contest one who manages a canoe or a boat, his attention strained upon the one issue, goes through an experience not unlike that of a fencer or of a wrestler. How often, when one is weary or "all out of sorts," one feels, and even says, "Everything seems to be against me." On the other hand, a happy child was heard to say, "I love everything, and everything loves me!" How fond we become of things that are closely associated with our hours of freedom and happiness, as in sports. A fishing-rod, a canoe, a camp ax, a bicycle, an engine that works well—we actually pet and fondle them! And the spots where our profounder happiness has come—the old home, the college, a scene of deep friendship or love—are "sacred," set apart from ordinary places, because our experience in them has become, as it were, a part of them. In short, emotional thinking tends to transfer the glow of our minds to the object of our thoughts. This is called in German *Einfühlung*. That which, to our cooler thinking, is only a "thing," becomes by *Einfühlung* friendly or unfriendly. Now, one has only to think of the greater extent to which this is characteristic of childhood, and then to consider that mind in its early stages lacked most of the knowledge of "mere things" with which we check our own emotional thinking, to get a clue to the functional origin of god-ideas.[1]

---

[1] The way in which emotional thinking calls for objects to express itself upon is illustrated by the story of a Shekyani chief, Ogwedembe, whose sister, married to a member of the Mpongwe tribe, had died. Ogwedembe, having come to the funeral, kept saying, "I wish my

Now and then a whole group of modern men and women, under a sudden shock or an excessive strain, seems to be transferred into a world of personal or quasi-personal meanings. The "Titanic" survivors who were rescued by the "Carpathia," so Stanton Coit, an eyewitness, relates, seemed not to be stunned and crushed but "lifted into an atmosphere of vision where self-centered suffering merges into some mystic meaning. . . . . We were all one, not only with one another, but with the cosmic being that for the time had seemed so cruel."[1] Still more significant is Professor James's analysis of his own attitudes and those of others on the occasion of the great California earthquake, which overtook him at Stanford University. "As soon as I could think," he says, "I discerned retrospectively certain peculiar ways in which my consciousness had taken in the phenomenon. These ways were quite spontaneous and, so to speak, inevitable and irresistible. First, I personified the earthquake as a permanent individual entity. . . . . Animus and intent were never more present in any human action, nor did any human activity ever more definitely point back to a living agent as its source and origin. All whom I consulted on the point agreed as to this feature in their experience. 'It expressed intention,' 'It was vicious,' 'It was bent on

sister had not been married to a Mpongwe, for it is not your custom to shed blood for this cause. But I feel a great desire to kill someone. If this had been a Shakyani marriage, I would have gone from town to town killing whom I chose." The Mpongwe replied, "But we have no such custom." He answered, "Yes, I know that; I only said what I would like to do, though your tribal custom will not allow me to do it."
—R. H. Nassau, *Fetishism in West Africa* (New York, 1904), pp. 311 f.

[1] *The Outlook*, April 27, 1912, pp. 894 f.

destruction,' 'It wanted to show its power,' or what not. To me it simply wanted to manifest the full meaning of its name. But what was this 'It'? To some, apparently, a vague, demoniac power; to me an individualized thing."[1]

With these clues in mind, let us imagine what the world must have seemed like to our early ancestors. What were the occasions of emotional excitement, and upon what object was attention likely to focus on each occasion? This object, whatever it may be to us sophisticated mortals, was to our ancestors a living thing, with desires and attitudes of its own. Animals, of course, were such objects, especially animals that were feared, those that were used for food, those whose special traits (courage, cunning, etc.) attracted notice, and those that were associated (in the mind of the savage) with important events, such as the revival of food-yielding plants in the spring. Where anxiety for the food supply is common, a food animal or even plant becomes a friend, perhaps a relative. To feel the reality of the totemic relationship was probably easier than it is for us to feel our racial unity with the African pygmies. To feel the wonder of an animal's courage or cunning was to attribute *mana* to him. If he was the totem animal, eating him at the tribal festival was a method of obtaining some of his *mana*. Further, since he was a relative, in the tribal dance that accompanied the meal men wore the animal's skin or head, or masks representing him. Just as a small child will shrink in terror from a man who, without any disguise, impersonates a bear by "going on all fours"

[1] Quoted by the *Boston Transcript*, June 6, 1906, from the *Youth's Companion*.

and growling, so to tribal men the mask-wearer was for the time being much more than an ordinary man: The human and the extra-human fused. Here we have all the elements and motives necessary for belief in exalted beings having qualities of both men and animals. These elements are consolidated into a tradition by the recurring festival, with its retelling of the old stories and its re-enactment of the ancient ceremonies under conditions, such as night, secrecy, and prolonged strain of attention, that favor the reinstatement of the emotion. What gives vitality to the whole is the feeling that great interests are at stake—food, health, all kinds of success, even unnamed and vague welfare and illfare.

In the general characteristics of emotional thinking we have the basis for spiritistic beliefs also. The origin of religion used to be sought in animism, or the belief that objects are inhabited by spirits. Such belief is, indeed, universal at certain levels of culture, and it has had an important part in the evolution of religion. The question is, What part? Clearly, animism as such is simply a general level of thought. It contributes something to the god-idea, but it is not of itself religion. We must still search for the motives, the life-issues. Moreover, animism is not a strictly primitive form, even of thought. It involves the notion of a difference between spirit and body, a notion that could have been achieved only through a considerable process. As the achievement of this notion is, of course, one phase of religious evolution, a preanimistic stage of religion is now recognized.

Let us try, then, to represent to ourselves how the idea of a spirit separable from the body arose. On the

converse side, this is the question how men first began
to think of body as separable from spirit. Not that all
objects whatsoever were at one time thought of as alive
and friendly or unfriendly; for objects habitually present without emotional accompaniments were probably
as colorless to early man as they are to us. But this
does not mean that early man thought of them specifically as not alive, as "mere" things; it means, rather,
that he did not raise the question. But any one of these
habitually colorless things might, merely by the laws
of mental association, become the focus of emotional
interest and therefore reveal itself as alive like a man.
Now, to be alive like a man was not, at first, to be compounded of soul and body, but just to have the breath
of life (*anima*). The Hebrew creation myth says that
God "breathed into his nostrils the breath of life, and
man became a living soul." The question, then, is how
this bodily soul came to be thought of as a spirit, that
is (primarily), a second or double capable of existence
on its own account and of uniting itself with bodies,
whether human, animal, or other. An old theory has
it that from the shadow that accompanies a man but is
intangible; from the reflection of one's face in a pool;
from dream memories in which one recalls having been
at a distance from the spot in which one's body certainly
lay; and from visions, at night or by day, of persons
whose bodies are at a distance or perhaps buried, men
inferred the existence of a man within a man, but separable from the tangible body. Wundt adds the experience
of trance, in which the body seems strange or "not here."
This "second" is still body, but intangible—a ghost
through which a sword may be thrust without wounding.

This notion, once reached in respect to man, could be extended to other things—the whole world could be peopled with flitting spirits or demons. Without doubt some such association of ideas occurred, but its effect was merely to render more precise and differentiated the thought factor already described as present from the beginning, namely, the self-projection characteristic of emotional situations. Spirits are at bottom not an intellectual "find"; they are rather a focalized representation of intense experience with its spontaneous *Einfühlung*.

Some important results flowed from the attainment of this notion. First, death received a fairly definite interpretation, at first a terrifying one—that the spirit of a dead man is a malignant power that lingers about the body for a time and then wanders abroad—but later, in the more progressive groups, the more constructive notion of continuity of social bonds between living men and their departed ancestors. Secondly, it became increasingly easy to attribute exalted human qualities to the superior powers. The vagueness of *mana* and the equivocally human nature of the totemic ancestor could not remain unchanged; they became conformed to the image of the human. But, thirdly, the unsocial tendencies of men were objectified in swarms of capricious, even malignant, spirits. There is no absolute dividing line between gods and such spirits; all have human qualities, all are projections of what men felt in themselves when they were excited. Even very great or divine spirits were often tricky, passionate, filled with the cunning of magicians rather than the wisdom and justice of magistrates. But as the larger, more stable interests of society came to be represented in certain spirits, who were approached by prayer and group ceremonial, so the more petty, less social interests were taken over by inferior spirits, who were in some degree controlled by individuals rather than worshiped by the group. Thus arises the opposition between religion and magic and the identification of magic with spiritism.

The prominence of sun, thunder, mountains, and the like in early god-ideas led many students to the supposition that these ideas sprang directly out of wonder at striking phenomena. No doubt there is a grain of truth here. Phenomena that excited strong emotion were doubtless taken as the presence of living things capable of friendly or unfriendly attitudes. But there remains the problem as to how experiences as commonplace as sunshine can awaken such emotion. We know definitely that early ceremonies in which sun, moon, rain, springtime, and autumn are prominent commonly have to do with the food supply. We may fairly infer that, though curiosity as to the causes of striking phenomena was never absent, the chief organizing interests, the ones that could produce recurring emotional excitement with reference to even these commonplace phenomena, were such obvious, vital issues as hunger, sickness, death, marriage, and war. The chief source of the god-idea is organic and social need; free curiosity is secondary.

A general answer can now be given to our second question, *What were men about* when they put all these factors together into god-ideas? It is clear that god-ideas attribute human qualities to the extra-human. This is sometimes called 'imaginative projection of the human self. But to early man there is no "projection" at all; the gods are simply realities of experience when it is most vivid. If he could have phrased his procedure, he might have said something like this: "I feel alive most intensely when with my tribe I wrestle with some sense of common need or rejoice in some common joy. At such moments I realize that our feeling is more than ours; it is something that overwhelms us; it is shared by those beings—ancestors, spirits, nature-powers—that are close to us in our struggle to live. They want what we want; they work with us to obtain it; and they that be with us are stronger than they that be against us."

In short, the genesis of the god-idea is a spontaneous, underived conviction that what is most important for us is *really* important, that is, respected and provided for by the reality upon which we depend. For early man the world of values is the real world.

CHAPTER VII

RELIGION AND THE RELIGIONS

In the earliest stages of culture religion is much the same the world over. The similarity is, in fact, so great that one inevitably asks whether communication has not taken place between the most remote and mutually inaccessible tribes. But religion develops into religions with contrasting or even antagonistic traits. Why this early uniformity and this later lack of it? For answer we must look to the broad general principle already explained, that religion is not a separate interest having a particular character of its own, but rather a way of dealing with interests, an organizing principle among all the values that are recognized at any stage of culture.

The almost uniform character of early religion does not point to a single origin of religious practices at some particular spot whence they have spread over the earth, but to the relative simplicity and uniformity of interests of all men everywhere who are still in the early stages of the conquest of nature. This principle applies to many things besides religion, such as primitive tools. It is not probable that the stone hammer, or the bow and arrow, arose at a single point, but at many points. Just so, the hunting and later the domestication of animals, and the gathering of wild seeds, followed by sowing and reaping, are to be traced to desire for sufficiency and certainty of food in a world that everywhere provides nutritive material of about the same sorts.

So with emotional attitudes; and so with ideas as to the forces involved, and the crude methods for dealing with them. The returning life of spring, for example, could not fail to be met with joyous ceremonies in many parts of the world, and these ceremonies would include many close similarities without any borrowing whatever. All this presupposes, however, some law of evolution whereby, under similar conditions, mental reactions of the same sort enter into the biological order.

On the other hand, growing differentiation of interests affected religion directly. For religion is not a thing by itself; it has no springs other than the impulse to live, to live well, to live a diversified yet organized life, and especially to live socially. To explain the rise of religions, then, we must study the particular factors in the experience of any people that led to specialization of interests. At the same time we must bear in mind tendencies toward organization and systematization that are common to mankind. Seven such factors and tendencies can be recognized:

1. *Geographic situation.*—For example, the Egyptian religion reflects a Nile valley consciousness; the Babylonian, that of the lowlands of the Euphrates; the Scandinavian, a consciousness of the northern forests and the rigors of the northern winter; the Hebrew, of the hill and valley land of Palestine, with its nearness to the great trade route between East and West and yet its possibilities of upland seclusion.

2. *Economic development.*—Herdsmen have one sort of religion, agriculturists another. The sacredness of the cow among the Todas is often adduced as an instance; the struggle between Jahwe worship and Baal worship

likewise. Great accumulations of wealth, as at Bethel in the days of Amos, produce results in worship and in ideals. It is not otherwise with us. Churches whose traditions relate them to an earlier economic order are laboring to understand the religious significance of factory production, with its massing of employees, its massing of capital, and its methods of distributing the product of labor. It is beginning to dawn upon the Protestant consciousness that the Christian religion has never been an independent thing merely acting upon the economic order, but that the religious order and the economic order are two parts of one indissoluble life.

3. *Social and political organization.*—As totemism was at once religion and tribal organization, so the formation of nations was the formation of national religions. Monarchy reflects itself in monarchic notions of divinity. Monotheism cannot arise until there is a large political consciousness. In one notable instance, that of the Egyptian ruler Ikhnaton, we can witness the idea of one only God, great and good, arising directly out of the thought of world-dominion. Ikhnaton's idealism failed to become a religion because the people were not prepared for it. It remained for the prophets of Israel to take up the task. With the battering down of Hebrew national pride by defeat and exile, some change had to take place in the idea of the national god. Some of the prophets, their political outlook broadened to international proportions, conceived the mind of Jahwe to be correspondingly broad—he was God of nations, not merely of one nation. Others, reflecting upon the inner qualities that make rich our social life (as Hosea's reflections upon conjugal affection, and Amos' analysis

of social justice), conceived of ethical tenderness or strength as belonging to the God of all the earth. In Jesus' notion of the Father there were contributions from family organization, national life, and international experiences.

4. *Interaction of peoples.*—The intermingling of peoples, whether by means of war, of migration, or of commerce, exercises an influence upon a people's religion as upon all other elements of culture. A god is taken over, or new forms of worship are adopted, or a dormant motive is stimulated into activity, or a doctrine is accepted. This applies not only to intentional syncretism like that at Rome, but even to would-be exclusive religions. A conquering religion may impose its gods upon the vanquished, but the vanquished faith is likely to mingle with that of the conquerors. This happened after the conquest of Canaan, and it happened with Christianity. Both Christian theology and Christian worship contain elements derived neither from Jesus nor from Judaism, but from the cults that surrounded the early church.

5. *Cultural influences, as philosophy, science, art.*— The earliest culture is not departmentalized as religion plus morals, plus law, plus philosophy and science, plus art and literature; rather, these interests are present without being differentiated from one another. The genealogy of science and philosophy as well as of theology reaches back to mythology. The beginning of the drama is in the so-called mimetic dance, which is a part of a religious ceremony. Another part of it, the chant, and the rude rhythm-making that accompanied it, have much to do with the origin of song and of instrumental

music. Carvings and drawings made for their supposed
magical effect gave rise to sculpture, painting, and writing. The effort to build a house adequate for a god had
much to do with the rise of architecture. Education,
finally, goes back to the initiation ceremony which, both
in itself and in its interim influence, constitutes a training
by society for social ends. It is only in recent times, in
fact, that control of education has passed out of the
hands of the church. But each of these (observation
and thought, song, poetic composition, etc.), broadening
its sphere, became more and more conscious of itself as
an interest *per se*. Where each had heretofore existed
only as a contributor to a whole that can best be called
religion (just because of its wholeness), each came to
assume independent control of itself. In a sense
"religion is the mother of the arts," and of the sciences
too.[1]

This differentiation from religion marks the arrival
of religion at self-consciousness, with specialization of
functions and organs—religious doctrines, literature,
art, priesthoods, and much more. We can now speak
of interaction between religion and the other parts of a
people's culture. The characteristics of religion in a
given instance will depend in part, for example, upon
the status of knowledge. A very accessible case is the
modification of even popular Christianity by modern
science and discovery. The larger world in which we
live is reflected in the idea of God, which has been
immensely enlarged and ennobled within the era of

[1] Hocking, chap. ii, makes some subtle observations on this fertility
of religion, and on the problem, What is left of religion when the arts
are all free?

great geographical, astronomical, physical, and biological discoveries. The influence of the aesthetic arts is more subtle because it works directly within the emotions; yet no one can doubt the religious effect of temple architecture—the solemn colonnade at Thebes, the graceful dignity of the Parthenon, the aspiring mass of a Gothic cathedral. Similarly, the investment of the ritual with aesthetic wealth in tone, color, and movement guides as well as expresses sentiment. When painters and sculptors became interested in the human figure as such, and not merely as a means of representing the gods, art acquired ability to soften and humanize religion, as it has done through a multitude of Madonnas with the Child. On the other hand, the absence of development in any branch of culture means always some difference in religious development. Limit education to a social class, and you will have a religion different from that which will appear in the same people if education becomes universal. The printing press, too, is religiously momentous. In short, we have in these interactions still further evidence that religion is not a separate and independent interest with a history exclusively its own. Even when it takes the form of a special interest it does not become wholly specialized, but remains responsive to all the movements of the arts and sciences that originally sprang from it.

6. *The institutionalizing of religion.*—Our first glimpse of religious origins shows us an institution—a ceremony firmly supported by custom. The sacredness of custom passes on to institutions like priesthoods, temples, systems of doctrine, and sacred laws and literature until in some cases civil government is paralleled in firmness

of organization, in dignity, and even in power by ecclesiastical institutions. Why religion gave itself institutional form is plain to see—important interests of a social sort appeared to require the correct repetition of the effective act, in the first instance some ceremony. But the mere fact that religion has been largely an institutional affair has had significant consequences, some of which are not so plain.

In the first place, it has helped to develop the notion of the secular as against the sacred. The temple and the priests are commonly supposed to be nearer to the gods than are the commonalty. In some instances this has resulted in two codes for conduct.

In the second place, institutions as such resist change. The very act of formulating and organizing anything carries in itself an assumption that here, at this point of time, something has been found that is worthy of preservation. Capital, labor, reputation, and dignity are therefore invested in it. The institutional leaders tend thenceforth to identify their own attitudes with those of the divine being, and thus finally demand the right to legislate for life in general and to exact obedience. The claim of ecclesiastical organizations thus to speak for the god is, historically considered, a demand that the religious spirit shall submit to one or more of its own ancient products.

But, in the third place, there is a much less understood side of the institutionalizing process. In spite of the conservatism of institutions, they are often organs, used in ways they know not of by the life-forces that produced them. Taboo applied to the property of the chief helps to found the general right of property. On the other hand, by establishing the intermediate idea of the ceremonially holy, taboo led the way toward feeling for the ethically holy and right. Ethical content has, in fact, seeped into many an ancient pre-ethical shell. From purification ceremonies intended to remove the effects of broken taboo grew the notion of a purification of the heart. Spells and incantations grew into prayers for favor; these grew into aspiration for universal righteousness. The shell that remains from the original ceremony, or verbal formula, becomes at last more or less consciously a symbol. Christian practice contains many a form into which fresh meaning has come. This is true of baptism (a residual of lustration); the eucharist (a residual of totemistic eating of the god); our processions and our bowing, kneeling, or standing in public worship; finally, a great part of our religious terminology. Even formulae that were originally intended to define the truth for all time cease, almost insensibly, to be definitions, and become instead symbols of truths or of group interests, the definition of which is elsewhere attempted. Wherever freedom prevails, creeds tend to become mere flags that remind the people of their group loyalties.

To assume, then, that the present meaning of an institutional form is the same as the earliest meaning is to make one's self liable to historical and psychological error. Institutions are more plastic than their external forms would lead one to suppose. Especially is this true of institutions that commit themselves to some high ideal, as the Christian churches have so largely done. The extent to which the progressive changes of Christianity have sprung from within the ecclesiastical bonds is rather astonishing. At the present moment, too, the faults of the churches are not more drastically exposed by the church's enemies than by loyal church people. It is safe to say, also, that no institution with a history has shown greater capacity for adaptation than the Protestant churches have displayed since the middle of the nineteenth century. The doctrine of evolution, the historical study of the Bible, the sudden expansion of the social consciousness, the transformation in people's ways through the growth of cities and of modern machinery—these things created a situation that would have been ominous for the churches if ecclesiastical institutions were really as inflexible as their external forms appear to be. Without attempting to say how far these churches have solved the problems thus thrust upon them, one can easily see that they have gone a long way in the assimilation of modern knowledge of a revolutionary character (as far as theology is concerned), that they have largely shifted their emphasis even with regard to the meaning of the Christian life, and that they have entered upon fresh practical tasks of the greatest difficulty.

7. *The influence of individuals.*—Several great religions and many minor ones take their start from individual leaders. It is an impressive and rather mysterious spectacle that we witness here. For in some cases the leader not merely starts something going, as a statesman, a warrior, or an inventor may do, but he attaches the people to himself personally with a loyalty or even affection that runs on for centuries after his death. There is nothing comparable, in other phases of life than the religious, to the attachment of millions of men

to Gautama, Jesus, and Mohammed. And these are but supreme instances; the masses respond, and have always responded, with a peculiar loyalty to many lesser lights. For this reason a chapter will be devoted to analysis of the mental traits of religious leaders. But it should be said at once that the influence of individuals in differentiating religion into specific religions is not limited to the leaders. Individual variation takes place, or may take place, in greater or less degree through a whole mass. The quick response that makes one an early disciple is an individual variation as truly as the quality in the master that evokes the response. So with the formation of parties for or against a new leader; the new issue, felt as such by large masses of men, is a sign that social evolution is going on by means, not only of "mutations" or large variations in a few individuals who lead, but also by accumulation of smaller variations in the masses that follow.

This list of the factors that give to each religion its special character does not include the mental traits of different races of mankind—what is sometimes called racial temperament. Differences between religions are, of course, to a considerable extent, differences between races also; but this does not prove that one is the cause of the other. Moreover, racial traits must themselves be accounted for. The most probable view of the matter is that mankind is a single species that originated at a particular spot, whence it spread over the earth, and that racial differences arose through the long-continued influence of special habitats. It is natural to suppose that causes that could produce the anatomical contrasts with which we are familiar might produce corresponding contrasts in mental constitution. There is, in fact, a popular belief that racial mental traits are passed on by the procreative process just as stature, or color of skin and of hair, or shape of nose is passed on. Yet everywhere we find the same senses, with few if any of the wide differences that were once supposed to exist; the same instincts; the same processes of mental organization. What is different is the objective interests with which men occupy themselves, and the degrees to which a given interest is followed up. But this kind of difference can be accounted for, in large measure, by the respective situations of different peoples, such as the kinds and degrees of action required by climatic conditions and the nature of the food supply, and the presence or absence of the stimulus that comes from the intermingling of peoples. In short, though a dogmatic denial of the existence of inborn racial temperaments would be rash, we cannot with assurance appeal to such temperaments as an explanation of the differences between religions. We are thrown back upon the assumption of minds substantially alike reacting in environments that do not offer the same stimuli, and therefore do not awaken the same desires and efforts. Hence, there are arrests of development in one quarter and particular types of development in another.

The differentiation of religions, that is to say, is primarily functional rather than structural. Differences in the thing that has to be done, or in the means for doing it, or in the groups that are related to the doing of it—in short, differences in the specific purposes of life and in the specific objects through which satisfactions are secured shunt thought to one track or another.

A need to think is primary, and this is none other than a need to organize the given environment, natural and social, so as to attain some specific aim, such as food, victory, health, or social justice.

When, however, such a thought process gets well started, it tends to develop an interest in its objects regardless of their relation to practical purposes. There is pleasure in developing a story, or in embellishing a portrait, or in reconciling and systematizing scattered concepts. Thus the initial differences in the thought structures of different tribes and nations are heightened until, growing from very similar types, we have the contrasting complexes presented by the theologies of the world.

CHAPTER VIII

RELIGION AS GROUP CONDUCT

That religion is a social phenomenon is already obvious. But the term "society" covers many kinds of groupings and many kinds of group enterprise. We must therefore go on to consider whether the sociality of religion may not be of various species. In particular we shall need to discriminate between the mechanism of group action (the structure) and the satisfactions that such action brings (the functions). In both the structural and the functional direction, in fact, we shall find important differences. They gather about certain types of group conduct that will now be described. Let it be remembered, however, that setting things apart for purposes of description does not imply any equal apartness in history. Differences develop for the most part gradually, so that types shade into one another. Moreover, contrasting types may live side by side.

Bearing in mind this caution as to the meaning of our classification, we may easily recognize three chief types of religious group conduct.

I. THE RELIGIOUS CROWD

1. *The type.*—Considered as social grouping and social enterprise, what is the difference between an old-fashioned negro revival and the Edinburgh Missionary Conference? A question like this reveals at once the existence of religious crowds as distinguished from other religious groups. The earliest religious group conduct

was undoubtedly of the excited, unreflective type. We have similar phenomena in the Crusades, in the mediaeval "dancing manias," in the "witchcraft mania," and in some revivals of the present day among both whites and blacks—to mention only a few instances.

2. *The structure of the crowd, or how the crowd form of co-operation is effected.*—What a man will do in a given situation[1] depends, not merely upon his original nature, together with the items that *might* be attended to in his present situation, but also upon the actual distribution of his attention over these items. If, upon looking at an autumn landscape, my attention centers upon the colored foliage, I act in one way; but if my attention centers upon the opening burrs of a near-by chestnut tree, I act in a different way. Now, attention may be distributed with a greater or less degree of what is variously called deliberation, analysis, and criticism. Deliberation consists in having within the focus of attention two or more objects or ideas that involve opposing tendencies to action.[2] An immediate result of deliberation is post-

[1] Students will find it worth while to accustom themselves to Thorndike's categories of situation and response. In order to understand an act, note not only what is done, or the "response" (beginning with bodily movements, then going on to vocal sounds, and finally to things said), but also the "situation," which includes the objects present, the bodily states, and what happened just before. Having analyzed thus both situation and response, one may raise the question, What in this act is due to original nature, and what to antecedent experiences of the individual?

[2] The apparently impulsive quality of ideas, sometimes expressed in the phrase "ideomotor action," as far as it is not directly instinctive, is a matter of habit. Whatever reinstates a part of a past experience tends to reinstate the whole of it; the presence of any idea involves a tendency to the reinstatement of any activity that has been associated with it.

ponement or checking of these tendencies. Hence, each idea that is thus attended to may represent to us an inhibition of a tendency represented by each of the other ideas. Deliberate action is response that takes place after, and in a form determined by, such preliminary inhibition or checking. To the extent that any response occurs without this preliminary inhibition we say that it occurs under suggestion as opposed to deliberation. Suggestion means, then, determination of the response by narrowing of attention so that inhibitory items present in the situation are at least relatively inoperative.[1]

Crowd action, in the technical sense of the term "crowd," is co-operation produced by suggestion, that is, the suppression of inhibitions. We shall soon see that co-operation can be secured also by the reverse process—by means of inhibitions. An example of crowd action is as follows: During a football game I stood with

[1] The art of the hypnotizer consists in controlling attention in the sense of narrowing it. What is the difference, it may be asked, between this narrowing of attention and concentration of mind in study or other enterprise? For practical purposes it is sufficient to answer that study holds on to differences, while suggestion lets them go. Theoretically, however, the matter is not so easy. The occurrence of complete mono-ideism is not demonstrable; attention always involves a field and a focus, that is, both multiplicity and selection. The selection that constitutes study and the selection that constitutes suggestion are, structurally considered, continuous. There is no precise dividing line between one's ordinary state and hypnosis. That a distinction, an inexpugnable one, remains, however, is clear. I surmise that the difference between the "normal" and the hypnotized individual, between waking and sleeping, and even between perception and hallucination, can be expressed only by reference to the distinction between greater and less self-realization. That is, the distinction goes back ultimately to the preferential functions. It follows, of course, that what is above designated as "the structure of the crowd" involves and depends upon a functional distinction.

many other persons at a certain part of the side line. We were all sympathizers with the home team. As the game grew exciting, we who were next to the rope grasped it firmly and pulled hard in the direction in which our team was struggling to go. We had no purpose in pulling, and most of us never discovered what we were doing. We were a crowd—that is, a mass of minds with attention narrowed to a single interest, and consequently acting as one. The unity depended upon lack of inhibitions.

Such reduction of inhibitions may occur precisely because men are together in one place. (*a*) The many, merely as sensory objects moving and making sounds, excite me and tend to dominate my attention. (*b*) The mere presence of others of my species awakens in me a gregarious response that is pleasurable—I thrill, fix my eyes upon them, move toward them, follow them about. The pleasure here involved also reinforces any other tendencies to action that may happen to be present. (*c*) Conversation, passing back and forth, further helps to fix the attention of the many upon the same things. (*d*) Some individual, either by design or under the excitement of the situation, makes a speech or expresses a sentiment or proposes action or initiates action that focuses attention still more completely. From this common focus of attention, which is excited and emotional, arises the common act.

Each sort of crowd action arises in the first instance spontaneously. But some sorts at least can be reinstated by a designed reproduction of appropriate conditions, as in football games, revival meetings, or primitive religious ceremonies. On such occasions an additional factor is the mental representation of previous crowd experience. What has happened before easily determines the present focus of attention and therefore the fresh response. Thus it is that fashions of crowd action arise.[1] There are styles in revivals—styles not only of singing, praying, and preaching, but also of response thereto. Dancing, shouting, and "the power" are renewed season after season in negro meetings. Similarly, different revival waves among the whites have produced different types of conversion. A study of laughter in these movements would undoubtedly show the prevalence of a fashion for a time, and then a shift, each fashion seeming to be most natural while it lasts. In the Billy Sunday meetings many church people of the present day, both laymen and ministers, lay aside their ordinary standards of taste, courtesy, reverence, kindliness, and theological consistency. The shock that this revivalist's standards once caused has now been replaced by habitual complacency—a crowd fashion has been created. By a parallel process the primitive religious crowd moved forward from what was spontaneous and unplanned to custom, specifically the punctilious ceremony.

Crowd action tends, in general, toward the simplicity of instinct, for unity is here attained by rendering individual variations inoperative. Nevertheless, habits that are common to the individuals in a group play a

[1] At the baseball games of a certain college I observed repeatedly a sudden and general increase of excitement on the bleachers when the seventh inning started. "The bloody seventh," it was called. This odd fashion appears to have had its origin in the fact that on one or two occasions the home team, after being outplayed in the earlier innings, made a marked rally in the seventh. Many other examples of crowd fashions could easily be found in our athletics.

part. How is it that such ideas as "Jerusalem," the "holy sepulcher," "Turk," "infidel," could start a crusade? It is because of certain already established habits of thought and of action. If crusades are no longer possible, it is because our background of habits is different. On the other hand, an individual's habits may be profoundly interrupted, as in many conversions, by his experience as a member of a crowd. What happens in this case is the arousal of a still more ingrained habit, or else of instinct itself.[1]

3. *Functions of the religious crowd.*—Our discussion of crowd structure has prepared us for the following brief catalogue of the satisfactions involved: (*a*) Satisfaction of the gregarious instinct. (*b*) Release from monotony and routine through fresh sensations and emotions. (*c*) Pleasurable sense of elevation, freedom, even sublimity. It arises from the unification of mind through the suppression of inhibitions. Hesitations, cares, responsibilities, vanish. One feels one's self bursting through limitations and becoming one with a great, not definitely bounded reality. Note that this sense of elevation is attained, not by solving problems, but by forgetting them. The physiological correlate is unification of motor discharge by simplification rather than by organization. A crowd cannot exercise skill. (*d*) Indulgence of other instinctive impulses, as those of sex and of pugnacity. The Roman bacchanalia, in which instinct assumed the throne, will serve as an example.

---

[1] When a crowd of Christians applauds a revivalist for picturesquely assigning to a savage hell persons who disagree with his theology, what happens is a flaring up of instinctive pugnacity—the same thing that makes men enjoy a dog fight.

(*e*) The primitive crowd, as the beginning of human co-operation, made the food supply more stable and social relations more dependable. The general efficiency was heightened by the massing of energy. (*f*) At any stage of civilization enterprises that do not require discrimination can be advanced by crowd action. Thus it is that revivals of the crowd type can reinforce common morality. For the same reason, however, they can reinforce the authority of dogma and help keep intolerance alive. But reconstruction of standards, as distinguished from enforcement of standards, requires deliberation.

Here we come upon a profound limitation of the term "society" as applied to a crowd. The fact that men act together is no guaranty that their acts are social rather than unsocial in motive and end. Crowds are notoriously cruel, notoriously unregardful of the moral standards that are the later and finer product of social evolution. If the leadership happens to be in the hands of a morally discriminating person, the crowd may, indeed, be led toward truly social ends, but power as a leader does not depend upon moral discrimination. Therefore the evolution of social standards, as far as this implies increasing regard of men for one another and disciplined action in behalf of this regard, depends upon supplanting the crowd form of organization by some other principle of integration.

II. THE SACERDOTAL GROUP

1. *The type.*—When a ceremonial system becomes well established, a new principle of group conduct appears. Co-operative action no longer waits for the

emotional realizations that mark the crowd. Whether such realizations are present or not, group action goes forward. A specialized control has been organized in such forms as priesthoods, traditions and sacred formulae, sacred scriptures, dogma (that is, authoritative teaching). For short, we may say that this type of grouping rests upon authority. The divine being makes himself known, not directly to the members of the group, but through a particular organ, and this organ not seldom enforces its authority by means of fears and even of physical penalties. For examples of the sacerdotal group, we may look to the organized tribal religions, to the national religions,[1] and to all churches that endeavor to enforce as final a particular form of worship, or of ecclesiastical government, or of doctrine.

2. *The structure of the sacerdotal group.*—How is the unity of the sacerdotal group brought about? Not by desultory crowd suggestion, nor yet by deliberation among the members of the group, but by systematized suggestion through sacrifice and sacrament, ritual, a code of commands and prohibitions, and religious education of a particular type.

The earliest religious rites were, from the standpoint of the people, actual participation by them in doing the thing that needed to be done. When, in the later temple sacrifice, the thing comes to be done for them, a new kind of control is set up over them. Through the priest the people approach the god; through the priest the god

[1] All national religions are perforce religions of authority. They participate in the exercise of sovereignty through taxation if in no other way.

approaches the people. Traditional lore, priestly wisdom, and political expediency become an organized authority, having a continuous life of its own. Its method of control is reiterated, systematized suggestion, primarily through such outward acts as sacrifice, around which common hopes and joys are made to center. Sacrifice gives way in many places to mystery-cult and sacrament, in which only a few material traces of their origins remain, as an ear of corn, a bit of bread, a cup of wine, a drop of oil or of water, a touch upon the head. But these are now the outward expressions whereby an articulated doctrine controls the people through suggestion. By suggestion from the priest the worshipers are assured, for example, that the god is present in the wine-cup that their eyes behold, or that some new relation to God is effected by a touch or by baptismal water. Thus the people, whether they betake themselves to the temple by two's and three's or by hundreds, are made one in the unity of a doctrine that exists independently of their will.

In sacerdotal worship the sacrament is reinforced by other parts of the ritual. Here the priest works upon the people by suggestion through what is recognized by them as partly, though not exclusively, symbolical. Pictures and statues, processions, kneeling, bowing, crossing one's self, the Latin of the mass, intoned psalms and prayers, the repetition of ancient creeds—these are one and all instruments of suggestion. They are not used because they promote reflection and deliberate action, but because they bring attention back repeatedly to the same point, thus renewing control by what is already authoritatively fixed.[1] Tendencies toward sacerdotal grouping can sometimes be discerned in a change from "saying" to intoning the Lord's Prayer, the Prayer of Confession, and the Creed; perhaps also in singing, instead of reading, the psalms. Here the content, which was at first an expression of discriminative thinking, not only ceases to awaken like thoughts, but becomes an instrument of suggestion whereby the worshiper's mind is bent to the ideas of the ecclesiastical authorities.

The sacerdotal group is kept together, in the next place, by a code of commands and prohibitions, which may include matters of belief as well as of conduct. In respect to conduct, ethical duties (which have to do with the social weal) stand side by side in all such codes with ceremonial prescriptions whose derivation from taboo is much more direct (as those that concern the superior sanctity of certain places, times, words, doctrines, and sacramental acts). The whole is enforced by the sanction of pains and pleasures attached to disobedience and obedience, respectively, by the will of a divinity. Here again suggestion, largely in the exceedingly effective form of direct command, is the mode of group unification and control. Reflection may be encouraged within limits, particularly in the way of defining and applying the prescribed rules, but the ultimate is always authority (as of revelation contained in an ancient literature, or uttered through a living priest).

[1] This does not apply to all use of liturgical forms or to all use of religious symbols. As the quiet of one's study, the presence of books, and the sight of one's desk stimulate intellectual work, so liturgical forms may be constructed so as to produce reflection and deliberation as distinguished from mere contemplation.

Therefore the ultimate psychological method of the sacerdotal group life is suggestion.

In the more developed sacerdotal groups perpetuity of control is sought through diligent instruction of the young. Instruction, one might suppose, would control less by suggestion than by awakening reflection. If we look, however, at ancient Jewish schools, or at Moslem schools, we shall see that drilling certain formulae into the pupil's memory is the central and essential thing in the work of the teacher; and in the sacerdotal branches of Christianity we shall find that habit-formation in thought and conduct, on the basis of direct command (whether it is fully expressed or not), is the essence of instructional method, reflection being employed only under the strictest predetermination of its main conclusions.

3. *Functions of the sacerdotal group.*—It is evident at a glance that religion in this form may contribute to any of the satisfactions of tribal and national existence. For example, in the wars of Israel, and in the European war that is raging as these words are written, religion strengthens the courage and solidifies the obedience of the soldiers. For each army feels sure that God is on its side. In both cases the soldiers are incited to a limited amount of reflection by having their attention called to the wickedness of the enemy; in both cases the individuals feel that they are freely devoting themselves to a cause; but in both cases the cause is chosen for them, not by them. That the method whereby religion here produces its social effect is suggestion rather than reflection might be inferred directly from the fact that the national point of view, *whatever it is*, is sure to be reinforced through the exercises of religion. Prayer, hymn,

mass, sermon, have the effect of removing inhibitions and narrowing attention upon a *predetermined* set of ideas and interests. Here sacerdotalism reveals its true and uniform kinship with the military type of social organization. The power of a regiment may be augmented by speech-making and exhortation, but these are not fundamental; they are only accessory to the basal ground of unity, which is that a few command what seems good to them, and the many obey. Just so, the religious group conduct now under consideration may include argument, persuasion, emotional revivals, and willing devotion on the part of individuals, but all these are produced by and on behalf of an authority that, in the last analysis, resides in one or a few persons who command what seems to them good. The relation between this "seeming good" to the authoritative few and the correlative "seeming good" to the obedient many constitutes the special problem of the functions of the sacerdotal group.

The processes of suggestion just referred to prevail also in various ecclesiastical groups that no longer fuse religious authority with the sovereignty of the state. The functions, however, are similar, namely, the reinforcement of any interest that presents itself by means of the organs of authority. These interests commonly attach themselves to some tradition or historical incident in which the authority of a god is supposed to be conferred upon a human individual or organization. Now and then a fresh revelation is claimed and a new sacerdotal authority set up, as in the cases of Joseph Smith, Mrs. Eddy, and John Alexander Dowie ("Elijah II"). These must be added to the more ancient instances of authority, whether in Israel, or in Islam, or in Christian history, if we would obtain an adequate notion of the satisfactions that keep alive the sacerdotal group. These satisfactions may be summed up as a sense of individual salvation through conformity to a fixed social standard, whether of belief or of practice. "Sense of individual salvation" is to be understood as including relief of functional disorders through faith or other conformity to authority; confidence that one is to succeed in business; victory over habits recognized as evil; release from fears (awakened to a large extent by the very authority that allays them), as from the fear of future retribution; enjoyment of prospective bliss in heaven; gregarious satisfaction, and the elevation already described in connection with the religious crowd. What distinguishes these functions from those of the religious crowd is the fact that, whereas in crowd action the self is inhibited, in the sacerdotal group it is recognized. On the other hand, what distinguishes the sacerdotal group from the deliberative group, which is now to be considered, is a difference in the sort of recognition given to the individual, and the consequences that flow from this difference.

III. THE DELIBERATIVE GROUP

1. *Type and structure.*—In deliberative bodies we find a kind of group conduct that is vastly different from the two types already described. For, as a preliminary to each common act the entire group pauses, the chairman saying, "Are there any remarks?" Then, as if challenging each individual to full self-expression, he asks, "Are you ready for the motion?" This procedure

has been devised so as to prevent action under suggestion.   Individual inhibitions are not avoided or
suppressed, but invited, spread out for inspection, often
acted upon separately by dividing the question or by
voting upon proposed amendments.   Moreover, provision is made for several alternatives besides yes and
no, as reference to a committee, laying on the table, and
making a special order for a future meeting.   The degree
and rapidity of variation are indeed restricted in most
such bodies by constitutions and by-laws.   Yet these
also come into being through deliberation, and they contain provisions for amendments—that is, they invite
individual initiative with a view to reorganization of
the group.[1]

Here, then, we have a group that achieves unity by
means of the very thing that might be expected to prevent united action, namely, the free variation of thought
and desire among its members.   The unity of a crowd
depends upon preventing its members from acting as
individuals; the unity of a sacerdotal group depends
upon prescribing in advance how the individual shall act;
the unity of the deliberative group is achieved by the
heightening and the freeing of individuality.

This structural principle appears in religion itself.
The Edinburgh Missionary Conference, for example,
which was regarded by the participants as a profound
religious experience, achieved its great religiousness precisely by frank recognition of the variant elements
present.   The range of deliberation, which was here

[1] One ecclesiastical constitution known to me has an article on
amendments that excepts from amendment a certain section of another
article.   But this section could be amended by first amending the article
on amendments so as to remove the restriction.

restricted by common consent, is theoretically unlimited in various religious meetings and bodies, both local and general, that choose their ends and their methods by vote of the members. These are religious groups; their enterprises are religious, and their proceedings constitute social religious experience.[1]

The structure of such groups may be summarily described as involving two principles: First, through pauses, incitements to reflection, and the pitting of desires against one another, the individual is stimulated to self-discovery—the discovery of what it is that he really prefers. Here is organization of a self, not suppression or mere manipulation. Secondly, by the same means the individual is stimulated to use the desires of others as data for determining his own preferences. He is listened to, but he also listens. In one and the same process he gets acquainted with others and with himself, and he forms a social will that is yet his own discriminative will.

2. *Functions of the deliberative group.*—Whereas in groups of the other two types ends are imposed either by instinct or by suggestion, in the deliberative group the membership as a whole freely chooses and defines its own functions. The ends actually chosen may and do include much that is derived from sacerdotal traditions. Instinctive satisfactions, too—as of the social instincts—are always a factor. Yet in the ethical group a fresh type of satisfaction secures an organ—the satisfaction of freely weighing and criticizing satisfactions.

[1] It involves no stretching of terms to say that listening to a statistical report from a church society is a religious act. For surely the point of view, the motive, and the meaning of the act determine its proper classification.

Since this weighing is a social act that looks toward the determination of social ends, it follows that the distinctive function of the ethical group is the criticism and reconstruction of society itself through the free acts of its members. Crowd action may assist social reconstruction, but only accidentally. Sacerdotal authority also may assist, but with equal right (which it fails not to exercise) it may close the doors of social criticism. But in the deliberative group we have a structure that arises and maintains itself precisely by inviting criticism and proposals for reconstruction.

The adoption of this reconstructive attitude, however gradually it may occur, and with whatever compromises with tradition, gives a new meaning to ideals and to faith. Under sacerdotalism an ideal is a pattern to be copied; the idealizing process consists in making the pattern vivid, and faith is acceptance of the authority that imposes the pattern. In the deliberative group, on the other hand, patterns are themselves judged, and there is provision for change that implies, if it does not assert, creative evolution in the social sphere. Here an ideal is not a set pattern, but a direction of movement, and faith is not conformity, but the will to idealize and to control the actual by means of the ideal.

Common worship, under such social standards, tends to acquire a character of its own. It stimulates the worshiper to reflect, that is, to have his own thoughts, to know his own mind, and to realize differences. Hence, in denominations that most approximate the deliberative type of government, there is avoidance of foreign tongues, of intonation, and of the spectacular. A larger proportion of words is used after the ordinary manner of communication rather than as symbols of something that they do not say. The minister in his prayer endeavors to represent the aspirations of the group. Finally, the sermon plays a larger part. The tendency of all this is to make the worshiper realize himself as an individual.

Conversely, the divine being who is conceived as the head of the group tends to be less and less a chief or king—even though a condescending one. Something more intimate seems to be required, some closer participation with men. Such participation is found in the special sort of ideals that the deliberative group commits itself to. The divine being, instead of merely giving commands, inspires the idealizing that judges all commands. He is the inner pressure that causes the questioning of standards. Therefore he is the chief worker in the group rather than a mere master of those who work.

In the deliberative society religious education also tends to acquire a quality of its own. Mere instruction and mere drill no longer suffice, for the end is not static. Mere drill, resulting in habit only, provides of itself for nothing but repetition of the past. Instruction, too, as long as it aims merely to transmit an existing body of ideas, lacks the forward impulse. Hence it is that religious bodies that tend most toward the deliberative type have insisted most upon personal assimilation, or upon a decision, or an experience of one's very own. Exact dogmatic formulae, accordingly, are less emphasized, and content, meaning, historical setting, and exegesis are more prominent. These groups accept, too, with less reserve, the educational doctrines of interest, initiative, and freedom.

CHAPTER IX

RELIGION AS INDIVIDUAL CONDUCT

The three types of religious group conduct that have just occupied our attention present to us the individual also in three typical religious attitudes.

First, we have the *impulsive* individual, who is saved from anarchy of desire by crowd integration. Neither instinct alone, nor yet external compulsion, guides and restrains him, but a new experience which by virtue of the presence of others brings fresh satisfaction.

Next we have, in the sacerdotal group, the *regulated* individual. Rules of conduct and of belief now serve as a constant corrective or restraint of impulse. One stops to consider what will happen if one acts in this way or in that. Foresight of rewards and punishments produces present satisfactions and discomforts, so that habits are formed with reference to what is remote as well as to what is near, and the individual attains a larger internal organization.

Finally, in the deliberative group we come upon the *self-emancipating* individual. He emancipates himself, not by destroying social control and organization of his acts, but by overcoming the separation between conduct and the ends of conduct that characterizes the sacerdotal group. Deliberation is the search for adequate ends, so that conduct may be controlled wholly from within itself; and "adequate ends" are those that have social validity.

Not a few writers have seen that religion is a mode of social control of individuals, but inasmuch as the varieties of such control have remained undescribed, distorted views of individual conduct have resulted. In particular, religion has been regarded as essentially restraint of individual variation. Reason, which is individual, tends to variation; hence religion resists reason, it is said.[1] Again, religion is an inner control that holds the individual to social standards when external social pressure is absent—a governing instinct.[2] According to this theory, religion does not create standards or determine ends, but is altogether ancillary thereto. It is simply a check to individual action, a postponement, which gives the more ancient, racial impulses an opportunity to come to the front. The religious reaction, since it is essentially repressive, is uniformly painful.

The facts that are offered in support of this theory are such as these: the prevalence of asceticism in religion; withdrawal from activity and from individual effort in prayer; and the muscular retractations that are characteristic of worship, such as bowing, kneeling, closing the eyes, and drawing one's self together in meditation.[3] The inference from muscular retractations rests upon the general principle that states of satisfaction are characteristically expressed by the expansor muscles, and states of dissatisfaction by the flexor.

---

[1] Benjamin Kidd, *Social Evolution* (New York, 1898), chap. v.

[2] H. R. Marshall, *Instinct and Reason* (New York, 1898). See also his article "Religion: A Triologue," in *The Outlook*, CIX (March 10, 1915), 587–93.

[3] *Instinct and Reason*, pp. 330 f.

That this theory contains a truth but distorts it will appear from the following considerations:

1. Religious rites have been very largely joyous, even taking the form of feasting, games, and various social pleasures, as at the awakening of spring or the ingathering of the harvest.

2. Intense individual religious experience very often exhibits two successive phases, strain and release. The strain may involve sense of sin, or some fear, or sense of incompleteness, or of divided self, or of world-mystery and world-pain; the release has the correlative forms of sense of reconciliation, confidence, unified self, power, a world-light that shines through the world-darkness. Here religion is release from repression.

3. In multitudes of cases religious experience involves no marked crisis of strain and release, but rather a reaching toward a goal, the enlargement of one's scope, the fresh discovery of one's powers and of one's world.

Before naming the fourth point it will be well to note that two authors, working from different angles, come to much the same conclusion as to the effect of religious experiences upon the individual. James, whose cases involved many a strain, comes to the conclusion that religious feeling is, on the whole, "a 'sthenic' affection, an excitement of the cheerful, expansive 'dynamogenic' order which, like any tonic, freshens our vital powers. . . . . We have seen how this emotion overcomes temperamental melancholy and imparts endurance to the subject, or a zest, or a meaning, or an enchantment and glory to the common objects of life."[1]

[1] *The Varieties of Religious Experience*, p. 505.

Delacroix's intensive study of several great mystics yields parallel results. The mystic's progress was found to include periods of intense strain but ultimate release. The movement in each case was from a relatively unorganized, obstructed, largely painful experience to serenity, steadiness, and increased power for action.

4. Many religious reactions use the expansor muscles, as processions and dances, song, laughter, the lightened step that follows prayer, the friendlier relations between men.

5. Many of the retractations mentioned by Marshall have acquired psychic connotations different from the original ones. It is no uncommon thing for meanings to flow faster than external forms. Think how the meaning of the following terms used in letter-writing has been transformed: "sir," "madam," "your obedient servant," "yours." Just so the bow, which was originally, perhaps, a sign of submission, is now something entirely different. So it comes to pass that kneeling, which may have originated as abasement before a conqueror, has become with many persons the posture of prayer in general, even the joyful prayer of thanksgiving.

6. Anyone who will take the trouble to watch persons who, withdrawing from the activities and from the sensory stimuli of our hurly-burly life, enter a church and assume the postures of meditation and prayer, will be convinced that the whole constitutes, on the muscular side, relaxation of strains. These strains are not the same as the contractions essential for muscular work, but rather contractions of muscles that have no work to do, or contractions beyond the requirements of the work in hand. They constitute on the physical side

obstructions and wastes, and their mental correlate is hurry, worry, distraction, and general discomfort. The act of merely "letting go" these tense muscles brings relief, an immediate satisfaction. There are probably several reasons for this satisfaction, but one of them is certainly contained in the general law that obstructed motor activity is disagreeable, but harmonious, unobstructed activity agreeable. Of much worship at least we can say that it is an organizing of the individual, and therefore agreeable. And the result is not merely increased confidence, but also actual increase of effectiveness through focalization of attention. In other words, postures that may have originated in repression are now means for releasing the individual and increasing his capacity for self-assertion.[1]

7. In the deliberative religious group we have a social force that not only does not repress the individual but even invites and stimulates him to self-utterance and to further self-discovery.

Clearly, then, the facts are over-simplified when religion is regarded as simply an instrument whereby society controls individuals. Neither society nor the individual is a static thing, either controlled or controlling, but both are in process of forming themselves. In the merely general statement that religion is a social phenomenon, we leave unmentioned on the one hand

[1] So well-marked is this aspect of worship that letting go one's tensions has almost become of itself a religion. I refer not only to books on psycho-physical hygiene like *Power through Repose*, but also to various episodes of the New Thought movement, particularly to teachers who promise their pupils, through mental concentration, not only peace but also power and plenty. One can, it is said, open at will a reservoir from which power will flow absolutely without limit.

the varieties of religious group and on the other the degrees and modes of individuality. To say that religion here and there represses individual action does not tell us enough; it is equally true that religion strengthens individuals against society. The whole truth is that religion has had a part in the entire evolution of both society and the individual. Let us see, then, if we can secure a general perspective of the individual side of this evolution.

Until very recently individuals were taken for granted, with little thought of a possible evolution of individuality itself. The political ideals of the eighteenth century, for example, assumed that society is some sort of aggregation of individuals, each of whom, in coming into society, gives up some of the freedom that is natural to him. Thus the individual was taken as the *prius* of society. Genetic psychology has shown, however, that individuality itself is achieved in the social process and not elsewhere. In other words, one and the same movement produces society and the individual. Looking at this movement from the standpoint of the individual, we discern the following significant facts:

We share with certain subhuman species gregariousness, parental regard, and sexual interest, each of which involves pleasure through the presence of others of our species, and at times conduct that is costly to the particular organism. But in merely instinctive responses we have neither individual nor society in the proper sense of the term. Individual and society cannot arise until a self appears.

But what is it for a self to make its first appearance? The answer is difficult. If, thinking of the event as an awakening, we recall our own experiences of coming slowly out of sleep, we get a little help; we notice a vague sense of well-being, or of ill-being, or of wanting something, which gradually becomes a clear realization of where one is and what one is doing. But in this awakening one uses a stock of memories to which nothing in the first beginnings of selfhood corresponds.

Concerning these beginnings we can say with some confidence, however, that they take place in connection with wants and satisfactions, and that at one and the same point arise the realization that these wants and satisfactions are *my own*, and an attitude of friendliness or unfriendliness toward objects associated with them. It has been many times pointed out that the moving, sounding objects associated in a baby's experience with feeding-time are early differentiated from other objects. Following Mead we may add that the baby's own moving hands and feet, and his coos and gurgles, are to be included among these peculiarly interesting objects. Thus the primal material for the idea of self and for the idea of *socius* is all of the same kind. Moreover, the "warmth and intimacy" of the sense of self attaches at first to all the moving objects that are regularly associated with the baby's satisfactions. It is, therefore, by differentiation from what may be called a protosocial consciousness that the individual self arises. The first self-consciousness is "we" more than it is "I."

This "social reference" of the ego abides, however distinct or self-assertive the ego may become. It is by co-operation and clash of wills that I come to assert my will as my own, and it is by thinking of myself from others' standpoints that I acquire an opinion of myself.

In this differentiation into self-judging selves communication by means of language plays an enormous part. One who should grow up without such communication would attain to only an indefinite and wavering selfhood; one who should grow up entirely without human companionship would never become a self at all, would never have a rational as distinguished from an instinctive mind.

Thus man is by nature social. Self-consciousness is *per se* social consciousness, and individuality is itself a social fact. Conversely, society, as distinguished from herds, arises in and through the individuating process, that is, through the increasing notice that one takes of another as an experiencing self. Neither term, then—society or individual—is static; neither merely imposes itself upon the other, but the two are complementary phases of one and the same movement.

When we say that religion is a social phenomenon, then, we should understand that it is *ipso facto* an individuating process. When we look backward from the standpoint of some assured individual liberty, as freedom of belief and of worship, any earlier social-religious order that denies such liberty has, it is true, the appearance of mere repression; yet the same thing, looked at from the standpoint of what precedes it, appears as the attainment of greater individuality.

Custom, which may be regarded as a precipitate of crowd action, is the first organized social control. It grips the individual with extraordinary power, resisting and organizing the discharges of even the most imperious instincts. But it is a psychical control, and it is one degree removed from instinct. It involves ideas more or less interrelated, to which attention is given when the original sensory stimulus is absent. The vague idea of *mana*, the crude mental pictures of spirits, and the emotionally real taboo, all are a stimulus and a support for an inner, self-realizing life.

Similarly, the development of sacerdotalism does not so much restrict pre-existing individuality as sharpen it. Fewer relations are regulated, and a secular sphere is set off rather sharply from the sacred. The closer concatenation of beliefs, the more spectacular worship, the codified instruction, the more exalted and more personal gods—all these have a sort of "Stop, look, listen!" effect upon the individual. Looking at the sacerdotal group broadly, then, we may say that it is not only a method whereby certain common goods are secured, but also a system of checks and pauses whereby men become more conscious of themselves as individuals.[1]

The individuality that is achieved in the deliberative religious group takes various forms and directions. A first and prominent direction is aspiration for an inner life as contrasted with external rightness of all kinds, whether ceremonial acts, or good works, or dogmatic assent. When effort centers upon "getting the heart right," the individual is required to be his own mentor and judge, and he has motive for fine and fundamental discriminations. This is true even when, as commonly happens, a group that emphasizes heart religion con-

[1] Therefore sacerdotalism faces a practical dilemma. If its checks and restraints are felt as such by the individual, he is likely to be stimulated thereby to reflect upon the validity of the commands that are placed upon him. This danger to sacerdotalism is partly avoided by restricting the range and the severity of the restraints, and by causing worship to approximate crowd action.

sciously attempts, in its early stages, nothing more than inner conformity to a tradition.

The individualizing effect of this effort toward inner life appears clearly in the sproutings and divisions that have taken place within Protestant Christianity. Nearly all of them, it is true, have assumed that they are conserving or restoring some ancient, authoritative standard; but whether they are right or wrong in this assumption, the new grouping arises through free, individual inquiry and taking of sides. The individualizing effect can be seen, further, in the respect paid to the spiritual experiences of the plain layman. When thousands of prayer and conference meetings invite men, simply as men, to tell their experience, to offer prayer, and to discuss the religious life, democratic individualizing of men proceeds apace.[1]

An impulse for education, almost a passion for it, has characterized some of these groups. A remarkable number of academies and colleges in this country has sprung from the religious conviction of the plain people and been nourished by their toil. The conviction that one may discern divine operations within one's self; that there is a divinely appointed place and work for everyone; that God will guide one to this work and help one to accomplish it—this conviction in a group brings to light abilities otherwise unguessed. It stimulates variation, and it is also a selective agency in that it encourages aspiring young people to go to school and college.

A second, closely related form of individual reaction in the deliberative group is directly intellectual. The

[1] The Methodist class-meeting, it has been remarked, has been the training school of a remarkable number of English labor leaders.

argumentative doctrinal sermon, which assumes that the congregation is judge; the private reading of the Scriptures with a desire to find proof texts; the discussion of doctrines in prayer meeting and Sunday-school class— these, though they invite crudity and dogmatizing, place the individual beyond merely external authority. Laymen who judge the soundness of their preachers are on the road toward free personality.

The establishment and maintenance of religious enterprises through the free decisions of laymen constitute a third phase of this individualizing type of religious group. A history of the relation of the home churches to the modern missionary movement would show the laymen first giving money to a far-away cause under the pressure of emotional appeals or of ecclesiastical loyalty; then studying missions, and here and there assuming responsibility for the support of a particular missionary; and, finally, beginning to accept the whole enterprise as their very own. Many other examples could be given of the broadening of the individual's horizon, the enlargement of his discretion, the increase of his initiative. We are apparently nearing a time when lay and clerical members of deliberative religious bodies will together take up the problem of the basis and the standards for social organization as a whole. In short, the religious freeing of the individual and the righteous reconstruction of society are tending to fuse into one process. The conclusion toward which these facts point is that religion, considered from the standpoint of the individual, is all in all a process of increasing individuation. It carries forward the ego-social differentiation. It confirms rather than depresses the sense of self, and this it does by being so profoundly a social experience.

What, then, is the psychological significance of asceticism? If we consider this question broadly, we shall see that asceticism, in the strict sense of self-inflicted pains and deprivations, is continuous with various self-imposed restraints that are not always counted as ascetic, such as submission to ecclesiastical authority and surrender to the will of God. We must take these as data, together with such conventional ascetic practices as retiring from society into solitude; renouncing marriage; denying the appetite for food; avoidance of ease and of pleasures (aesthetic enjoyment included); reflection upon disagreeable subjects, like death, hell, and one's own sins; inflicting positive pain upon one's self, as by means of the hair shirt, by scourging, by denying one's self sufficient sleep, or by not removing such sources of distress as vermin and filth.[1]   Our problem lies in the paradox that men should take satisfaction in thwarting such natural functions as these: the food instinct; the sexual instinct; the gregarious instinct; the parental instinct; and nearly the whole list of preferential functions, especially multiplication of objects, communication, and aesthetic contemplation. Why do these men want to restrict their wants?

The most obvious part of the answer is that in a large proportion of cases one factor is the idea of individual salvation—the supposedly necessary price is paid for the greatest or most enduring satisfaction, such as

---

[1] One of the best psychological analyses of such phenomena is that of James. See *The Varieties of Religious Experience*, Index, under "Asceticism."

heaven, or escape from hell. To this extent the real problem of asceticism is this: How do repressive conceptions of the gods or of salvation secure social currency ? Granted these conceptions, voluntary self-repression follows as a matter of simple practical wisdom on the part of sensitive natures that feel and aspire greatly. Our sure clue to this problem lies in repressive forms of human government. The individual has had to cringe and abase himself before irresponsible monarchs; his property has been taken by an irresponsible taxing power; he and his sons have had to risk their lives in fighting, without opportunity to decide for themselves the conditions of war or of peace. Just so, to get on the safe side of an ethically irresponsible god, or to accumulate merit with him, is a large factor in asceticism.

But it is not the only factor. Asceticism (under which I include the types of submission already mentioned) has too great emotional power, too great attraction, to be based upon a mere calculation of benefits. There are direct instinctive factors also, and even an element of self-emancipation.[1] Correlative to the instinct of mastery, there is an instinct of submission that brings actual satisfaction in surrendering to an obviously more powerful being.[2] It is as if by complete abnegation of self-will one became a sharer in the greatness of the master; he is placated, I become a part of his conquering retinue, and thus, by "having no will of my own," I gain significance.

---

[1] I speak here of factors that are not pathological. In some individuals, doubtless, abnormal organic sensibility, or a mental derangement involving a fixed idea, plays a part.

[2] See E. L. Thorndike, *Original Nature*, pp. 92 ff.

But discomfort can yield satisfaction without regard to any other and greater being. A common practice of children consists in experimenting with their own ability to endure pain or exertion without flinching.[1] Grown-ups boast of the hardships they have endured in sickness, in camping or exploring, and in exhausting labor. Mythology abounds in admiration for those who suffer without being conquered. How is it that such apparent defeat of desire is turned into victory? The explanation is in two of the preferential functions: to be conscious, and to unify the objects of consciousness. Consciousness may be heightened by increasing the intensity of a sensation, even though it be from any other point of view disagreeable; and self-realization may actually be promoted by incorporating the discomfort into the conscious unity of one's will. To face the coming blow, to take it without flinching, and then to contemplate it without whimpering—this victory *over* self is a victory *of* self. It takes that which breaks into the self, and uses it to effect a firmer organization thereof. A strained situation sometimes loses its strain as soon as one "knows the worst." Peace may come precisely through a clear, unfaltering recognition that one's feverish desires are finally defeated. The ascetic, without doubt, finds a part of his satisfaction in the freshness and the intensity of his experiences and in the self-unification that he achieves.

Another factor in much asceticism is clearly ethical. It is an effort to subdue individual impulses that oppose

---

[1] I have seen boys run pins almost full length into their own muscles. If the muscle was kept motionless there was little pain, but the act was nevertheless a test of "grit."

or seem to oppose the social standard. Here the central conflict concerns the sexual instinct. The substitution of marriage for promiscuity, and the founding and maintenance of the monogamic family, have involved human individuals, particularly the males, in the greatest of all ethical strains and struggles. The individual is required by social tradition and by social penalties to accept a standard against which the most powerful instinct rebels. Appropriate educational processes might perhaps guide this enormous impulsive energy toward the maintenance instead of the destruction of marriage and the family. But up to the present time education with respect to this moral issue has commonly lacked any such constructive method. The social standard and the individual impulse have simply collided, and the individual has been left to resolve the conflict, for the most part, by his own resources.

The typical ascetic saint goes through an inner conflict with what he regards as evil. He seeks complete victory; he will not be satisfied with anything short of the death or final quiescence of the troublesome desires. That is, he seeks to make himself as perfect as the socially evolved standard. Usually, however, he abstracts the standard from the social end or good in the interest of which it originated. He imagines that he can be good within himself, regardless of his contributions to the social good. He even withdraws from society into solitary places, or enters a narrow, monastic group of like-minded seekers after holiness. Not able to abandon wholly the social basis of the good, however, he seeks intimacy with the divine being. God now becomes partly abstract and unsocial like the ascetic himself, but partly a substitute for human fellowship. The sympathy, the friendship, even the conjugal and the parental affection upon which the ascetic has turned his back, now assert themselves toward God, or the suffering Savior, or the child Jesus, or the Virgin, and by a process of autosuggestion the saint feels his affection reciprocated. Thus asceticism finally supports itself upon the very wants and satisfactions, rooted largely in bodily functions, that were at first denied in the interest of something supposedly more sacred.[1]

[1] It should be said, too, that surrender and self-abnegation differ according to the conception of God. The asceticism of India, among the enlightened, seeks a genuine and final emptying of the self, because the supreme being is without predicates. But the Christian idea of a positively benevolent God carries into Christian asceticism the constant possibility of interpreting surrender and self-denial as the substitution of social purpose for selfishness. Hence the frequent union of austerities with philanthropy.

CHAPTER X

CONVERSION

Self-realization within a social medium has now been established as one important phase of the religious experience. When this religious self-realization is intense, and is attained with some abruptness, the change is called conversion. The convert looks upon himself as having passed from a lower to a higher level, as having attained to real life, or as having come to himself, or as having "found" God. The present chapter will attempt an analysis of this experience, both as to its structure and as to its functions.[1]

Recent publications, as those of Starbuck and James, have made particular cases of conversion so accessible that we may here take the primary data as in large measure already known. To avoid ambiguity of lan-

[1] "Conversion" is used in at least six senses: (1) a voluntary turning about or change of attitude toward God; this is the New Testament sense; (2) the renunciation of one religion and the beginning of adherence (doctrinal, ethical, or institutional) to another; similarly, a change from one branch of a religion to another (as Roman, Greek, or Protestant Christianity); (3) individual salvation according to the evangelical "plan of salvation"—repentance, faith, forgiveness, regeneration, sometimes with assurance; (4) becoming consciously or voluntarily religious, as distinguished from mere conformity to the religious ways of one's family or other group; (5) Christian quality of life as contrasted with an earlier, non-Christian quality—a "really converted man," for instance; (6) any abrupt transfer, particularly a very rapid transfer, from one standpoint and mode of life to another, especially from what the subject recognizes as a lower to what he recognizes as a higher life.

guage, however, the term "conversion" should be understood, in this discussion, to refer to experiences that
seem to the subject of them to have the following marks:
(1) The subject's very self seems to be profoundly
changed. (2) This change seems not to be wrought by
the subject but upon him; the control seems not to be
self-control, the outcome not a result of mere growth.
(3) The sphere of the change is the attitudes that constitute one's character or mode of life. But one's whole
world may acquire new meaning; or there may be a
sense of divine presence; or there may seem to come
new insight into a doctrine or into a whole system of
doctrine. (4) The change includes a sense of attaining
to a higher life, or to emancipation or enlargement of
the self. Not seldom there is victory over habits that
brought self-condemnation. Now and then there is
recovery from moral degradation and helplessness. The
interest of these cases for us springs from the impression
on the part of multitudes of converts that here the
Divine Being can be discerned laying his hand, as it
were, upon men.

The general setting of these experiences includes
three significant facts:

1. In point of abruptness these religious changes
are paralleled by experiences in every other sphere of
human interest.[1] Intellectual problems are solved in a
flash, as in the case of Sir William Rowan Hamilton's
discovery of quaternions; whole subjects of study that
have been dark and meaningless have become suddenly
luminous; in some fortunate glance of the eye nature
becomes for the first time appealing and intimate; or

[1] Starbuck has a collection of instances in chap. xi.

one discovers that one is already in love with a person of the opposite sex.

2. Conversion is continuous with religious growth in both process and content. The "growth cases" in our current evangelical Protestantism, as Starbuck showed at length, arrive at the same general type of religious attitude as the "conversion cases," and the rapidity of the change has all degrees.

3. The distribution of the phenomenon is significant. Conversion is by no means coextensive with religion. Those who say that a sense of sin is a universal mark of the religious experience are seriously wide of the facts. It is true that religion almost everywhere allays some sort of anxiety, but not until the social standard takes the form of an inner ethical demand—a demand to be right and not merely to obtain goods—do we find in any large degree the victorious sense of self-realization with which we are now dealing. There seem to be traces of conversion (as in Isaiah) when the failure of Israel's sacerdotal conception of Jahwe forced thoughtful minds to reflection and self-examination. The earliest followers of the Buddha, who proclaimed that the root of evil is in ourselves and not in something imposed upon us, are represented as coming suddenly into the light with all the emotional marks of the evangelical Christian conversion. There are signs that the mystery-cults among the Greeks and the Romans awakened personal religious experiences of the conversion type.[1] The history of Christianity, with its emphasis upon the value of the

[1] See F. Cumont, *The Oriental Religions in Roman Paganism* (Chicago, 1911), pp. 26 ff.; W. A. Heidel, "Die Bekehrung im klassischen Altertum, mit besonderer Berücksichtigung des Lucretius," *Zeitschrift für Religionspsychologie*, III (1910), 377–402.

individual, has been rich in conversions of eminent men like Paul, Augustine, St. Francis, and Luther. Mystical sects like the Friends of God[1] cultivated the experience as a privilege of the common man. The great modern revivals, from those of Wesley and Whitefield down, have presented abundant cases. In the evangelical movement, particularly in Methodist and Baptist circles, the prevailing sentiment has been at times that the conversion experience should be universal among Christian believers. It is to this end that various systems of revival technic have been devised.

But all this represents only a slight segment of the history of religion. Even in Christianity conversion experiences are the exception, not the rule. Communions that have aimed at a converted membership only have not been able to maintain any such standard of admission for a long period. For the conversion of parents tends, by bringing religion into the home, to produce in their children a natural religious growth through nurture, and therefore to prevent conversion. Further, the contrast effect necessary for the abrupt experience cannot be made continuous; it implies occasionalism, whereas organization in religion, as in anything else, aims at continuity. Each revival "burns over the ground,"[2] so that an interval must elapse before another can arise in power.[3] The one statistical study thus far made of

[1] See R. M. Jones, *Studies in Mystical Religion* (London, 1909), chap. xiii.

[2] A phrase actually in use in revival circles.

[3] As a consequence of all this, in religious bodies that attempt to make conversion a standard experience for candidates for membership, the following conditions are common: (1) Confused use of the term "conversion." The term has to be let down to fit the experiences that are

the relation of revivals to the growth of church membership through a considerable period tends to show that the increased rate of accessions at the time of revival is offset by a decreased rate afterward, and that possibly the effect of the revivals is not to increase the total accessions, but rather to hasten certain additions, so that the curve of accessions takes the form of wave motion, with high crest and deep depression alternating.[1] Further study is needed of communities in which an effort has been made to incorporate evangelistic methods into an ordered program, as "decision day" in the Sunday school, and a regular annual revival. Here the tendency appears to be to produce occasional conversion experiences within a process that is, as a whole, a crude kind of religious education.

Turning, now, to the structural aspects of the abrupt experience called "conversion," we shall find: (1) traces of mental reproduction of the individual's own earlier experiences; (2) fresh sensory elements; (3) certain instinctive impulses; and (4) a law under which these elements are characteristically combined.

1. The ideational factors are predominantly reproductions from antecedent experiences of the convert

actually produced. What sort of fact, for example, is back of Sunday-school statistics, or evangelistic campaign statistics, that report a certain number of conversions? (2) Confusion, morbidness, and negative reactions on the part of would-be Christians who do not have the standard experiences. (3) Professional revivalism grows shallow. Unable to produce a satisfactory number of conversions of the standard type, it substitutes therefor almost any act that has a religious coloring. A "convert" is one who signs a card, or holds up a hand, or shakes hands with the evangelist, for example.

[1] Samuel W. Dike, "A Study of New England Revivals," *American Journal of Sociology*, XV (1909), 361-78.

himself. His notion of the "higher" life has been formed under the influence of standards present in his environment. He is converted *to* something, the idea of which he has already met, as at home, or in Sunday school, or in preaching, or in his reading and reflection. If the conversion experience includes consciousness of the presence of the Christian God, it is because Christian rather than, say, Brahmin ideas of God have already been acquired.[1] Only so does Christian "assurance" or "the witness of the Spirit" occur in any articulate sense. Only so does articulate insight suddenly arise in any sphere. A vast mathematical experience lay behind the discovery of the quaternions. Just so, preceding the sudden rise of interest or meaning in a field of learning, there is some acquaintance with the field.

2. On the other hand, fresh sensory elements often play a part in conversion. The tone of a preacher's voice; the rhythm, melody, and volume of revival songs; repetition of a given impression; the sight of others performing a religious act; organic sensations, such as thrills, tingles, shudders; very possibly now and then sexual sensations not recognized as such; and the entire sensory mass that constitutes physical tone, particularly fatigue and similar states in which excitability as distinguished from discriminative sensibility exists—all these have to be reckoned with. The "twice-born" type, which is characterized by acute and persistent feeling of powerlessness to unify one's life, with consequent yielding up of self to some supposedly external

---

[1] Revivalism can do no more than reinforce antecedent educative processes. To the extent, therefore, that revivalistic methods interrupt religious education, or separate themselves therefrom, they are parasitic—they rob the source of their own life.

"redemptive" person or principle (all of which is distinguished from growth from within), is probably determined by some persistent, though not yet defined, physiological depression.

Here is a vast field in which we are sure that certain elements are present, though they have not as yet been measured. It is clear, for example, that a bold, commanding tone and manner on the part of some preachers produce an effect over and above what they say. Pathetic, pleading tones, on the other hand, produce a specific response of their own in the form of tender emotion. Revival music is obviously different in ideas, in melodic character, and in rhythm from the music that is most enjoyed in other situations. The unification of an audience by means of sharply accented rhythms and by the repetition of refrains; the emotionally melting effect of what may be called "personal reference songs" (I-me-my songs), and the reinforcement thereof by sentimental melodies—all this is clear, though we do not yet know just what part a given key, cadence, or kind of rhythm has in producing a given emotion. The significance of rhythm, repetition, and the languorous love music that is sometimes used will be discussed in later paragraphs.

An important side light upon certain sensory factors in conversion comes from an experience occasionally reported as having occurred in connection with anesthesia.[1] The type is well represented by a gentleman who, in a conversation with me, described the event substantially as follows: Upon awakening from ether anesthesia

[1] See, for instance, James, *The Varieties of Religious Experience*, pp. 387-93.

in connection with a surgical operation he recalled that
he had witnessed, as it were, the solution of the profoundest problems of life. It was as if all the contra-
dictions of existence had risen before him and then been
brought into wondrous unity—an experienced unity.
Before the operation he had been losing his religious
hold by reason of difficulties growing out of his college
and university studies, but his anesthetic experience had
given him a religious footing that it seemed to him
nothing could ever shake. I inquired what doubt had
been laid, and what specific answer had come to any
specific question. He replied that there was no definable
intellectual content in the whole experience; he could
not even now give a philosophical resolution of his old
philosophical doubts; yet he had become immovably
sure that there is a good meaning in existence as a whole,
and his daily life had gained in confidence and moral
firmness.

Here a reversal of attitude toward life as a whole
was initiated by a physiological process, the psychical
correlate of which must be regarded as primarily sensory,
namely, kinesthetic sensations of muscular rigidity
followed by those of muscular relaxation.

In general, an anesthetic acts first as a stimulant and later as a
depressant. The final and complete relaxation of the muscular
system is frequently preceded by tonic muscular rigidity. The
psychical effects of such a change will hardly be realized by anyone
who has not become familiar, in his own person, with the relation
between muscular tension and anxiety, restlessness, and a divided
self on the one hand, and that between muscular relaxation and
calm, poise, and self-reconciliation on the other. When everything goes wrong and you cannot adjust yourself to yourself or
your work; when you find yourself doing under high tension what

ought to be easy; when you cannot let go your cares or secure restful sleep, then hunt for tense muscles and relax them. In forehead, jaws, fingers, legs—somewhere you will find a physical basis or condition of your unrest. Relieve the tension and yourself and your world will be less divided and contradictory; you will experience in some degree the very unification that the mystic looks upon as a revelation. Relaxation has always been one feature of mystical practices, in fact. It is not strange, then, that here and there a medical patient gives a mystical interpretation to the change from tension to relaxation under an anesthetic.[1]

This total *mass of relief* was *his* relief; it was a coming to himself after dispersal and distraction. The emotional massiveness of the relief, under the recognized principle of perseveration,[2] was carried over into the waking state. Put into articulate terms it was: "All is well; I have nothing to fear; I am part of a system that is good." This is already an attitude, a sort of self-assertion. Note, now, that it fulfils two of the conditions that are favorable to habit-formation, namely, strong initiative and strong satisfaction. Thus it is that the old doubts are overcome. The habit of self-repression in the presence of certain notions is replaced by a habit of self-assertion. Henceforth, instead of postponing one's selfhood or making it dependent upon a single branch of its own activity (the logical), the self boldly asserts itself as an integer, assuming in advance the ultimate success of its particular enterprises.

The order of events here is *sensation* (of tension and release), *emotion* (of peace or of joy), *reorganization of*

[1] G. A. Coe "The Sources of the Mystical Revelation," *Hibbert Journal*, January, 1908, pp. 366 ff.

[2] Ladd and Woodworth, *Elements of Physiological Psychology* (New York, 1911), pp. 586 f.

the self (including ideas of its relations to its world). This ought not to seem strange to us, for it is simply the opposite of well-recognized experiences in which physical conditions induce worry, self-distrust, and dejection. Thus it is that sensory factors may be one, or even a chief, determining condition of religious conversion.

3. Instinct plays a part in conversions. Many revivals are instances of gregariousness, that is, of a coming together because the mere presence of others gives satisfaction. Then, disapproval from others produces distress, and approval produces satisfaction, altogether apart from any judgment that one might form on other grounds as to one's own conduct or character. Thus the group standard passes over into individual conviction and determination partly by an instinctive route. Further, instinctive submission in the presence of superiority is often here—submission to the assertive personality of an evangelist, or to the church as greater than the individual, or to the overpowering greatness and goodness of God. Some persons take instinctive pleasure in sinking their own will in one that they regard as superior. A few years ago a revival song-book set multitudes of persons singing:

> O to be nothing, nothing!
> Only to lie at his feet,
> A broken and emptied vessel,
> For the Master's use made meet.

That the nonsense of the second couplet did not promptly dawn upon the people is probably due in part to the instinctive satisfaction of feeling utterly submissive. Possibly the rather sharp contrast between the "once-born" type and the "twice-born" arises in part from individual differences with respect to "mastery and submission," both of which are instinctive. The "once-born" may be those who instinctively tend more toward mastery, the "twice-born" those who tend toward submission. This hypothesis does not exclude but may be combined with the hint already given that some sort of physiological depression probably underlies any persistent sense of helplessness.

What the convert regards as coming to himself is at the same time a conscious adjustment to an objective order of a social or at least quasi-social sort. He finds his place in a system of duties; or he becomes more sensitive toward his fellows (early Buddhist literature offers an example); or he lays hold of a god who sympathizes with men; or, at least, he finds some law that seems to secure the possibility of a satisfactory destiny for both himself and his fellows. Thus his conversion consists in taking a human point of view for himself and his world; his self-realization is a realization of society. Starbuck holds that in the group studied by him the basal characteristic is a change from individualistic self-centeredness to a social center for the self.

The impulsiveness and convincingness of this change point back to parts of our instinctive social endowment. Underneath the attitudes toward one another that we designate as respect for human life, regard for the interests of others, and affectionate regard are certain ultimate tendencies, not only to take notice of other individuals, but also to take their pleasures and pains as our own. In the evolutionary order this kind of interest in others makes its first clear appearance in the relation of mother to child. But it is instinctive in both sexes.[1] When we behold a helpless or suffering individual, especially one smaller or weaker than ourselves, we find ourselves spontaneously taking his point of view and desiring *with* him. This taking-the-other's-point-of-view-as-worth-while-for-us spreads outward from the parental relation until it becomes the broadly human principle of benevolence, respect for persons, and, finally, ideal justice. Now, the conversion experience includes, all in all, a movement in this direction. To come into communion with a god of love, for example, is to take for one's self the god's broadly human point of view. It is to give play to our own parental instinct.

The fact, now well known, that adolescence is the period of life in which evangelistic influences have their maximum effectiveness, points to a connection between adolescent conversions and the sexual instinct. The connection is both indirect and direct. The physiological change has an *indirect* effect because the general state of restlessness or excitement induced by the intrusion of a new (or largely new) set of organic sensations makes it easy for youth to acquire new interests of almost any kind. The sexual instinct plays a *direct* part also in that it increases attention to persons (both one's self and others), and in that it extends and deepens tender emotion.[2] Thus the instinct of sex joins with that of

[1] On the nature and classification of instincts see E. L. Thorndike, *The Original Nature of Man* (New York, 1913), especially chap. vii. A brief summary of Thorndike's main conclusions will be found in his *Education* (New York, 1912), chap. v. See also W. McDougall, *An Introduction to Social Psychology* (Boston, 1909), especially pp. 60–81.

[2] It is true that sex attraction as such does not seem to include regard for another's interests; nothing can be more ruthless than the sex instinct, in some of its manifestations, at least. Yet it does not

parenthood in establishing in conversion a more social attitude. This is the direct influence that adolescence has upon abrupt conversions.[1]

How does the delayed instinct of sex enter thus into the texture of adolescent character? (*a*) Obscure, not clearly localized sensations of a new order occur. (*b*) This interferes with the habitual sense of self, which depends in large measure upon a mass of common or unlocalized sensations. (*c*) The strangeness of one's self, the experience of being jogged out of habitual adjustments, has as its motor correlate restlessness and yearning. (*d*) Its idea-

generally exist "in and by itself" in the human species. The fixation of attention upon another, the vivid realization of his presence as this particular individual, which is characteristic of sex attraction, has an important consequence. We individualize one another by *Einfühlung*—that is, by imaginative putting of one's self in another's place—so that we reciprocally feel one another's satisfactions and discomforts. Now, sex attraction, as well as parental instinct, strongly individualizes its object. Therefore we may assume that sex makes a direct contribution to the appreciation of benevolence and justice. Something very like the parental attitude also appears between lovers—the attitude of protection, intense response to every sign of pain, cuddling.

[1] Typical of the adolescent impulse to interpret existence as a whole in human terms is Mary Antin's account of her first acquaintance with the ocean at the age of about twelve: "So deeply did I feel the presence of these things that the feeling became one of awe, both painful and sweet, and stirring and warming, and deep and calm and grand. . . . . I was alone sometimes. I was aware of no human presence; I was conscious of only the sea and sky and something I did not understand. And as I listened to its solemn voice, I felt as if I had found a friend, and knew that I loved the ocean. It seemed as if it were within as well as without, a part of myself; and I wondered how I had lived without it, and if I could ever part with it."—*The Promised Land* (Boston, 1912), p. 179. Tagore has recognized more clearly, perhaps, than any other poet of religion the inner connection between human affection and the attractiveness of God. *The Crescent Moon* (New York, 1913), which is concerned with parental love; *The Gardener* (New York, 1913), which has conjugal love as its theme, and *Gitanjali* (London, 1913), which is an offering of songs to God—these three are variations upon a single theme.

tional correlate is mystery. The strangeness of the self spreads out over one's world. The world cannot mean the same simply because that *to which* it has meaning is different. (*e*) New pleasure is experienced in the mere presence of persons of the opposite sex even though reference to sexual union is completely excluded. The sex interest, that is, expands into a social interest that sustains itself merely as such. (*f*) New pleasure is experienced also in the society of persons of one's own sex. Witness the gangs, sets, teams, clubs, that characterize the period. The reason is that the changing sense of self calls for material for self-interpretation. Further, the strangeness of the self to itself makes social support almost indispensable. Even a timid person can act confidently as one of a group. (*g*) This new social self-realization can be more or less deep, more or less expansive, and it is almost certain to meet resistance from the habitual narrower self. Two levels of life can thus appear within the same life, two opposing directions of desire, both grounded in instinct. The mystery of both one's self and of one's world may, however, yield before the experienced reality of society. The adolescent doubter rarely doubts the validity of ethical principles that formulate the rudiments of respect for persons.[1]

[1] We must warn ourselves against ambiguity in discussions of "the" adolescent. Discrimination is necessary between emotional strains induced by our high-pressure modern life, by school conditions, by bad habits, or by a particular religious environment, and the natural unfolding of adolescent interests in situations that provide wealth of experiences without overstimulation. On the other hand, it must not be assumed that we can find adolescent nature in situations that provide no wealth of experience. That the social impulses of adolescence are largely thwarted and misdirected in large sections of our population cannot be doubted.

The reasons for the attraction of adolescents to religion now become clear. (*a*) Religion commonly presents itself as a fellowship—a congregation, a church, a historic cause or party. (*b*) Religion commonly presents itself as fellowship with a superior being who has, or can be induced to take, the human point of view. In some of the higher religions direct communion with such a god is held out as the privilege of the individual. (*c*) In general, religion represents a contrast between the ordinary or habitual and something deeper and broader—a contrast closely like that between the adolescent's narrower, habitual self and the broader self that strives with it.

4. So much for the elements involved in conversion. Under what characteristic laws, if any, do they here combine? Premising that "abrupt" is not a strictly determinate conception, we may summarize the process where it is most abrupt as follows:

First, the elements already noted (sensations, ideas, motor tendencies, instinctive desires) are combined into a new and satisfying whole by the process of suggestion.[1] Conversion is promoted by anything that narrows attention to two contrasting levels of life, as the reiterations, pleadings, and commands of a preacher; congregational singing; the mere presence of an expectant congregation; community sentiment; private conversation (personal evangelism); reflection and reading. Rhythm plays an interesting rôle. From early times drumming, hand-clapping, swaying of bodies, chanting, and dancing have been used as means of inducing the type of hypnosis popularly called trance. Entirely independent of the

[1] A short exposition of suggestion will be found on pp. 120 f.

fatigue effect produced when these exercises are greatly prolonged is the tendency of rhythm, as of other repetitions, to bring wandering attention back to one and the same point. Here we get light upon the usual tactics of the song-leader in revival meetings and also upon the rhythmical character of revival melodies.[1]

But, secondly, only a part of the work of reorganization is done thus suddenly. Another part, which is more gradual, precedes the climax. Suggestion, the mere narrowing of attention for a few minutes, does not profoundly reverse one's likes and dislikes unless a preparatory process has taken place. The convert himself may not be able to give any account of such a process; his experience may seem to him like an explosion. Yet we know that new points of view do mature, new attitudes do take root, before their presence is clearly recognized. One may see an object, and even react to it, or reverse an opinion, or change one's attitude toward a person without being able to recall the steps involved— one wakes up to find that the deed is already done. This is the sort of fact that necessitates some such term as the subconscious. Reserving to a later chapter a general exposition of the subconscious in religion, we note merely that a maturing of this type underlies the conversion phenomenon. It is what makes possible

[1] Conversely, we get light upon the rhythmical utterance or sing-song that characterizes many persons when they speak under what they regard as inspiration. A Quaker preacher who in his preaching commonly felt himself controlled by the Spirit confided to me that his high sing-song seemed to *come upon* him; it even embarrassed and humiliated him. Here the lack of variety is strictly parallel with the loss of facial expression and the reduction of vocal emphasis when one is approaching hypnosis.

depth of response to the suggestion that precipitates the crisis.[1]

To immediate suggestion plus the subconscious we must add, finally, a third law, that of habit-formation. At the Water Street Mission in New York, for example, it is not assumed that a down-and-out is really on his feet as soon as a conversion climax has occurred. No; his surroundings are looked after; he is helped to get work; friends accompany him to and from work so that he may be sure not to yield to the old saloon habit; he is brought to the mission every night and made happy there; he is set promptly at the task of helping other down-and-outs. In short, he is given the experience of a new external as well as internal world, and he is drilled in definite social acts with pleasurable associations until good conduct becomes habitual. Thus he continues to build his new self and his new world after the climax, just as it was partly built before. Wherever converts "stick" it will be found that habit-formation, particularly through a new social fellowship, follows the conversion crisis. Yet popular thought commonly attributes the results of this habit-formation to the crisis itself.

There remain for analysis the functions of the conversion experience. The convert experiences the change as the attainment of "new," "true," or "real" life. What does this mean? Before answering, let us make sure what the question is. It is not, Do we ourselves regard the new life as higher than the old? Functional psychology neither approves nor disapproves the satisfactions that it investigates. It seeks rather to discover

[1] S. H. Hadley is said to have remarked that the down-and-outs converted at the Water Street Mission in New York are men who were formerly under the influence of religion in their childhood homes.

what it is in any situation that makes it satisfying to the man who finds it so. To do this we must attend to the points of view that men occupy in their likes and dislikes. The existence of such points of view, which is obvious enough, implies (a) satisfactions, (b) discrimination between satisfactions, (c) preference for certain satisfactions as against others, and (d) at least a potential scale of preferences. Our present concern is with these scales of preferences or—since our definition of a value is "a discriminated satisfaction taken as a mark of an object"—with scales of values. Let it be repeated that our question is not, Which scale is the best? but, What scales are actually used?

To say of a man that something is good from his point of view is to say that he is acting, or tends to act, as an integer. In human experience, as a matter of fact, satisfactions are not merely accumulated. A man may be dissatisfied because he enjoys something that he does not approve. He may seek to acquire new capacities for enjoyment, as when he trains himself in the appreciation of poetry or of music. The peculiarly human way of dealing with satisfactions is to relate them both to objects and to the self, and to judge both. It follows that, when scales of values are concerned, we must see a person's preferences through his own eyes or we shall not see them at all.

If we assume in advance that the convert's satisfactions conform to the scale that we ourselves prefer, or that they conform to types, biological or other, that take no account of the conversion experience itself, we proceed by an a priori rather than empirical method. In order to be objective and empirical, we must let converts tell us what values they experience; we must inquire whether there is a consensus of testimony, and if there is a consensus we must, in the absence of positive disproof, accept this consensus as representing an actual part of the order of nature.[1]

[1] The doctrine that nature has no preferences is not empirically founded. It is either (a) a principle of method, in which case the doctrine exists because it is itself preferred, or (b) a bit of a priori speculation. There is good reason for ignoring preferences in certain parts of research, but there is also the best of reason for recognizing them in other parts. Whoever says that nature has no preferences, or that if they exist science should ignore them, exhibits in his own person a case of preference that has scientific interest. For scientific method itself is an expression of preferential functions—the functions of multiplying objects of experience, of unifying them, and of communication. It involves recognition of individuals by one another, each of whom agrees (so to say), in consideration of the mutual benefits to be received, to look through the others' eyes as well as his own. Nothing is a fact for science until several persons, each from his own point of view, have perceived it. The organic law of science might be formulated somewhat as follows: "We the undersigned mutually agree that in the assemblies and the publications of this society we will postpone all our other likes and dislikes in order that we may indulge together our liking for analysis; and in order that the judgments of each of us may attain to objectivity, each of us agrees to listen respectfully to what every other member has to say." We do not depart from scientific method, then, if we go on to ask what are these postponed likes and dislikes, and also what is the kind of value that each scientific man attributes to every other scientific man. Let it be noted, too, that communication of points of view from person to person is fundamental in every science.

The "psychologist's fallacy," which consists in attributing the ways of one's own mind to the mind that one is studying, appears in a peculiar form in some discussions of functions. For the assumption is made that the biologist's or psychologist's point of view in the analysis of a given satisfying situation is the point of view of the situation itself, as if what all men are *really after*, all the things that they *can* enjoy, are those that fit into the chosen scheme of the investigator. It is often said that the researcher must interrogate his facts. It would seem to be a rather happy circumstance that some facts are able, in articulate language, to answer questions about themselves!

Postponing for a moment the points at which the testimony of converts has been proved to be untrustworthy, let us see whether we can formulate any reasonably certain functions of the conversion experience.

1. Conversion certainly involves, not merely new satisfactions measured upon an old scale, but also and rather the adoption of a more satisfactory scale. There are, then, various scales to which different degrees of satisfaction attach, at least in these cases. Here a large problem opens out, namely, whether these cases are representative of any general law of satisfactions. Some light on this question will appear in the next paragraphs.

2. Conversion is a step in the creation of a self—the actual coming-to-be of a self. The language of the parable of the Prodigal Son, "he came to himself," is scientifically accurate. In conversion the pronoun "my" acquires meaning that it did not have before; mere drifting, mere impulse, are checked; my conduct and attitudes attach to me more consciously; I stand out in a new way, judging myself and my world, and giving the loyalty of articulate purpose to the cause with which I identify myself. This achievement of a fresh self-realization is generally a permanent gain, not merely a momentary ebullition. From the testimony of Starbuck's respondents it appears "that the effect of conversion is to bring with it a changed attitude toward life which is fairly constant and permanent, although the feelings fluctuate."[1]

3. Conversion is generally, perhaps always, a step in the creation of society. The heightened realization of the self involves the refusal of desires merely as mine.

[1] P. 361.

A distinction is made between a lower, illusory self and a higher or valid self; and this validity appears to be always a social self-assertion. Just as the scientifically valid proposition is the "common to all" as against the "particular to me," so the religiously valid self is the one that reaches out into a fellowship, actual or imagined.[1]

The sense of emancipation is a sense of being where free selves are at home; the convert's new world has the standpoint of the convert himself; it is suffused with the self-enlarging, self-emancipating principle. This is the case not merely in Christian conversions following upon the preaching of God as love, but in other religions also. This is, no doubt, what should be expected in view of the account that genetic psychology gives of the rise of ego-consciousness, but it is of considerable importance that we are able to witness the same social principle at work precisely where the ego feels itself to be most completely emancipated.

The early Buddhist legends exhibit the principle rather remarkably. The Buddhist theology, in its fundamental doctrine of the nature of evil and of salvation—that suffering arises through desire, and is to be overcome by extinguishing desire—has no trace of a social conception of the ego or of salvation. For no distinction is made between egoistic and social points of view. Desire as such is represented as engendering evil, and the evil engendered by desire is represented as having its seat precisely where the desire is. Nevertheless, the conversion experience of both the Buddha and his first disciples is represented as followed by a burning

---

[1] It should be noted that the scientific "common to all" is, to a considerable extent, "common to" an imagined "all." That is, science as well as religion, has its ideal society.

desire to tell others and thus rescue them from their suffering! That is, one kind of desire did remain, the desire for *mutual* self-emancipation, but this desire, instead of enslaving the individual, appears as taking part in emancipating him.

4. There is no psychological dividing line in the social self-realization of the convert between fellowship with men and fellowship with the divine. Conversion is a faith-creating process, specifically social faith. The new world of the self is a world of its own kind; it feels itself in and into (*einfühlen*) whatever it conceives. Its values define its real objects. Thus it is that conversion not seldom makes real or brings near to the individual what he has previously accepted merely as instruction from others. Heretofore he had, to use James's distinction, knowledge about God, but now he has acquaintance.

The process here can easily be misinterpreted. The convert does not come into his fellowship with God by inferring from the phenomenon of conversion to a personal cause of it. His experience of self-emancipation is to him, *per se*, a satisfying social experience; it is direct acquaintance with an adequate *socius*. In the testimony of converts there is a general consensus as to the immediacy of this certainty. We, as psychologists, noting that the language of each convert reproduces the instruction that he has received from a particular religious communion, are certain that there is a mediate element in what the convert feels as wholly immediate. We know that in accordance with the law of suggestion he experiences what he is told to expect. He may thus become certain of doctrines that may or may not be true. He may misjudge himself, thinking his motives to be purer and simpler than they are, or that he is firmly established when he is still weak and liable to fall. But alongside of this mediate factor there is a factor of immediacy also. Granted that his training has prepared him for the crisis, and that conversion puts him under the control of existing social standards and ideas of God, the fact remains that conversion makes these things real to the convert. Heretofore he had "knowledge about" them; now he has "acquaintance with" them. The world or God has meaning *for him* and makes response *now*. Here is no mere repetition of the past, for the individual is a new and unique one, and this experience *as his* is as fresh as the creation morn itself.

The recognition of this immediacy does not commit us, as mere observers, to the affirmation that the convert's sense of divine communion has ultimate validity. Validity implies the possibility of a social judgment as contrasted with the impressions of an individual. The impressions of the convert are to be tested by actual experiment, on the part of the many, with the conditions for realizing a self and for realizing the presence of other selves. Such experimentation is going on in the whole of our social intercourse as well as in religious conversion processes, so that the problem of validity becomes not merely, Can the conversion experience be repeated? but, What is the relation of the "self-and-*socius*" experience of converts to the whole evolution of "self-and-*socius*" in the race? The point that we have now reached is that religious conversion is, all in all, a particular instance of the differentiation of the individual consciousness, which is also social consciousness, the beginnings of which were referred to in the last chapter.

CHAPTER XI

MENTAL TRAITS OF RELIGIOUS LEADERS

Of the common qualities of leadership, which are found in religion as in other affairs, there is no occasion to speak. But religious leaders, at least those who attract most attention, have long been distinguished from other men by what seem to be certain peculiar traits. We shall now inquire what these traits are, whether they are, in fact, peculiar, and why they influence other men so powerfully.

First, however, it is advisable to discriminate between different types of religious leaders and of religious leadership. Nothing is easier, or more speciously fallacious, than to characterize religious genius by a few selected experiences that happen to fall within the range of one's scientific specialty. If I am a specialist in nervous diseases, I am bound to notice the frequency of hallucination and other signs of nervous instability among prominent religionists, and consequently I shall be in danger of a narrow characterization of religious leaders as neurotics. Medical men have not always avoided this error. It is parallel to the attempt of certain writers to make sexual passion the fundamental motive in religion. The frequency of sexual interest and of neurotic symptoms is not to be denied, but rarely does either of these suffice to characterize a man or woman who attains great religious influence. Other qualities are prominent and influential in the same men and women, and, as we shall see, in much religious leadership these things play little part or none at all.

There has been, in fact, an evolution of religious leadership that is part and parcel of the evolution of religion. Three broad types of leader are distinguishable, the shaman, the priest, and the prophet, and these three reach the climax of their respective influence in this historical order—the climax only, for evolution does not separate things as a staircase separates different levels by a vertical rise. Shamanism persists in all religions, though not in all religious individuals, and seeds and sprouts of late-maturing plants can be discerned early in the evolution. Further, the terms "shaman," "priest," and "prophet," as here used, should not be taken as full and adequate description; they are merely centers around which to gather bodies of related facts.

1. *The shaman.*—Practically everywhere in early religion we find religious specialists who correspond in important ways to the persons among us who are called "psychics." The shaman is supposed to learn and reveal hidden things, such as the future, or the whereabouts of a lost object, or the doer of a secret act, such as theft, and to influence the mysterious forces, all by processes that we recognize as subjective. A typical shamanistic procedure is the trance. By dancing continued to the point of exhaustion, or by exhausting sweating in a sweat lodge, or by mental numbing brought on by monotonous music, prolonged torture, or the use of narcotic drugs, the shaman gets himself out of his usual grooves, is shorn of his habitual inhibitions, and passes into autohypnosis or trance. This condition involves unresponsiveness to

the generality of stimuli, with focalized responsiveness to some particular sort of stimuli. The shaman now acts from suggestions, some of which, based upon tribal traditions and upon previous experience of his own, he took with him into the trance, and others of which are derived from the immediate situation. His response to these suggestions is likely to take the form of visions— he sees the enemy, or the god, or the supposed culprit, or the issue of the impending battle. Sometimes he speaks automatically, that is, the impression of the moment passes directly into involuntary speech. To the beholders, and largely to the shaman himself, all this is the direct expression of *mana* or of some more definite being, such as a spirit, by which he is "possessed."

According to the tribe's theory, the shaman is a leader because of this super-something that is in him. In reality his leadership is due to at least three factors: First comes the impressiveness of the trance phenomenon itself, and the fact that this individual experiences trance more than his fellows. He is likely to have a special aptitude for trances; that is, to be nervously unstable, a neurotic. Certainly spontaneous trances in someone are the necessary antecedent of the cultivation of trance states. Yet, since most normal individuals can be hypnotized, the automatisms of a given shaman may have been induced entirely by training administered by previous shamans. Nevertheless, it is safe to assume that a neurotic tendency, if it is not too extreme, is a help to religious influence at this stage of religious evolution.

A second ground of shamanistic influence is success in doing the thing that the people desire. Undoubtedly shamans—and here we may include the oracles—are sometimes wise. They are wise, not merely because they know how to avoid issues, or surreptitiously to gather information, or to give forth ambiguities that can be interpreted in accordance with the event, but also because the abstracted mind sometimes gains in truth even from its oversimplification. It seems clear that the reducing of inhibitions, the dropping of things from attention, not seldom makes the really important fact seem important. Successful guesses at character, or solutions of problems, or prediction, doubtless do thus occur now and then, redounding to the glory of the shaman, and overbalancing any number of weaker performances or failures. And the shaman is sometimes helped unwittingly by others. If he scrutinizes the faces of the whole assembled group in an effort to find which one has committed a theft, the culprit will be likely to wear a telltale facial expression. Reading excited faces is a well-developed art practiced by some who pose among us as mind-readers. Again, the encouragement that he brings to the anxious, adding to their actual power as well as comfort, is secure ground for the shaman's influence. The mere prediction of victory in battle might produce the courage to win it.

A third ground of the shaman's influence is wisdom gathered from habitual dealing with public interests. For he acts for the group, and therefore accustoms himself to men, to the graver problems, and to causes and effects (however inadequately he may analyze them).

These are the foundations of the shaman's power in his group. The cornerstone of the whole is automatisms interpreted as intercourse with the superior powers.

The shaman himself shares this basal belief with his group. Nevertheless, because he discovers that matters can sometimes be helped along by mixing certain voluntary performances with the automatic, he becomes a trickster as well as a "psychic." The case is parallel with that of some modern psychics who make a livelihood by fortune-telling or by securing supposed communications from the dead. If we detect such a person committing a fraud, we are likely to suppose that he is consciously fraudulent all the way through, whereas he may still believe that "there's something in it" because of the presence of a genuinely automatic factor to which he knows not how to give any but a spiritistic interpretation. What we call fraud is thus in part his way of helping on what he believes to be genuine intercourse with superior powers.

We have here the clue to some modern phenomena in the sphere of religious leadership. Even the founders of some of our newest cults exhibit traces of shamanistic procedure. This is true of Joseph Smith, of Mrs. Eddy, and of Mr. Dowie, though in unequal degree. Each of these leaders mixed shrewd calculation with what gave itself forth as inspiration, and none of them acknowledged the mixture, but claimed superindividual authority for the whole. The question is often asked whether they must not therefore be regarded as, to this extent, conscious impostors. The extent and audacity of Joseph Smith's inventions are amazing. Yet mental ability to carry through his plots by his own unsupported designs was not his. He was in all probability inwardly upborne by what seemed to be a power beyond himself. His very frauds were thereby, we may well suppose, sanctified in his eyes. This inner support, in turn, gave to his acts the force and sureness that made them impressive to the people—his fellows took him at his word partly because he believed it himself. Mr. Dowie and Mrs. Eddy, though each represented a type far removed from that of Joseph Smith, experienced, nevertheless, a parallel inner support for their respective inventions. It is this that gives impressiveness to a certain oracular or magisterial tone that would otherwise appear as spiritual impudence. But, as with shamanism, so with Mormonism, Dowieism, and Christian Science: the spread of the movement is due partly to the added fact that it met real needs—it bore desirable fruit that the people could experience for themselves. In all three instances temporal blessings were achieved, either improved health or improved economic conditions, and in all three there were engendered inner strength and consciousness of moral triumph.

2. *The priest.*—If the central item in the shaman's function is to lay hold of fresh power by psychical means, the corresponding item in priestly functions consists in conserving by institutional means whatever has been attained. This, too, is leadership, and it has a creative aspect; though it is conservative rather than radical, it is not mere petrifaction. The priest, seeing to it that the ceremonies are duly observed; that sacred places, times, objects, and persons are kept sacred; that the traditions are accurately handed down from generation to generation and ultimately committed to writing, not only repeats the utility acts which the shaman originated, but also makes an immeasurable contribution to the organization of a firm society. Priesthoods train men

to the idea of law, even to law that enforces itself by inner rather than outer force, as taboo, divine favor or displeasure, and post-mortem rewards and penalties. The priestly régime likewise trains men to act and to feel together. Tribal consciousness and, at its beginnings, national consciousness are inseparable from the circle of ideas and practices over which the priesthood presides. In his own way, then, the priest is a religious leader, and his mental traits deserve attention.

Historically the shaman and the priest shade into each other. Yet the shaman type yields in time to the priestly type. For automatisms are not easily organizable into a permanently controlled system. The tribe must repeat again and again the acts that secure the help of the superior powers, but fresh intercourse with these powers by the way of "possession" cannot always be guaranteed. Besides, early acts that appear to be useful become hardened into custom, so that the ceremony tends to go on, whatever be the psychical outcome of fresh resort to the unseen beings. The priestly mind, accordingly, is the mind that observes times and seasons, holds to exact forms of approaching the gods, systematizes, creates orthodoxies, and finally sets up mental kingdoms and empires that rival in real power the civil and military authorities. Not self-abandonment to fresh impulse, not intuitive certainties, but the logic of consistency, with an ever-present assumption of the validity of the past—this is priestliness. Hence, among other things, the punctilious writing down of the exact formula for the sacrifice, the effort to preserve the very words of religious founders, the interpretation of national history in terms of religious doctrine—in short, the birth of sacred literatures. Here, of course, is opportunity, much used, for dead formalism, mechanical routine, and lazy revenues (the priest's portion of the sacrifice, etc.), yet all in all the priestly mind has shown upon occasion aggression and resistance and organizing ability.

3. *The prophet.*—The term "prophet" is used in two main senses. On the one hand it is made to cover all of the more directly psychical, as distinguished from priestly and ceremonial, methods of intercourse with the gods. Thus the shamanistic performance of Israel's bands of soothsayers, of Saul when he fell into a trance, of Elisha when he called for music as a means to insight— these on the one hand—and the ethical preaching of Amos and the statesmanship of Isaiah, on the other hand, are all called "prophecy." But at times prophecy means specifically the experience that sets such men as Isaiah and Amos apart from both the priests and the sooth-saying types of so-called "prophets." In this restricted sense the term will be used here. It points to the fact that from time to time, in various religions, leaders have arisen who have gone directly to the sources of religious life, thus setting themselves in contrast with the priests and the priestly system; it points also to a second fact of the first importance, namely, that this going to the sources, though it is continuous with shamanism, never-theless transcends it, and contrasts with it not less strongly than it contrasts with priestliness.

The most accessible and illuminating instances are the great prophets of Israel. "I hate, I despise your feasts, and I will take no delight in your solemn assem-blies," says Amos, speaking in the name of Jahwe. "Yea, though ye offer me your burnt offerings and meal

offerings, I will not accept them: neither will I regard
the peace offerings of your fat beasts. Take thou away
from me the noise of thy songs; for I will not hear the
melody of thy viols" (Amos 5:21–23). Here is the
prophetic protest against the ceremonial or priestly conception of Jahwe's dealings with Israel, a revulsion from
orthodox institutionalism toward the primal sources of
religious feeling. But this is less than half the story.
The spiritual lineage of Amos goes backward, in important respects, toward shamanism. For he feels himself
to be the immediate mouthpiece of Jahwe; he experiences a kind of possession. But the contrast with shamanism is as great as that with priestly institutionalism.
It is no return to shamanism that Amos desires. "Let
judgment roll down as waters, and righteousness as a
mighty stream" (5:24); "Hear this, O ye that would
swallow up the needy, and cause the poor of the land
to fail, saying, When will the new moon be gone, that we
may sell corn? and the sabbath, that we may set forth
wheat? making the ephah small, and the shekel great,
and dealing falsely with balances of deceit; that we may
buy the poor for silver, and the needy for a pair of shoes,
and sell the refuse of the wheat" (8:4–6). Here at last
is religious leadership that, conceiving God predominantly as ethical will, regards ethical conduct as the
service of God and the prophet's own ethical fervor as
divine inspiration. It is true that the great prophets
experienced dreams and visions; it is true that these
automatisms were interpreted as divine possession after
the manner of shamanism; but the complementary
truth is that a distinction was made between true and
false prophets upon the basis of the content of their

respective messages. The true prophet must speak ethical truth without compromise. "The prophet is a fool, the man that hath the spirit is mad!" Hosea's hearers seem to say, and he retorts, "It is for the multitude of thine iniquity, and because the enmity is great" (Hos. 11:7).

Here is a transition point in religious leadership, the rise of a fresh conception of the leader's intercourse with the god. Inspiration or divine possession is now evidenced by ethical fervor. This is too simple a statement, it is true, to represent the whole historical situation. It was a complex made up partly of shamanistic, in some cases more or less priestly and nationalistic, assumptions. But the idea that ethical communion with the divine being is the essential religious experience did reach the surface in this prophetic movement, and this is *the* distinctive mark of this most remarkable group of religious leaders. That their proffered guidance was accepted at the time in only a minor degree, the nation turning rather with renewed devotion to priestly ceremonialism and orthodoxy, does not detract from the claims of these ethical prophets to a place in the world's list of its greatest leaders. For the sacerdotalism that fastened itself upon the people wore out, while the prophetic message gained in power through the centuries. It was the prophetic, not the priestly, element in Judaism that attracted Jesus and formed his character and the basis of his message; and Paul, in spite of his legalistic training, and in spite of a strong tendency to automatisms, was conquered by it.

The career and the writings of Paul present an extraordinary instance of the coexistence in one individual of the qualities that underlie all three types of leadership. In the first place, he had a luxuriant experience of the sort of automatisms that might have made him a great leader of the shamanistic type. He had visions, fell into trances, spoke and wrote under conscious inspiration, spoke in "tongues" abundantly (an automatic phenomenon that will be described in the next chapter). But, in the second place, there was much of the priest in him, both by reason of his training as a strict Pharisee and by reason of the natural qualities of his mind. A maker of distinctions, a systematizer, a lover of precedent and of consistency, an organizer, a ruler of his followers—think how all this, added to the whole body of assumptions involved in his training as a Pharisee, fitted him to be the originator of a rigid priesthood. Yet both the shamanistic and the priestly tendencies within him were resisted and transcended, though not at all extirpated, by the influence upon him of the prophetic spirit of Jesus. Paul's immortal ode on love is a direct and specific comparison of the values of the shamanistic and the prophetic principles respectively. He is dealing with the extreme, disorderly automatisms of the circle at Corinth. He expresses a wish that all the Corinthian Christians might speak in tongues (I Cor. 14:5). He thanks God that he himself speaks in tongues more even than anyone there (14:18). He believes, with shamanism, that this experience is actually a divine taking possession of one's vocal organs, yet, unlike shamanism, he is ready to judge it by its fruits. As far as it leads to disorder, it is to be condemned, and anyhow, he exclaims, "In the church I had rather speak five words with my understanding, that I might instruct others also, than ten thousand words in a tongue" (14:19)! Further, he prefers "prophecy," or inspirational speech in the language of the people. He prefers it because it can be understood, and also *because it can be controlled by the speaker* (14:1–33). Without completely reconciling these various supposed sorts of direct intercourse with God, Paul actually attains the notion of sitting in ethical judgment upon anything that offers itself as a divine message. Process is to be judged by content and tendency. In principle this asserts that true communion with God is had in our ethical impulses, judgments, decisions, and actions. He summarizes his position on another occasion thus: "Quench not the Spirit; despise not prophesyings [the automatic]; scrutinize all things; hold fast that which is good; abstain from every kind of evil" (I Thess. 5:19–21). This is the setting of his ode on love. He contrasts love with the whole wonder-awakening group of automatisms, and even with knowledge, dear as knowledge is to his extraordinary intellect, and leaves us with this ultimate principle: The supreme and normative experience of God is ethical love.[1]

The fundamental trait of our third type of religious leader, then, is a broad and intense sociality that transcends mere institutionalism because it *individualizes men as objects of love.* The leader is now, in a high ethical sense, the lover, and he is able to lead because he loves, and therein represents God. This is the open secret of Jesus' influence upon men. The records of his life are

---

[1] By ethical love I mean the broader social will—broader, that is, than conjugal fondness, parental regard, or the partiality of a narrow friendship.

too meager to enable us to speak in much detail of his mental traits, and the critical questions that still gather around the Gospels involve, to some extent, the interpretation of his mind and of his attitudes. Nevertheless, it can be said with confidence that he represents a reaction against the sacerdotal conception of divine communion, and that, though he appears to have experienced some automatisms that he interpreted as special divine impartations, these were not the staple of his reliance either for himself or for others. That is, of shamanism there are only minor traces even in the records, which are themselves interpretations and not portraits, and sacerdotalism is directly opposed. That he was a wonder-worker, a healer of diseases by what we recognize as suggestion, does not indicate that he occupied the standpoint that I have called shamanism. He healed the people because of his overwhelming sympathy, not as a means of dominating them. How he wrought his cures was obviously insignificant to him, compared with the joyous fact that the people were lifted out of their distresses. He was not a shaman, but a servant of the people.

Even if criticism should prove that he held to an extreme catastrophic view of the coming of the Kingdom; even if we should be obliged to believe that he was ultimately a disillusioned idealist (that is, that he expected to be accepted during his earthly lifetime as the promised Messiah), what has been said still holds true of his mental traits, and it contains the explanation of his power over men. His simple trust in a Father who understands us and brings good to pass even through seeming ill; his equally simple valuation of human life, as if ungrudging, unsparing helpfulness were the most natural thing in the world; his penetrating conceptions of right and wrong, as if he simply gazed upon the thing he talked about; a certain moral irresistibility because he reduces the problems of conduct to simple issues of ethical love—these are the grounds of his influence. In some important respects his influence resembles that of Lincoln. Jesus had the same homespun feeling for "folks," the same appreciation of friendship, corresponding directness of perception and picturesqueness of speech, quiet courage, a more than full measure of patient endurance, something even of the same humor. This is the sort of leadership that describes itself in the old saying, "We love him because he first loved us."

These examples, though they are drawn from a single stream of religious tradition, are representative of religious leadership as a whole. There are types of leadership, as there are grades of culture. It is a narrow view that thinks to explain the influence of Paul, of Jesus, of the Buddha, or of Mohammed by saying that each was more or less neurotic, or even epileptic, and that the people took his abnormalities for divine possession. In two of these cases at least the neurotic hypothesis rests on slight ground. That Jesus is said to have had a vision or two, and the Buddha a sudden life-enlightening conversion, by no means proves them neurotic in any useful sense of this term. Such experiences come to minds that function so capably that only under the exigencies of some overworked theory can they be called "abnormal." To characterize as neurotic any mind that experiences a well-marked automatism is to make the term "neurotic" scientifically useless. The ultimate test of mental morbidity, whether of the extreme sorts, called "imbecility" and "insanity," or of the milder sorts, called "neurotic," is one's ability to fulfil one's functions as a member of society. Neurasthenia, for example, is to be classed as a mental disorder, not because it involves a mental process that is peculiar to neurasthenics, but because certain processes that are common to all men are here present in so excessive or one-sided a way as obviously to interfere with the carrying on of life's business in co-operation with others. Neither Jesus nor the Buddha was made weak or inefficient by automatisms that he may have experienced; neither trafficked in them after the manner of the shaman; neither relied upon them as the basis of his certainty of the principles that he taught, but each rested the authority of his teachings either upon analysis of life or else upon the practical self-evidence of basal ethical ideals; neither was separated from men by any mental peculiarity, but each was drawn to men and drew men to him by compassionate helpfulness. Finally, though each was a dissenter from the existing social-religious order, each dissented, especially Jesus, in the interest of a wider and deeper sociality. That the shamanistic features added by tradition to the picture of each of these prophets, and the so-to-say "rabbinical" doctrines that offered themselves as the historical story had influence with succeeding generations, is undeniable. Antagonistic elements mix in any evolutionary process. But the specific ground of the personal influence involved, the reason why tradition selected these particular men as first among the sons of men, cannot have been either a shamanistic or a priestly element in the men themselves, but rather the element of ethical prophecy, the fresh resort to new and ethically higher sources of religious experience.

Signs of neurotic mental make-up are far more abundant in Paul and Mohammed. Mohammed's visions and auditions were numerous and apparently vivid. A true shamanistic touch appears, moreover, when he has visions that seem as if made to order for the obvious purpose of carrying his point in certain disputes. That these automatisms helped to give him sanctity and authority in the eyes of the people need not be doubted. The remaining question is whether the messages that he uttered had a prophetic character, and, if so, what part they had in making Mohammed the great leader that he became. His general capacity for vigor and persistence in action is sufficiently .witnessed by the way in which he organized his followers and led them to victory against great opposition. What is more significant is that he was a religious and social reformer. His message, seen in the light of contemporary religious crudity and social unintegration, was of the prophetic type. It was to a relatively exalted conception of God that he called men, and to certain progressive, though limited, notions of social duty. These, rather than the automatic form that his originality took, are his distinguishing marks. There were ten thousand men who could have visions to one who could conceive such thoughts, but it was this one to whom the people clave.

Our study of what makes one a leader brings us, of course, to a consideration of what it is that the people desire, or at least are ready to follow. That grounds of religious leadership evolve, as we have now seen, implies that parallel changes occur in the springs of action in the whole religious body. Here opens the wide problem of wherein mental evolution consists. In what sense, if any, does human nature remain the same, and in what sense does it move? Postponing this question to subsequent chapters, let us close the examination of the elements of religious leadership by a word concerning the more obvious relations between the leaders and the led. It is obvious that religious evolution is a movement in which both the leaders and the led are *carried along*. The notions, once seriously held, that religion was largely invented and imposed upon the people by priestcraft or statecraft, are, as we now see, so unhistorical as to be preposterous. A leader does not manufacture religion any more than a gardener makes a rose. In religion as in floriculture there is a fundamental, spontaneous process which is guided more or less toward specific products by individual action.

To be more specific, there are three sorts of thing that religious leaders may do. First, a leader may embody, focalize, and render effective an already germinating standpoint of the people by bringing it to conscious definition. He makes them see what it is that they already want, or he guides them in a particular procedure for obtaining what they want. The revealing of men to themselves is what gives such apparent self-evidence to the greatest prophetic messages, and this is also one ground of the impression that God himself speaks through the prophet. Secondly, a leader may bring victory to one of two or more competing attitudes, policies, or beliefs of society. He may do it by superior definition, argument, and emotional appeal; or by organizing a party; or by presenting some apparently supernatural sanction, whether from tradition and precedent, or from some fresh divine interposition. Thirdly, a leader may be thus not only a lens through which light already shining from some large portion of the population is brought to a focus, but also the one through whom a particular ray enters the social complex. Originality in the full sense of insight that has not before existed in the race is implied, of course, in the general progress of knowledge. Each item of this progress begins with some individual who sees something that his predecessors did not see. Similarly, ethical progress in any direction is initiated by some individual or individuals whose satisfactions and dissatisfactions are different from those of other persons. This is ethical originality, which becomes creativeness whenever it effectively organizes and propagates itself. How far a particular genius focuses existing light and how far he emits an original ray is generally hard to make out, but the fact of such original radiation of light, and the other fact of great differences in the amount and color of light radiated by different individuals must be recognized. The religious genius, like other geniuses, is always in a true sense a product of his time and of his people, though he is more than a mere product thereof. Granted a genuine mental evolution, together with genuine differences between individuals, the way is open for a reasonable recognition of originality in any degree. The degree of it in a particular case has to be determined, as well as may be, by historical study of the entire situation.

CHAPTER XII

RELIGION AND THE SUBCONSCIOUS

In an earlier chapter reference was made to the fact that certain attitudes that seem to introspection to be entirely new are nevertheless the result of an unrecognized ripening process. There are, in fact, multitudes of experiences in which an apparently ready-made mental product makes its appearance, giving an impression that, though it is "within me," it is not altogether "mine." This "something more" yields the general problem of the subconscious.

Religious experiences that involve this "something more" readily lend themselves to the following preliminary classification:

1. Visions and voices that seem to the one who has them to embody or convey information, as of the divine presence, the divine will, or the future.

2. Impressions that something is true, as that a certain person is or is not sincere ("discerning of spirits"); that a certain event is to take place; that this or that is one's duty; that God is personally present, though he is invisible and inaudible; that he has a certain attitude toward one (as "condemnation" and "witness of the Spirit"); or that this or that is the correct interpretation of a passage of Scripture.

3. Involuntary muscular reactions of many sorts that give an impression that one's body is being partly or wholly controlled by a will other than one's own. A

minister who participated in the great revival in Kentucky in 1801 gives the following classification of cases that fell under his observation: the falling exercise; the jerks; the dancing exercise; the barking exercise (grunts in connection with jerks); the laughing exercise; the running exercise; and the singing exercise.[1] "Getting the power" seems to have been a popular designation in some parts of the country for extreme loss of muscular control, manifested by falling and lying prone for a period. In one direction these phenomena reach a climax in "speaking in tongues," which is involuntary movement of the speech organs through which they form sounds, sometimes articulate syllables, supposed by the subject to express meanings in a tongue that he has never learned. Sometimes, in our day as in New Testament times, "another interprets," that is, gives in the language of the assembly the supposed meaning of that which has been spoken "in a tongue." The interpreter of tongues obviously follows impressions in the region of ideas, so that his experience falls under the second classification, and is parallel with that of the "inspirational speakers" who appear at meetings of spiritualists. Just as the vocal apparatus may come under this apparently foreign control, so may the apparatus for writing, as happens with many mediums. On the other hand, some writing mediums say that they control their hands in the usual way, but that the ideas are given whole and not "thought out."[2] Thus, the sort of internal dialogue

[1] *The Biography of Elder Barton Warren Stone, Written by Himself* (Cincinnati, 1847).

[2] Quoting Montgeron, *La Verité des Miracles* (1737), Marie and Vallon point out that the Jansenists were sometimes able, in one and the same discourse, to discriminate three degrees of inspiration: (1) ideas

in which we do our ordinary thinking, which is recognized as an inner talking to one's self, may be displaced by an inner dialogue in which one or both of the conversers seem to be other than one's self.[1] The "inner voice" or voices, too, may take the aspect of actual sounds instead of a give and take of ideas merely, in which case we have an audition (see 1).

4. In addition to these three sorts of rather well-defined reaction there are inner realizations of a more general or even vague kind that seem likewise to the subject of them to be "something more" than the "mine." As many an adolescent has suddenly discovered an inexpressible meaning in such familiar sights as the starry sky, or a forest, or the sunset afterglow, so a state of elation or of depression has often seemed to religious persons to be a communicated insight, not merely a mood. The case of anesthetic revelation reported in the chapter on "Conversion" presents merely an extreme instance of the practically universal objectifying of the affective qualities of our experience. Even the general urge of life that makes men take the side of hope rather than of despair, and to trust that the world is more rational than it seems from the angle

take hold of the speaker in a manner that he feels to be supernatural; (2) though at first he uses his own language to express them, there comes a time when the expressions themselves are internally dictated to him; (3) finally, the vocal apparatus speaks involuntarily and without any apparent previous thought (A. Marie et Ch. Vallon, "Des Psychoses religieuses," *Archives de Neurologie*, II, No. 12, 429).

[1] A small boy was heard to pray as follows: "Now I got a favor to ask you, and you sure to do it: Take the goodest care you can of M. and N. YES, I WILL! For Jesus' sake, Amen." The "Yes, I will," uttered in stentorian tones, was undoubtedly the child's dramatic participation in the supposed response of God.

of our partial experience, is taken by many as the utterance "within us" of an ultimate truth.

What, now, is the problem that psychology has to face in such facts? That a problem arises here at all is because much experience, to say the least, is given as the experience of individual selves. Even if we should become convinced that mind-stuff exists beyond and between the focal points called selves, or that sensations and desires could float about as isolated psychic states, we should still have to take individual selves into account, regarding *this* experience as belonging to A, while *that* belongs to B, and sooner or later asking how far A's and B's possessions respectively extend. It is important to note that the possessive "my" stands for a phase of experience as it is *given*. It is a datum, not a derivative through analysis or through association. We can, indeed, pull apart the items that we call mine, as my clothes, my body, and my pains and pleasures. But we cannot arrive at a "mine" by the reverse process of adding together items which to start with are merely "this's" and not already "my's." Each "my" is a unique datum, each self is an individual.

But it does not follow that selves are isolated and mutually exclusive atoms. Whether or not any item in my mental life is exclusively or wholly mine is not determined by saying that it certainly is mine. Joint ownership is a possible conception. As the same umbrella may shield two persons from rain, so one brain might conceivably be "mine" to more than one self. Moreover, several selves might have the very same thing—as sun or moon—as "my" object, and the very same end in view as "my" end.

As a matter of fact, no atomic exclusiveness anywhere appears. My own "my," along with my birth, is not a matter of my own devising; it arises

Out of the deep,
Where all that was to be, in all that was,
Whirl'd for a million aeons through the vast
Waste dawn of multitudinous-eddying light.
—Tennyson, *De Profundis.*

Moreover, this rising "out of the deep" is not merely a single event at the dawn of my consciousness; every pulse of my self has the same character. The "mine," that is to say, is always more than mine, even a part of the vast ongoing that some call nature and others God. My most private experiences, those most intimate to me, are thus, in some sense, overindividual as well as individual. If I try to think of myself in a purely numerical way as a discrete unit, the result is the abstract notion of unity, not this self of mine experiencing this and that. All "my" "this's" and "that's" occur as parts of a wider whole. The actual, concrete "my" is thus conjunct, in its inmost nature, with the "more than mine." A dividing line, on one side of which is the "mine" and that only, and on the other side of which is all else, simply does not exist.

The problem of what constitutes individuality is further complicated by the fact that different individuals know one another as "present." When I am challenged to say what I mean by your presence, my first impulse is to measure the inches that separate us. But this throws little light upon what it is for you to be present. At most it names a condition under which this experience arises, the experience itself being some sort of conjunction of "my's." Just as a moment ago we noted the immediacy of nature in our consciousness of the "my," so here we come upon the fact of social immediacy. We shall have to deal with it more at length in a subsequent chapter. But at this point we must note at least this: that the "my" is falsely construed whenever it is thought of as having only external relations to the "thy." Atomistic notions of "I" and "thou," as if each were inclosed within an impenetrable wall, do not describe our social experience. We are more intimate to one another by far. To the analysis of this intimacy genetic psychology has made two contributions. It has shown that the "my" does not arise in child consciousness before the "thy," but coincidently with it, and that the "my" construes itself throughout by reference to "thy's." Comparison of mine and thine, and give and take between me and thee, are included in the stuff of which my "me" consists. That is, social communion is the very experience that gives the "me" any meaning at all. Any actual, concrete "my" is already a "my-thy." Thus the individual self is conjunct, not only with nature, but also with society.

Clearly, then, we cannot escape the "something more" that is within and yet not merely mine. What we must do with it is to seek ever-closer definition of its, or their, ways. To this end our first task with respect to any wonder-awakening "something more" is to establish, as far as we can, identity of process between it and ordinary psychic events. Only thus shall we learn whether the subconscious has any laws peculiar to itself, and, if so, what they are. If we should conclude that it has no peculiar laws, the effect would not be to explain away any phenomenon, but rather to necessitate a more than usually rigorous analysis of our ordinary life.

Let us ask, then, first of all, whether the sorts of phenomena that were catalogued at the beginning of this chapter are limited to religious subject-matter or religious motives. The answer is a decided negative. Visions and voices that seem to be veracious, and are sometimes proved to be so, occur in any sphere of life. Convincing impressions, particularly as to persons, are common and useful even in business. So, also, involuntary muscular reactions that seem to express knowledge may concern any subject-matter. We need not resort to mediums for instances. Thus a young woman, upon being asked the most important question that a man can put to a woman, started to give the favorable reply that she supposed was dictated by both heart and judgment, but was astonished to hear herself say the exact opposite of what, as she relates in a manuscript in my possession, "I thought I was saying." But she records that "Once spoken—astonished as I was—the words stood, and I held to them as the days and weeks went by." It turned out that on the road that she meant to travel, but was thus prevented from traveling, sorrow lurked. The man was not what she had supposed. She was rescued, in fact, by this unexpected use of her vocal apparatus. She herself had no doubt that it was somebody's knowledge that uttered itself thus.

That the inspiration process in religion is in no sense separate or peculiar will be clear to anyone who will examine literary and other artistic inspirations and then note the parallel ways in which new ideas arise in the common life. Thus oratory now and then exhibits the phenomenon of ideas seeming to control the speaker rather than the speaker his ideas. Henry Ward Beecher said:

There are times when it is not I that is talking; when I am caught up and carried away so that I know not whether I am in the body or out of the body; when I think things in the pulpit that I could never think in the study; and when I have feelings that are so different from any that belong to the lower or normal condition that I can neither regulate them nor understand them. I see things and I hear sounds, and seem, if not in the seventh heaven, yet in a condition that leads me to apprehend what Paul said, that he heard things that it was not possible for a man to utter.[1]

Poetic composition is another fruitful example. From Bryant, who claimed no inspiration, yet admitted that his thoughts sometimes seemed to be hardly his own,[2] to Goethe, who believed that genuine creative work is always a gift from above, there are all grades of conviction that one's ideas are given rather than achieved. Here are Goethe's own words:

All productivity of the highest kind, every important idea, every great thought which is followed by fruit and has consequences, is in no one's control, and is elevated above all earthly power. Such things men receive as unexpected gifts from above. In such cases man is often to be regarded as a tool of a higher world-government, as a vessel found worthy to receive the divine influence.[3]

Emerson says:

It is a secret which every intellectual man quickly learns, that beyond the energy of his possessed and conscious intellect

[1] *Beecher's Patriotic Addresses*, edited by J. R. Howard (New York, 1887), p. 140.

[2] Bigelow's *William Cullen Bryant*, p. 153.

[3] Otto Harnack, *Goethe in der Epoche seiner Vollendung*, 3. Aufl. (Leipzig, 1905), p. 32; cf. pp. 143, 160.

he is capable of a new energy (as of an intellect doubled upon itself), by abandonment to the nature of things."[1]

The frequency with which poets take poetic invention as a theme for a poem is rather remarkable in itself, but still more significant is the unanimity with which they represent the poet's mind as an instrument upon which "something more" plays. What we call most original with them they regard as given to them.

Yet, as Emerson remarks, all are poets to a greater or less degree, and, as Holmes points out, every association of ideas is a case of something wrought in us rather than by us.[2] The subconscious, whatever it is, is surely an everyday affair. Thus, there "pops into my head" the solution of a problem that has puzzled me. My memory testifies that the last time I thought about the question I had no answer for it. But now the complete answer is present, with all its parts fitted together, just as if I had found them one by one and built them into a designed whole. Or to take an instance from the realm of volition: whereas yesterday I was pulled hither and thither by conflicting desires with respect to a certain matter, this morning, after a night's rest, my will is at peace with itself. Some of the things that I craved I no longer desire at all, and I now desire some things to which I was antagonistic or indifferent. A third ordinary sort of experience is the adjustment of conduct to conditions the existence of which we do not seem to

[1] Essay on "The Poet," in *Essays*, Second Series (Boston, 1898), p. 30.

[2] Among the best popular descriptions of literary invention are those of Oliver Wendell Holmes in *The Autocrat of the Breakfast Table* (Riverside Press, 1891), p. 191, and *Pages from an Old Volume of Life* (Riverside Press, 1891), pp. 283 ff.

know. Here is an instance that was recorded by the subject at the time of its occurrence:

I have just been writing several New Year's greetings, dating each at the bottom, "December 31, 1911." Just as I wrote this date on one of them I had a feeling that I had not written it correctly on the preceding one, and that I had probably written "11" instead of "31." This proved to be the case, but I was not sure until I looked to see.

Here the process of correcting the error was started without apparent knowledge that the error existed.

It is therefore impossible to give a psychological account of the subconscious in religion without some attempt to weigh the general theories of the subconscious as such. The nature of the problem will be somewhat clarified, possibly, if we note that the subconscious is not a fact of observation but wholly an inference. That the notion arises at all is because memory and introspection are baffled. One of the clearest examples is this: The well-known illusion of length produced by converging lines is produced also when invisible shadows are substituted for certain of the lines. Here we infer that *something like* perception has occurred, although the subject can give no account of it whatever.[1]

Three types of theory exist: (1) The neural theory, which holds that all deliverances called subconscious are due to restimulation of brain tracts that have been organized in a particular way through previous experiences of the individual. According to this view, there is no subconscious elaboration or ripening, but only plain reproduction. (2) The dissociation theory, which, start-

[1] K. Dunlap, "The Effect of Imperceptible Shadows on the Judgment of Distance," *Psychological Review*, VII, 435.

ing with the fact that the field of attention includes a penumbra as well as a focus, holds that the penumbral items of experience can be combined and elaborated while remaining within the penumbra, and thus, when the focus of attention shifts to them, can appear as ready made. (3) The theory of a detached subconsciousness. This phrase was devised, I believe, by a persistent critic of the theory, the late Professor Pierce. It covers all views that assert that each of us has a "double" or secondary self, or an understratum of psychic existence, possessed of powers and character of its own that outrun and are separate from the ordinary. Here belongs the notion, widespread of late, that God is present to us as this substratum of our self or as an obscure second self.

Whatever may be said of the third theory, the first and the second certainly contain at least a part of the truth. Let us begin with the neural theory. It insists that inspirations, however new they seem to be, are in fact reproductions in the same sense in which the materials used in ordinary thought-processes are reproductions. Here, even if we reserve our judgment as to what the brain finally is, we find a true analysis of such facts as these: Many a man supposes that his words are new and original when in fact he is quoting or paraphrasing what he has heard or read. Thus it is that words from a language that one has never learned, but only heard casually, are sometimes spoken. An unlettered old Scotch woman came to her pastor declaring that she had a message from the Lord. Thereupon she delivered in English, a tongue not ordinarily at her command, a truly eloquent passage about the Dissenters. Her ordinary self was not capable of such thinking or of such diction.   Inquiry proved that as a young woman she had been housemaid to an eloquent minister of English speech who had a way of rehearsing his sermons aloud at home, and whose sentiments concerning the Dissenters were those that the woman supposed that she was delivering from the Lord.[1] Even if we should be obliged to hold, as I think we must, that newness or originality (whatever this is) belongs to some subconscious deliverances in the same sense in which it belongs to ordinary thinking, the main mass, at least, of the ideas that are attributed to the subconscious arrive at the focus of attention by the ordinary route. This is the reason why none but those who study and practice poetry get poetic inspirations that count. Only a musician has the sort of inspiration that musicians recognize. Mathematical solutions come by inspiration to none but mathematicians.[2] One must first be familiar with mechanical devices before one can invent new ones. Just so, those whom religion counts as prophets arise within religion, and they employ in their prophecies both traditional ideas and the results of their life-experience.

But the dissociation theory, which accepts the notion of subconscious elaboration and therefore newness, cannot be dispensed with. Something of the nature of fresh perception, and organization of the fresh percept into an idea-system, may take place so far from the focus of attention that, when the focus shifts toward it, the

[1] This case was communicated to me by my colleague, Professor G. A. Johnston Ross, to whom the old woman brought the message.

[2] Sir William Rowan Hamilton's account of his discovery of the method of the quaternions will be found in the *North British Review*, XLV, 57.

product seems to be wholly new and at that moment injected into consciousness. A homely example of penumbral perception is as follows: I "awake to the fact" that my telephone bell, which is in another room, has been ringing for some time, though I cannot tell when it began to ring. Similarly, I may "awake to the fact" that I have a formed opinion on a certain matter, or a formed attitude toward a certain person. Most of our opinions and prejudices are, in fact, built up casually, that is, in a region of dim attention. Hence it is that we are so much more certain *that* our views are true than *why* they are true. One may be a shrewd judge of men, and yet flounder when reasons for a judgment are demanded.

Our own thoughts may thus come to us as not ours. They simply "pop into our heads," surprising us by their appropriateness; or they may appear as an insistent emotional restraint upon what we regard as our opinions or our attitudes; or they may appear as inner speech, or, finally, as fully sensory presences—visions or voices, for which the psychological term is "hallucination."[1] Thus it is that a "sense of duty" restrains; that a "sense of divine condemnation" oppresses; that "assurance" or "witness of the Spirit," and certainty that one is being divinely guided, arise. Back of the individual realization there are elements of religious tradition which the

[1] That is, sensation through stimulus of a brain center from within the brain itself instead of through a nerve current initiated at a peripheral sense organ. Central stimulation may be accomplished by narrowing attention upon a mental image. Hence, in dreams, in hypnosis, in emotionally tense situations, or in any situation in which attention is narrowed and inhibiting ideas are absent, the mild stimulation involved in having a mental image may be raised to the intensity involved in sense-perception.

individual acquires in the usual way and then gives back to himself as not his own. It is not improbable that the young lady whose lips rejected a suitor whom she intended to accept had already accumulated a body of congruous but not clearly defined impressions unfavorable to him, so that an opinion-forming process had been going on in the ordinary manner. If need for immediate action had not arisen, the opinion might have matured without a hint of mystery or surprise. Here is an important clue to the wisdom of oracles and sooth-sayers.[1] Not less is it a clue to the wisdom of the great prophets, and to the surprise that they felt when the burden of prophesying fell upon them. The prophet's message reflects the prophet's interests; it employs the materials that religious tradition and his own past offer; it is worked up as other convictions are worked up, though the steps may be obscure to the prophet himself, so that he disclaims authorship altogether.

It is true, as Browning says, that—

> There are flashes struck from midnights, there are
> fire-flames noondays kindle,
> Whereby piled-up honors perish, whereby swollen
> ambitions dwindle;
> While just this or that poor impulse, which for once
> had play unstifled,
> Seems the sole work of a lifetime that away the rest
> had trifled.
>
> —*Christina.*

[1] Cotton Mather, having interrogated certain fortune-tellers as to how they got the ideas that they gave forth, received the answer that "When they told *Fortunes*, they would pretend the Rules of *Chiromancy* and the like Ignorant Sciences, but indeed they had no Rule (they said) but this, *The things were then Darted into their minds. Darted !* Ye Wretches; By whom, I pray? Surely by none but the Devils."—

It is true, likewise, that now and then what seemed to be a fair structure of moral purpose suddenly tumbles into ruin. Yet these moral self-revelations or reversals are rarely if ever a mere explosion of a previously inactive impulse, but rather a coming into the foreground of what had been growing in the background by repeated but forgotten reactions. Thus it is that converts now and again find themselves on the side of religion without knowing how they got there.

The third theory, that of a detached subconsciousness, appeals to the popular mind more than it does to psychology. It has got its vogue largely by heaping up supposed marvels instead of patiently taking them to pieces. The medical mind, too, with its traditional "disease entities," and with imperative motive for immediate action, sometimes finds it convenient to hypostasize mental abnormalities.[1] To persons who are emotionally inclined toward occultism, the notion of a detached subconsciousness is more comforting than any doctrine of mental continuity can be. Likewise, religious thinkers who reluctantly yield the physical world to natural law find it possible to make a last stand for supernaturalism by referring to supposed divine communications delivered in the mysterious twilight of the

Cotton Mather, *The Wonders of the Invisible World* (reprint, London, 1862), p. 20. The process here is similar to that of all thought. One fixes attention upon a topic, and ideas simply come. The marvel, if there is ground for it at all, rests, not in the process, but in the usableness of the product.

[1] And then dogmatize about them! It is noteworthy, however, that Morton Prince, when he finally faces this problem, declares that there is entire continuity between the conscious, the "co-conscious," and the "unconscious." See *The Unconscious* (New York, 1914).

subconscious. Indeed, the doctrine of a detached sub-consciousness reproduces in refined form the ancient religious notion of possession.[1]

It behooves us to be humble as well as incredulous in the presence of such widespread, persistent impressions. Time and again they have been found to have "some-thing in them," after rational criticism had declared them to be delusions or frauds. The range of perception is certainly far wider than the psychology of fifty years ago was ready to admit. There is something in witch-craft, in clairvoyance, in mediumship, that is worthy of careful scientific analysis. To declare unthinkable the possession of one individual consciousness by another, or the use of one person's muscles by another person, would certainly be rash. The mental life is a complicated intermeshing that has the prima facie look of a tangle. Just which thread is which and just what constitutes a thread are problems. If psychology could wholly ignore

[1] That any Christian theologian should regard it as a gain for religion when men look for God in the dim, outlying regions of con-sciousness rather than at the focal points called "I" and "thou," is rather surprising. If there is one thing that distinguishes Christian thought from all other theologies, it is the extraordinary value that has been ascribed to the individual ever since Jesus declared that one person outweighs the whole non-personal world. Yet not a few Chris-tian writers of our day find the focus of religious experience in the self's continuity with nature rather than in the self's interaction with society. Certain details of this theological situation I have discussed in "Religion and the Subconscious," *American Journal of Theology*, XIII (1909), 337–49. To the theological publications there referred to should be added the subsequently published works of Professor W. Sanday, in which he suggests that God was in Christ as his subconsciousness. These works are: *Christologies, Ancient and Modern* (Oxford University Press, 1910), and *Personality in Christ and in Ourselves* (Oxford University Press, 1911).

psychic individuality; if what we have to deal with were separate states which combine merely in the sense of touching one another at their surfaces, as marbles in a bag, or bricks in a wall, then there would be no problem of the subconscious. But since our mental life is given largely as intercourse between individuals, we have to face questions that concern the nature of such intercourse, including the question as to how we identify another individual as present.

Two considerations that are urged in favor of the doctrine of a detached subconsciousness deserve attention. First, the "something more" sometimes exhibits high organization. Connected discourse flows from the pen of some automatic writers who afterward declare that they have no memory of having written anything. In cases designated as alternating personality the physical organism, through speech and conduct, expresses now one coherent set of ideas and attitudes, now another, the two being as different as those of two ordinary members of society. Secondly, the "something more" is believed to be an effective source of knowledge, of wisdom, of artistic excellence, of moral reinforcement.

The second consideration is palpably based upon picked facts. The shallow repetition, the misinformation and misguidance, the ignorance and stupidity that proceed from the same source, must be weighed against the relatively few happy hits. This statement is true of religious inspirations as it is of spiritism and occultism generally. It is never difficult to secure the authority of inspiration for anything that is believed, desired, or feared, and any sort of stupidity can be thus sanctified. Mohammed's ability to secure inspirations that assisted

his desires is well known.[1] All in all, the farther back
we go toward periods confessedly of ignorance and delusion the more clear-cut is the impression of the divinity
as revealing himself by the detached route. In short,
the products of the religious subconscious have multi-
tudinous marks of the primary personalities with which
they have been associated. What we are obviously
dealing with here is the whole human welter of things
wise and things foolish, things known and things guessed
or hoped for, things good, bad, and indifferent. It is
probably our very selves that we give back to ourselves
when we think we are possessed.

The facts of multiple personality do strongly suggest
a detached subconsciousness. Yet even here there is
no such complete break as is popularly supposed. The
secondary personality depends upon and uses the mental
acquisitions of the primary—uses its language, has its
understanding of common sights and sounds, has its
memories as its own. Hence, even if the primary per-

[1] Guillaume Monod (b. 1800, d. 1896), announcing himself as
Christ, the redeemer of the world, gathered about himself a sect that
looked upon him as a revealer. When some of his predictions failed of
literal fulfilment, he saved his claim by pointing out that biblical predictions failed in the same sense. Similarly, he found biblical parallels
for his lack of omniscience, for the fact of his human ancestry, his
mortality, and even for a period of insanity. See G. Revault d'Allonnes,
Psychologie d'une Religion (Paris, 1908). Among the writings produced
in the interest of what I venture to call "psychic" theology is a book by
H. C. Stanton that bears the following suggestive title: *Telepathy of the
Celestial World*. ("Psychic Phenomena here but Foreshadowings of our
transcendent Faculties hereafter. Evidences from Psychology and
Scripture that the Celestials can instantaneously and freely communicate
across distance indefinitely great") (New York, 1913). Chap. iii argues
that the method of communication among the three persons of the god-
head is telepathy.

sonality were totally unable to recall experiences of the secondary, nevertheless the usual sort of psychic individuality is here in large measure. But inability to recall the secondary has been exaggerated. There are apparently all degrees of memory lapse, not just one characteristic and complete sort. The popular notion that hypnotized subjects upon being wakened have no memory of what has occurred during hypnosis is erroneous. Sometimes there is full recall, sometimes partial recall, sometimes apparently complete amnesia. Even a subject who declares that he cannot recall anything is sometimes, at least, mistaken.[1] The sundering, in short, is best interpreted as a phenomenon of attention and memory. It is a dissociated individual consciousness with which we are dealing, not two individual consciousnesses related by a subconscious bond.

There is no manner of doubt that painstaking analysis of particular cases of the subconscious in religion has tended with great regularity to transfer more and more of the mysterious "other" to the account of the "mine" or of the ordinary "not mine."[2] The particular content of the inspiration and often the very form of the seizure

[1] To such a subject I said, "Try hard to remember! Try!" To which he replied, "I heard something." "What did you hear? Try to remember!" I said. "I heard music," he answered. Further questions that gave no suggestions but only helped to hold attention to the problem elicited a complete account of the hypnotic hallucination. Here, then, was a subject whose first, positive declaration seemed to indicate an utter break, whereas the ordinary bridge between one's present and one's own past was there. There was the full appearance, but not the reality, of a detached consciousness.

[2] Occasionally something like a crucial experiment is made, as when certain tongue-speakers, believing that their gift prepared them to preach the Gospel in non-Christian lands without preliminary study

are parts of some tradition, or group movement, or individual history, that are reproduced and worked up by the individual himself in precisely the same sense in which he reproduces and works up the things that he more readily recognizes as his own.

The significance of this conclusion for our general conception of religious consciousness is as follows: Individual self-consciousness, as we have noted, includes within itself, even as such, a reference on the one hand to nature, on the other hand to society. Out of the relative vagueness of infancy the self grows by defining itself more sharply in both directions. In the terms of natural law I recognize a connection, even continuity, between my very self and my muscles, my brain, my food, the weather, external nature as a whole. On the other hand, in terms of ethical regard I recognize connection, even continuity, between my very self and other selves. Now, the general tendency of religion has been to interpret what we have come to call "nature" in terms of other selves, or, as the case may be, another self. Yet the evidence, namely, cases of supposed "possession" and the like, has been undermined by the increasing definition of our nature-ward connections. The progress of the natural sciences has involved a progressive dislodgment of anthropomorphisms of the "possession" type, until at last the science of psychology threatens, to say the least, to give the coup de grâce to the whole idea of "possession."

of the native languages, actually undertook such a preaching mission. They had a rude disillusionment. See F. G. Henke "The Gift of Tongues and Related Phenomena at the Present Day," *American Journal of Theology*, XIII (1909), 205 f.

Yet man is fundamentally social, and religion is, all in all, his most considerable attempt to express this side of his nature. There is a certain social insistence even in the idea of "possession" and in anthropomorphism as a whole. At some points, however, social insistence focalizes at the opposite pole, namely, where selves are most clearly individual and most clearly related to one another—where human wills clash, and problems of righteousness and mercy arise. The most potent single influence in this direction, the life and teachings of Jesus, sprang directly out of religion under the pressure of adversity. It was the manward bond, not the natureward bond, that controlled his thinking. This ethical tendency has been reinforced in our Western world by the pressure of the sciences against other things upon which religion had relied. Christians find themselves more and more obliged to fall back upon their ancient doctrine that "He that abideth in love abideth in God, and God abideth in him." That is, religious experience tends to focalize itself where individuality is most pronounced, not at its obscure outer edges; where self-control is at its maximum, not its minimum; where the issues are those of society as a deliberative (or potentially deliberative) body.

True, our very selves are enmeshed in the mechanism of nature as well as in other selves. The growth of culture makes men more and more acutely conscious of this bi-polarity, more certain of a deep contrast between the ethical regard for persons by which we define ourselves as members of society and the impersonal diagrams by means of which the sciences describe the order of nature—an order that is within each of us as well as round about us. The more poignantly we realize this cleft within our very selfhood the more does it appear that the problem of social living does of itself lead on to the question of a possible unity or reconciliation between the natural and the social. To this problem our discussion of the subconscious contributes a single item, to wit: There is no probability that the cleft can be filled up or bridged over by the hypothesis of beings or processes intermediate between individual selves and nature, or by psychic processes of a subsocial sort.

CHAPTER XIII

THE RELIGIOUS REVALUATION OF VALUES

That the notion of evolution applies to all human experience, religious experience included, has been assumed in the preceding chapters as a matter of course. Some particular applications of this assumption must now be examined. Since any general law is a description of observed facts, we are not to assume that laws of evolution based exclusively upon experience other than the religious must be adequate to express also the facts of the evolution of religion. Rather, we must first observe the facts, and then ask in what sense or manner an evolution here occurs.

The distinction between mental structure and mental function leads, in fact, to a peculiar and neglected problem concerning the evolution of the human mind. If we were to think of this evolution in an exclusively structural sense, we might figure the totality of mental process as the movement of a set of blocks with which a child is playing. At first the blocks are merely shuffled about; then simple structures appear, such as one block placed upon another; afterward there are more complicated structures, in which one part corresponds to or depends upon another, as towers, houses, and bridges. From a purely structural standpoint these results, one and all, consist in growingly complex rearrangements of blocks, each of which has a predetermined size and shape. Now, it is true that in the most elaborate human mind we can discern the very elements that appear in primitive human reactions and in our animal ancestors, such as sensations of the various kinds, and instinctive tendencies to action, with their correlative satisfactions and dissatisfactions.

This point of view gives rise to the doctrine that, just as the child's blocks are unchangeable, so human nature is everywhere and always the same. Note, however, that this doctrine, in its most common application, concerns human motives. Underneath our most civilized and ideal undertakings, it is said, are the old, fundamental desires that we share with the savage and with the brute. But this statement involves a shift from structure to function, or else confusion between the two standpoints. Most often it is confusion that we meet in declarations of the unchangeability of human nature. For the assertion that developed mind likes and dislikes the very same objects that primitive mind likes and dislikes would be prima facie false—we are too obviously endeavoring to make ourselves unlike savages in matters of taste!

How, then, is it that we who pride ourselves on our unlikeness to the savage nevertheless assert that our nature is identical with his? The most common way is this: We invent the notion of *generalized desires*, saying that in spite of specific differences there is generic identity, and then we identify these generalia with the specific instinctive desires that first appear in evolution. Thus it is that the fundamental and all-inclusive motives are said to be those of nutrition and sex. Here we first look for the truly real, just as many mediaeval philosophers did, in the general or class notion; but we then proceed to identify this "truly real" with a particular instance of it. We pick out these two instincts for this honor because we are under the influence of a popular evolutionism that naïvely regards the early members of an evolutionary series as somehow more significant than the later members.

We fall into this logical quagmire partly because we do not clearly distinguish between the evolution of structure and the evolution of function. We may properly speak of an evolution of mental functions because preferences actually change. Human development does not consist merely in finding new varieties of food with which to satisfy primordial appetites, but also in achieving new wants, genuinely *new wants*. The possibility of classifying a new want under some general notion that includes old wants does not in the least imply that the new is not really different from the old. Such classifications, however, do suggest the possibility of finding laws of functional change.[1]

[1] Freud's psycho-analysis, when it undertakes to dissect the mental life of ordinarily healthy individuals, appears to assume that the real motive is always the crudest that the situation permits us to suspect, the one most nearly corresponding to savage or animal or pre-moral conduct. As Morton Prince has pointed out (*The Unconscious*, pp. 214 ff.), where any one of several possible motives may be present, Freud picks out one on the basis of theory alone and declares it to be the actual one. This opens the way to amazingly arbitrary interpretations of conduct. Why did I forget my umbrella when I left my physician's office? Because I had a secret wish, all unknown to myself, to remain and to return soon (*Psychopathology of Everyday Life* [New York, 1914], p. 239, note). Why did I hand the beggar a gold piece when I intended to give him only a copper coin? This was not mere carelessness or preoccupation; no, unknown to myself I wished to perform an act of sacrifice to mollify fate or avert evil (*ibid.*, p. 192)! Upon such interpretations there is no check whatever, once the point of view and the method are accepted;

The proposition that human nature changes, or that desires and motives become in the strictest sense different from those of our ancestors—the proposition, in short, that human functions evolve—meets another obstacle in a habit that grew up when the doctrine of evolution had to win its way by debate. A moment's reflection upon the notion of evolution will show that it implies change as well as continuity, and that change is not accessory to continuity but as fundamental, as real, as continuity itself. Yet change has received far less attention. The opponents of Darwinism, though they did not accept the idea of universal movement in nature, were entirely certain of immense differences, which were construed as breaks. In the early days the argument for evolution had as a chief task to prove that these apparent breaks are not breaks after all. The great point to be established was continuity of life. When Darwin undertook in *The Descent of Man* to show that the human mind is derived, along with the body, from animal ancestors, he addressed himself to likenesses between the human and the subhuman mind. To fill in the apparent gaps and thus demonstrate continuity became the distinguishing enterprise of evolutionary psychology. Theological prejudice, pride of species, and actual defects of data all had to be overcome. Thus it is that "mental evolution" came to be habitually thought of as "mental continuity," whereas difference and change,

there is nothing here to distinguish psychology from psychological mythology. Many Freudian analyses may be, as a matter of fact, correct; help may be brought to disordered minds by means of analyses both correct and incorrect. The point is that the system cannot discriminate, by means of its own principles, between actual motives and fancied ones.

which are just as fundamental, have remained in a sort of hazy background. We know far better what we have in common with brutes and savages than what it is that separates us from them.

The most obvious continuities in mental evolution are those of structure. By taking to pieces even as exalted a mental product as a poem or a mathematical discovery we can prove that it contains primitive elements. What more natural, then, than to think of minds as differing simply in degrees of complication among elements that, like a child's blocks, are unchangeable? But, even apart from difficulties inherent in the notion of mental "elements," there are reasons why an exclusively structural view of mental evolution cannot be sufficient. For changes have to be thought of in some sort of dynamic terms. Mental changes imply, prima facie, some doctrine of mental dynamics. This prima facie necessity is reinforced by considerations that concern the influence of mind in the struggle for existence and for better existence. If mind is a favorable variation in the total vital process it is because mind, as such, does something and is going somewhere—it has specific functions of its own. What happens depends in some measure upon what is desired.

As the clearest continuities in mental evolution are those of structure, so the clearest changes are those of function. On the functional side, too, there is continuity; our desires have much in common with earlier orders of life. Yet desires change; there is an evolution of functions. If this is denied by the doctrine that human nature is always the same, the denial rests upon confusion of problems or upon inadequacy of data. The man who utters this doctrine would regard it as a horrible fate if his own capacity for desiring and enjoying were to be limited for the rest of his life to that of a savage.

A scientific challenge of the popular doctrine of the fixity of human nature has come from at least three writers. In an article already referred to Lovejoy shows that, as a matter of fact, self-consciousness brings new desires. Henry Rutgers Marshall, examining the assumption that, since war is an expression of human nature, we must expect the indefinite recurrence of tragedies like that which now shakes the world, argues that desires have already changed in humanitarian directions to such a degree that the doctrine of the unchangeability of human nature is simply contrary to fact.[1] Thorndike's minute analysis of the original tendencies of human nature reveals not only this and that readiness to respond to a particular stimulus, but also tendencies to deal with the response itself.[2] In this dealing with his own responses man reconstructs his wants and acquires a new nature. Thorndike's statement of this point is as follows:

The original tendencies of man have not been right, are not right, and probably never will be right. By them alone few of the best wants in human life would have been felt, and fewer still satisfied. . . . . Original nature has achieved what goodness the world knows as a state achieves order—by killing, confining, or reforming some of its elements. It progresses, not by *laissez-faire*, but by changing the environment in which it operates and by renewedly changing itself in each generation. Man is now as civilized, rational, and human as he is because man in the past has changed things into shapes more satisfying, and changed

[1] *War and the Ideal of Peace* (New York, 1915).

[2] *Original Nature of Man* (New York, 1913), p. 170.

.parts of his own nature into traits more satisfying, to man as a whole. Man is thus eternally altering himself to suit himself. His nature is not right in his own eyes. Only one thing in it, indeed, is unreservedly good, the power to make it better.[1]

Mental functions evolve, then, and the tendency to functional as well as structural evolution is a part of man's original nature. This phase of evolution is, on the one hand, mind's increasing discovery of what it wants to do, and therefore of what mind really is. On the other hand, this discovery goes forward through conflict with what we are. Purposes, as contrasted with impulses, and the increasing organization of life through ideas, are achievements. They require the redirection of old desires, and redirection involves resistance. You cannot make a river grind wheat until you check the current in some measure. Human nature, then, is not merely a current that flows by reason of the law of gravity; it has also the peculiar property of resisting and redirecting its own flow. If, now, we could determine what is resisted, and what is the direction of these redirections, we should thereby formulate laws of functional evolution. In the nature of the case such laws could not be deduced by analysis of primitive mind alone; the whole cultural history of mankind also would have to be surveyed.[2]

[1] Pp. 281 f.

[2] Possibly the question will be raised whether my use of the terms "evolution" and "development" is accurate. Should not both terms be restricted to structural changes? And is not "growth" the proper term for what I have called evolution of functions? In reply I would point out the following facts: (1) The idea and the term "function" play such an extensive part in biology that we may reasonably doubt whether anybody would be satisfied by a description of evolutionary changes in purely structural terms. Functions, as biologists see them, certainly

The bearing of all this upon the psychology of religion is direct. For the points at which the sharpest conflicts occur between new functions and old are the points at which religious consciousness is most acute. Here the religious experience itself is a revaluation of values, a reconstruction of life's enterprise, a change in desire and in the ends of conduct. Consider the evolutionary significance of prophetism of the ethical type. The prophet calls upon the people to like what they do not like, and in the long run he makes them do it. His own generation

evolve. (2) The inclusion of mental functions within the concept of evolution was accomplished long ago in the recognition of mind as a favorable variation. (3) Whether mental functions, thus included in the concept of evolution, are all of a kind, or whether there are several kinds; and if there are several, whether they all appear at a single point (remaining thereafter a constant) or whether they appear successively— these questions must be determined by empirical inquiry. (4) Such inquiry must include among its data the manifestations of mind in the cultural history of man. To stop where biology leaves off would be an arbitrary procedure, and it would settle important questions by an a priori rather than an empirical method. (5) The evolutionary process might conceivably be or become self-guiding in part or in whole. The human species may yet deliberately control human reproduction so as to select, by thought analysis, the variations that are to be perpetuated and accumulated. In such a case a new desire would appear, a new mental function which would in some measure displace natural selection. A eugenist who employs argument as a means of producing a better species should be the last person to question the proposition that mental functions change, and that the term "evolution" applies in the strictest sense to such changes. (6) It follows that the cultural heritage of the race may be more than an accumulation of instruments organized and directed by merely primordial impulses. As a matter of fact, education aims, as Thorndike points out, "to make men want the right things. . . . . We have to make use of nature, to co-operate with each other, and to improve ourselves" (*Education* [New York, 1912], p. 11). Education is always selective. It never seeks to transmit the whole present social purpose, but only certain parts of it that are regarded as worthy of being strengthened as against other parts. Therefore the cultural history of the race is not a record of "growth" merely, but also of changes in the directions taken by the whole racial movement. The appropriate designation for such changes seems to be "the evolution of functions."

.may stone him, but a later one builds him a monument. The prophetic spirit, in both the leader and the led, is the human spirit attempting the hard thing where the easy thing might seem to suffice. In the Jewish-Christian form prophetism "takes trouble" about the oppressed, when this means loss of profits. Men are attracted, in spite of themselves, toward a vision of brotherhood that will take away many a hard-won social advantage. They accept a social-ethical thought of God that causes discomfort to those who seriously entertain it, for it makes them condemn themselves. But men must like even this; else would they not build monuments to the prophets!

Our discussion of religious groups and of religious leadership shows that in much religion the prophetic spirit is not clearly in evidence. Yet the extent of it is by no means small. Where is there an instance of a religious leader whom the world calls great who has achieved his influence with the people by maintaining existing standards, much less by lowering them? Certainly Zarathustra, Gautama, Jesus, and Mohammed were reformers of standards. Every one of them took the harder road, every one of them was attractive to men because of the very thing that made the road hard.[1]

[1] A fine example of the process may be found in the earliest Gathas or hymns of Zoroastrianism. Zarathustra the prophet feels himself called to deliver to the people ("the kine") a message which he realizes will go against their inclinations. The content of this message brings together the following ideas: economic needs; protection from enemies; the sin of shirking work; the sin of lying; free choice between good and evil, and the determination of destiny by such choices; the duty of joining with the god of light and truth, Ahura Mazda, in his contest with Ahriman, the spirit of evil; clear recognition that this contest between good and evil exists also within ourselves; the ultimate overthrow

An oft-repeated phenomenon of the prophetic consciousness is shrinking in the presence of an overwhelming
task.[1] But afterward the prophet is sustained by the
very greatness of his cause.

At points like these mental evolution is not motion
in the line of least resistance; it is the evocation of
resistance; it is the creation of problems and of difficulties—it is the clearest sort of creative evolution.[2]

of Ahriman and the triumph of the good. Here we behold ethical
idealism growing out of the soil of daily labor—idealism that requires
self-conquest and preference for the hard task, yes, participation in an
undertaking of cosmic import. See *Sacred Books of the East*, XXXI, 1–90.

[1] "Ah, Lord Jahwe! behold, I know not how to speak; for I am a
child," pleads Jeremiah (Jer. 1:6), and Isaiah cries, "Woe is me! for I
am undone; because I am a man of unclean lips, and I dwell in the
midst of a people of unclean lips" (Isa. 6:5).

[2] To a rather surprising extent the founders of minor religions and
of sects, as well as the great founders and prophets, get their influence
with the people by giving them something harder to do. Alongside of
insistence upon a particular dogma, form of worship, or mode of ecclesiastical government, even alongside of desire for health, or for wealth,
or for social recognition and power, we find self-denial, ethical austerity,
a fine growth of gentleness and of mercy that cost self-discipline. A
good recent example is John Alexander Dowie. He was a healer, a
dogmatist, a shrewd organizer of a great economic enterprise. Yet
I have heard him preach ethical standards with definiteness and power
such as I have rarely witnessed in the sermons of other preachers. It
was apparently the aspiring, self-overcoming factors in his movement
that gave it a chief part of its power with people.

A similar remark applies to Mrs. Eddy, though with modifications.
To the question, Why do so many persons follow Christian Science?
the usual answer is that desire for health is the essential motive power
of the whole movement. Another motive, no doubt, is desire for peace of
mind in a restless age. But discipleship requires also a sort of daring, a
letting go of old supports (whether drugs or public sentiment), and no
little self-discipline. It is almost inconceivable that Mrs. Eddy could
have attained her remarkable influence by her healings and her mental
anodynes alone. There had to be the self-overcoming element also.

The obverse of the prophetic spirit is the sense of sin in the stricter meaning of this term, that is, disapproval of one's self in the light of a law or of a divine command that one freely approves. Paul's classical description represents it as disapproval of and struggle against the very thing that one likes. This should be distinguished from the so-called "sense of sin" that consists essentially in discomfort in the presence of something that one wants to escape. In Paul's case the sinner desires to cling to the very standard that causes the distress.

One sometimes hears the statement that the sense of sin is a universal mark of religion. This is not true unless "sin" be taken very broadly, as is done in translations of early religious literature that use this term for such things as offending an arbitrary god whom one scarcely loves or admires or approves at all. The offense called sin may even be accidental. The term "sin" is used, likewise, to name violations of a ceremonial code, as by entering a holy place, or by touching a tabooed object. Here the "sense of sin" is little more than fear of approaching calamity, and "repentance" is a sort of running to cover. The worth-whileness of the divine will or of the law that makes the trouble is scarcely considered at all, but rather avoidance of the trouble.

Yet even these crude fears, by virtue of their anthropomorphism, their sympathy with the offended spirit or god, contain the germ of a more exalted experience of sin and repentance. It is remarkable to see the sinner exalting the moral character of the offended divinity, and then taking his side, as in the Fifty-first Psalm. Here is actual desire that the god's point of view, which condemns and gives pain, should prevail. Then comes a realization that human nature requires reconstruction. This idea, already present in the great psalm of penitence, reaches its classical expression in the cry of Paul, "What I hate, that I do. . . . . Wretched man that I am! who shall deliver me out of this body of death?" Theoretical interest in this phenomenon turned, unfortunately, to the problem of the origin and the mode of transmission of "original sin." Men fought over the relation of it to Adam, but they failed to see that human nature's recognition of its own defects, wherever this recognition occurs, is part of a reconstructive process that has already set in, a part of the evolution of mental functions.

In our day the sense of sin has become, in an appreciable degree, a realization on the part of individuals that they participate in a social order that is in large measure unjust. Looking backward to Jesus' ideal of a loving society—a divine-human family—and then at the ways in which contemporary society prevents men from learning to love one another, and at the actual exploitation of men, women, and children—body and soul—for profit, many a Christian has come to realize that salvation cannot consist for any of us in establishing a private relation of harmony with God. Our sinfulness is conjoint, co-operative, and our salvation accordingly must be wrought out in a reconstruction of society. We are in the act of achieving a social conscience by revaluation of our values.

A little way back a hint was given that by comparing new wants with old we might conceivably discover laws of the functional evolution of mind. Certainly some of the differences between the wants of civilized men and those of savages can be defined. Aesthetic wants, for example, have disengaged themselves from the primitive utilities that gave them their first sustenance. Likewise, desire for knowledge has been enfranchised, for learning does not have to prove its usefulness. We express this by saying that beauty and truth are valuable in themselves. This is as much as to say that over and above appetite, above all that is unreflectively instinctive, we have acquired wants that utter themselves in free contemplation, reflection, and judgment. This is what makes us persons—this achieving of some freedom from our impulsive selves which is also a demand for new and larger self-realizations. Men are most clearly conscious of the process in the form of ethical conflict and achievement—the overcoming of hatred and of indifference toward one another, and the displacement of compulsion by reflective loyalty and love.

Here are traces of a law of the functional evolution of mind. The relation of religion to it is most intimate. The connecting thread between primitive religion and the religions that are counted as developed is the anthropomorphism that begins by peopling everything with friends and enemies, and culminates in faith that at the heart of things, as at our hearts, there is regard for persons. Therefore our preliminary description of the religious consciousness as the effort to complete, unify, and conserve our values may now be rendered more precise by noting that, though this effort takes many forms, even conflicting forms, there is a characteristically religious way of choosing between them. Religion is, indeed, insistence upon having enough of what is desired, but it is also criticism of desires. Revaluation of values, it is true, is not equally present everywhere in religion, nor does revaluation anywhere advance with even pace. Yet this is the function that characterizes the confessedly great turning-points of religious consciousness in individuals and in groups, and the direction of this revaluation, its central tendency, is toward the placing of increased value upon persons. "What shall it profit a man if he shall gain the whole world, and lose his own life?" The reverse side of this valuation of persons is valuation of society, which is the organized regard of persons for one another.

The conclusion, thus far, is this: Mental functions are in process of evolution. The law of this evolution is that wants are reintegrated in terms of personal-social self-realization. This law is most acutely revealed in the religious revaluation of values that is characteristic of prophecy, the sense of sin, the attribution of ethical character to God, the hope of life after death, and faith in the possibility of a fully socialized society.

CHAPTER XIV

RELIGION AS DISCOVERY

We have taken as the most significant mark in religion—at least the most interesting for us—a certain aspect, tendency, and process of values and valuations. When we speak of this as religious experience we assume that here, as in other types of experience, some sort of reality reveals itself as present, that some phase of the real world is here and now becoming defined. Religion is *realization*.

This proposition brings us to a new set of problems. What they are will become clear if we reckon first of all with a misunderstanding. The standpoint of function or value is supposed by some persons to reduce the whole of religious experience to mere subjectivity. "When you make the essence of this experience desire, attitude-taking, enterprise, values," the objector says in substance, "you make it appear that the reality of any object—divine beings, for example—is a matter of religious indifference, whereas interest in the objectively real lies at the heart of religion." It must be confessed that functions and values have been handled by some writers in such a manner as to give prima facie ground for this objection. It does not hold, however, against the value standpoint as such, but only against a particular interpretation of it.

If reality were discovered and defined altogether by some non-valuational process—as, for instance, by a supposed "pure" reason or by a supposed "pure" empirical science—and if religion were merely a consciousness of getting along with realities thus known, merely a set of satisfactions arising in situations antecedently *given*, then, indeed, religious self-realization would be a subjective shadow or epiphenomenon—whatever this may be. But no one who is familiar with the main lines of psychological progress needs to be told that any such notion of the cognitive process is archaic. Psychology knows no "pure" reason and no "pure" science. Intellectualism, whether a priori or empirical, has been replaced by dynamic views of the whole mental life. Mind in its actuality is interest, satisfaction-dissatisfaction, desire, action, enterprise, as well as idea, memory, judgment, and thought system. Neither *mere* facts nor *mere* values are found among our data. On the idea side every datum includes attention, which is selective. Thinking includes a "will-to-think." Observation attends to "this-rather-than-that," and "takes-it-as-so-and-so." On the other hand, we have no such value datum as "satisfaction-in-general" or "as-such." A value is a discriminated satisfaction taken as a mark of an object. Thus, on the one hand, cognition is no mere mirroring of the "is-ness" of things, and, on the other hand, the inner world of desire and action does not whirl upon a merely subjective axis. Desire, attitude-taking, and enterprise, whether religious or other, are at the same time idea, thought-organization, and discovery of the real. For reasons of convenience we abstract now one aspect of mind, now another, as the idea aspect (intellect) and the action aspect (will); but if we then go on to treat any such aspect as if it were a thing, or even as if it were a datum rather than a derivative from a datum, we begin at once to move in a fog.

This dynamic conception of mind, necessitated by analysis of particular processes, is reinforced by more general considerations that are involved in the evolutionary, natural-history point of view. Mind lies for us wholly within the objectively real world-order called Nature—not partly within and partly without. Mental process is process of the real in relation to the real. This we may safely take as an axiom of present-day science, even though the implications of the axiom be not yet fully defined.[1]

[1] Our hesitation with regard to this point—for the sciences are nowhere more cautious—is not due to lack of affirmative grounds for regarding mind as a real part of nature dynamically considered, but to foresight of difficulties in applying the notion. We are cautious about a possible return toward animism, for instance. Nevertheless, the most complete and penetrating critique of the mind-body relation thus far vouchsafed—W. McDougall's *Body and Mind* (New York, 1913)—accepts the doctrine of real interaction. Biology hesitates to admit among the real factors in evolution anything not involved in the simplest possible notion of living body, but at the same time the obvious continuity of biology and psychology acts as a constant pressure toward the inclusion of mind within biological dynamics. The general situation may be described as follows: first, the hypothesis that getting what we want is in no sense due to the fact that we want it is so rash that scarcely anybody is willing to adopt it; secondly, we have a science of psychology that is objective in the same sense as other sciences (that is, it is based upon observations and experiments that can be repeated and thus become a common possession); thirdly, the facts with which psychology deals are obviously continuous, in some sense or other, with the facts of other sciences, especially the biological sciences; fourthly, psychology is increasing our control of nature in many directions, as in education, therapeutics, and even business; fifthly, we are increasingly aware of the historical significance of social experience. But, finally, we do not see how to relate any imponderable psychical realities to our supposedly closed and self-conserving physical system, and, besides, we fear a return to speculative and imaginative interpretations of experience. On the whole, however, mind takes its place in our scientific conceptions of nature, leaving us the task of working out details as best we may.

Adding to this axiom what has already been said concerning the relation between facts and values, we shall now take mind as the name of a real ongoing, a real doing, that is attaining to definition of both itself and its world. It reaches this twofold definition in one and the same process. Self-realization and world-realization are correlative phases of the same experience. The question—so often puzzling to students—of how we get from our own minds to objective reality is to be answered by denying the presupposition of the questioner. The mind lives, moves, and has its being within reality; it *is* reality. What it moves *from* in the progress of knowledge is not mere subjectivity, but reality indefinitely or confusedly aware of itself and its environment, and what it moves *toward* is clearer definition of both, with corresponding focalization of functions.

This general conception of mind applies to religious functions exactly as to others. Like commerce, government, or education, religion is a process in which the real produces definition of itself. Each of these phases of life is enterprise and discovery in one; each uses ideas derived from all sorts of sources, but in using them modifies them; and, just as each draws from many sources, so each contributes widely in turn. This is obviously the case in regard to early society, where religion is inextricably intertwined with ceremony, myth, industry, social organization, and ethical standards. A parallel relation appears in the historical connection between theology and philosophy, and between religion and morals. Religion is never merely an "aside"; it is a "live issue"; and the liveness of it is manifested, not merely in those who are recognized as devotees, but also in culture generally—in the literature, the plastic arts, the world-view, the moral ideals, of a people. One cannot write a truly realistic history of mind without recognizing the religious enterprise as a fundamental factor therein.

If at the present moment the work of discovery seems to be a monopoly of the sciences, the reason is not that any actual monopoly exists, but only that attention for the moment happens, because of certain historical incidents, to be focused upon scientific processes and products. Mind *as a whole* is enterprise, and enterprise is discovery. The sciences are *a part* of this enterprise, and they do experimentally uncover fresh data; but they also accept, and work within, data uncovered by interests other than scientific. Valuational changes that are going on even in this day of ours are transforming the very foundations of much scientific thought. For the real world of the modern man is nature *plus society*, and society is discovering itself, not chiefly through the scientific enterprise, but in other ways. The conditions of modern life—industrial, civic, educational—have caused us to feel the presence of one another in new and acute ways. Again and again, when we have assumed that the mechanism of an enterprise included all its essential factors, we have found ourselves checked by the personal element. Pausing to analyze this personal element in order to control it, we have come to value persons in a new way, whereupon the enterprise has changed its character. For example, we decide to apply efficiency tests in a factory. At the outset we assume that labor is simply so much power to be directed, and we think of it as continuous with the power of our steam engines. But sooner or later we discover that "labor" means persons who must be reckoned with as something other than a part of the machinery. Humanitarian ideas then seep into the ledger and the balance sheet. If at first we justify humanitarianism in business on the ground of selfish profit-seeking, later we become ashamed of this narrowness; we feel a presence greater than the data of our fiscal calculations, and through this feeling the horizon of our enterprise, and therefore the horizon of our real world, moves outward.

The modern recognition of persons, which is discovery, affects our thinking in ways as profound as they are subtle. We have a new interest in certain facts—nay, that we discover them as facts at all is because interest runs that way. Points of view are shifted toward social values in whole ranges of investigation—in history, economics, psychology, general logic, or theory of the sciences, for example. Hence whole bodies of particular discoveries are suffused by an antecedent sense of reality which arises in our social valuations, our fresh regard for others.

Let us not conceal this factor in discovery by misconstruing the significance of "points of view," as, for instance, the social. They are general determinants of the sphere or phase of reality with which a particular science deals. When, for example, the sciences undertake to analyze experience from the point of view of phenomena only, they take the perceptual process as real. A generation ago many a man of science dreamed that by defining the sphere of the natural and physical sciences as phenomena in contrast to reality we should at last escape the entanglements of metaphysics. But phenomenalism in science does not escape the problem of the real; rather, it makes acute the question of what we mean by a perceptual process really occurring. So the growth of social "points of view" in the sciences connotes a movement in our sense of reality; it means that a new recognition of persons is finding scientific ways of expressing and of feeding itself. Thus a fresh feeling of social values blends with the special sciences in the discovery of man.

It is thus that religion is discovery. It does not, indeed, establish any body of doctrine that is immune to the ordinary norms of judgment; rather, it is a root that goes on living when criticism withers our systems of doctrine. Religion survives religious doctrines because the adventure of life is large, and because in its very largeness as adventure it is an original acquaintance with the real. This assertion rests for the most part upon general considerations, just stated, concerning the nature of mind. But we must not stop with anything so general. We must go on to answer two questions of an entirely specific sort: What kind or phase of reality is coming to light in the religious consciousness? and, What is this "coming to light" that is so different from rational criticism? In other words, what is the content, and what the process, of religious realization? The second of these questions will occupy the next chapter.

We have seen that all sorts of wants appear as religious at some time or other, but we have seen also that religion is a law of mental evolution, in accordance with which wants tend to be reintegrated in terms of personal-social self-realization. This reintegration, we shall now see, is the discovery of society. In the strict sense of the term, "society" means, not any and every aggregation of individuals, not mutual dependence as such, but consciousness of one another as individuals having worth in themselves because having experiences of their own. Society is a reciprocal attribution of value to "I's" and "thou's"; it is a matter of persons. Now, in all strictness and literalness, persons are a gradual discovery in the course of human history. At the totemic level, the bond that men feel uniting the group is bodied forth to thought as an animal, a plant, or other object that to us is non-human. The totem object is sacred, has value in itself, but no like value is attributed to men. The ceremony is performed with a punctiliousness that is genuinely conscientious, yet conscience requires no similar respect for the feelings of one's fellows. Instinctive affection of parent for child is here, of course, and gregariousness or pleasure in the presence of others. These are partly offset, however, by what seems from our point of view to be extreme callousness, not only toward strangers, but even toward one's own flesh and blood. As to rudimentary social organizations, we have seen that though men "hang together" in groups that have some firmness, the cohesive principle is not feeling for the worth of the individuals who compose the group.[1] The sacredness of life, the rights of man, the immeasurable worth of the individual, are ideas not yet achieved, though the instinctive energy for this achievement be present. Such convictions arise—are now in our day arising—in and through fresh feelings that accompany growing and changing contacts of men with one another.

[1] See p. 125.

The gradualness of the discovery of man by man is often concealed from us by the tools with which we study the past. Such terms as "person," "individual," "family," "society," "co-operation," which derive their connotation from our relatively advanced life, have to be used to describe a period to which such connotations do not apply. It is a mistake to assume that even as instinctive a thing as parental affection is the same at all stages of human evolution. It cannot be the same if parental notions of children's capacities change, as we know they have changed. In social evolution, not only does the range of acquaintance and of co-operation increase, but what men are to one another—the very concept of man—likewise changes. To revert to a typical fact already mentioned, the change from tribal to national organization included revision of the notion of justice, which is the notion of man. In the figure of the ideal monarch, and in that of the national god, we behold a fresh step in men's discovery of one another.

The anthropomorphism of early thought, and the dissolution of it by criticism, are sometimes interpreted as a movement from a personal to an impersonal point of view. But this is less than half the truth. The earliest worship is not directed to personal gods. *Mana* is not an individual at all; early spirits are as unstable as mists that appear to gather from nowhere and to disperse into emptiness; even when a divine name first becomes a firm possession, it signifies no firmly organized divine personality, but rather something that may be on occasion a man, a sacrificial animal, a great spirit, a nature-power. The personal god, the correlative of personal as distinguished from institutional religion, is a late arrival. Men must think of themselves as persons if they are to have a personal god, and they think of themselves as persons only when they both individualize one another and think of the other's experience as having value in itself. Only a personal god, we may say, is fully anthropomorphic. In this sense the movement of religion, in most areas, has been toward rather than away from anthropomorphism. Wherever such a god is worshiped, there the discovery of human persons and of human society is well advanced.

It is true that religious institutions have practiced toward persons all manner of cruelty, repression, and disrespect. But the severest condemnation therefor springs from the lips of prophets who speak for a personal god. Such prophets feel that spiritual values—that is, persons—are values from no mere angle of approach, or particular position in time, but in some final, eternal, and cosmic sense.

It is true, also, that religious thought in one great branch of the race has issued in the doctrine of an impersonal ground of the world. How, it may be asked, can this prominent fact of religious evolution be reconciled with the identification, just now made, of the inner principle of religion with that of the discovery of persons? For answer, four facts and phases of the situation in India may be noted: First, her religious philosophies do not define the popular religion. The people worship gods who have definite characteristics, good and bad. Secondly, the *motive* of these philosophies does grow out of an increasing sense of personality—the mind thrown back upon itself by the pain and mystery of life. The reason why a solution of the problem was sought

in an impersonal absolute, with the practical corollary
of the extinction of personality, is that the *social* significance of persons was missed at the outset. Society,
and society only, is the sphere of personal self-realization.
When, therefore, the Brahmin thinks to discover the
real world by introversion, ignoring the social reality
that is immediately before him, he excludes from his
data the only experience that can sustain his sense of
his own reality. Philosophical Brahmanism and Buddhism are less a development of religion than a sort of
self-suffocation. Thirdly, it is the Brahmin's non-social
point of view that leads to his doctrine of *maya*, which
asserts that the whole finite world is an illusion. As
social participation in one another's experiences is the
only corrective for dreams, so also it is the only sure
bridge between the abstracta of reflection and the concrete world-order. Knowledge is co-operation. Science
knows no private fact, no unshared truth. It is in
society that real objectivity arises and has its meaning.
Where there are no social purposes to be achieved, there
no stable meanings exist. Does our Western world
realize how closely its superior objectivity of mind,
which makes possible its success in research, is bound
up with our occidental sense of the reality of persons?
Fourthly, no doubt India's backwardness in practical
matters that concern co-operation and social justice is
due in part to the fact that her thinkers, from whom
social leadership might have been expected, have committed themselves to a non-social view of individual
experience.

In view of these four considerations, we shall not be
indulging in arbitrary or subjective criticism if we con-

clude that the whole situation as respects philosophical Brahmanism and Buddhism presents an arrest rather than anything that is typical of religion as such. All in all, the evolution of religion is to be witnessed where social integration is proceeding, most of all where custom is becoming reflective loyalty, where loyalty is coming to understand itself as love (which particularizes individuals), and where love asserts itself as demand for justice (which is the recognition of persons as finalities for thought and action). Religion is the discovery of persons.

Those who say that the present social movement is essentially religious are following the only adequate clue to the repentance-and-conversion process that has set in on so large a scale. Yet some distinctions are in order. It will not do to identify all sociality with religion—for instance, sociality so instinctive or so mechanized as not to feel the reality of persons. Further, the very point of religion at a given historical period may lie in the opposition of a fuller toward a less full realization of society. At the present moment in the western world the glow of religion is found in our sociality chiefly when it becomes radical, so radical as to accept the principle of justice as unqualifiedly valid. Social wholeness or health, under unqualified justice, requires that the utmost value that individuals attribute to one another shall be realizable by them. There are, to be sure, social enterprises of great worth that properly ignore the question, What would satisfy the reciprocal good-will of men toward one another? But this is precisely the sort of question that religion insists upon facing. As a result it finds itself in the profoundest discontent with things as they are. The discovery by Christians that *to love enough we must be just*, and the corresponding transformation in their thought of God, leads on toward most radical demands. Justice cannot measure welfare by averages; it cannot forget, as science often must, the individual in the general. A fully socialized religion, which is none other than religion, is therefore the most dangerous thing in the world for institutionalism and for rights that attained their full growth in some period already past. By a natural spiritual gravitation our most radical social groups, as far as they are conscious of a positive human goal, tend to recognize their emotions as religious. For religion, to quote an old prayer-meeting phrase, "laughs at impossibilities, and cries, 'It shall be done!'" It refuses to take human nature as a static datum eternally resistant to social ideals, but insists upon the possibility of fundamental changes, and sets us the task of building a new race, a regenerate race! It goes so far as to face the apparent defeat of life by natural processes that entail defect, weakness, and death, and it insists that this, too, is a problem of justice in the radical sense. Religion becomes so ultra-radical in its sociality as to raise the question whether there is justice in the cosmic order itself, and to undertake social enterprises of cosmic scope, such as the promotion of a universal democracy of God.

Our discussion has treated the evolution of faith in divine beings as all one with the discovery of human persons. This treatment is necessitated, not by any supposed logical implications of human selfhood, but by the forms actually taken by the historically growing social self-realization. At the totemic level men's realization of one another as constituting a social unit is *per se* consciousness of, or faith in, a real totem. Tribal and national gods, likewise, are no mere addenda to the social objects; rather, in god-ideas the tribe or nation articulates its own social insistency. Stated in abstract form, faith in divine beings is social valuation asserting itself as objectively valid, that is, as not mere wish but also as law or movement of reality.

So it is with our present most open-eyed social idealism. It knows itself to be more than a subjective preference; it is the fulfilment of a destiny; it is the working out of some cosmic principle through our preferences. Duty is for us not a mere imposition of the mass will upon the individual; it is reality in the large making itself felt in the parts.[1] Intense devotion to the social welfare takes the form, without any addition to itself, of reverence, self-realization through unreserved self-giving, and desire that all men should reach this same height of realization. Society at this, its highest, would be no mere aggregate of arbitrary preferences, but escape from the arbitrary into law, escape from the seeming into the real.[2] This feeling of a cause that has us as its agent leads spontaneously to the use of religious phraseology. If the approach is through the notion of moral law, we get such terms as "ethical religion" and

[1] "Morality, truly interpreted, does bring man into contact with the final nature of things." The law of duty "is not made, and cannot be changed by God or man; it belongs to the nature of things." See W. M. Salter, *Ethical Religion* (London, 1900), pp. 84 f.; cf. F. Adler, *The Religion of Duty* (New York, 1909), and *Life and Destiny* (New York, 1903).

[2] Cf. G. Haw, "The Religious Revival in the Labour Movement," *Hibbert Journal*, XII, 382–99.

the "religion of duty."[1] If the approach is through a keen sense of men as worthful objects, the term becomes the "religion of humanity."[2] If the emphasis is upon society as completely organized upon the principle of justice, we hear of the "religion of democracy."[3] If the social impulse attaches itself to the idea of production, the command, "Be a producer," may assert itself as religious.[4] In short, the modern social movement, where it is most reflective, is religion, and as such it is also discovery of the real as against the seeming.[5]

As we have already noticed, this does not imply that there are two separate and independent kinds of

[1] See references in the second preceding note. In an argument addressed to ethical societies against giving up the term "religion," the late W. L. Sheldon said: "We hold to the assurance that in spite of all the necessary transformations that may occur in human emotions, in forms of worship, or in beliefs about the supernatural, we can retain the hallowed associations we have had with this phrase. It is not right that we should consent that the deepest feelings connected with it should be regarded as belonging to any particular creed or body of men. If we surrender this word we are liable to be driven to surrender the feelings connected with it. . . . . Religion implies the surrender of one's will to ideal or sacred principles which are to him the expression of the true destiny or worth of the human soul."—*Ethical Addresses*, First Series (Philadelphia, 1895), pp. 47 f., 62.

[2] E.g., E. H. Griggs, *The New Humanism* (New York, 1904), chap. x.

[3] C. Zueblin, *The Religion of a Democrat* (New York, 1908).

[4] T. N. Carver, *The Religion Worth Having* (Boston, 1912).

[5] The authors named in the last six notes are only a few of those who reveal this characteristic tendency of present social thinking. Other typical names are as follows: Stanton Coit, "The Humanity of God," *International Journal of Ethics*, XVI, No. 4 (July, 1906), 424–29; H. D. Lloyd, *Man the Social Creator* (New York, 1906); G. Spiller, *Faith in Man: the Religion of the Twentieth Century* (London, 1908); H. Jones, *The Working Faith of the Social Reformer and Other Essays* (London, 1910).

discovery, the scientific and the religious. The two procedures are continuous without being identical. The
sciences are a part of the total adjustment process which
in its totality is discovery. We are discovering ourselves,
in short, through the reintegration of our wants, scientific and other, in terms of personal-social self-realization.
And this is religion.

It will be asked, perhaps, whether we are discussing
religion as a whole or only at its best. Have we not
idealized it ? Is not most religion, after all, institutionalism, traditionalism, conformity ? Does it not commonly
reinforce the "powers that be" in their resistance to
change ? Has it not given the authority of supposedly
supernatural sanctions to what is natural, temporary,
even arbitrary ? Are not these alleged discoveries of
persons and of society simply instances in which religion
has drifted with a general historical current ? Has
religion, then, contributed anything at all to discovery ?
These questions deserve an answer; they deserve it most
of all because they call attention to historical facts.
What is needed is to get the facts into perspective.
When this is accomplished we shall see that the whole
evolution of mind is discovery, and that the defects just
mentioned inhere in the whole discovery process, whether
religious or scientific. The history of science, as well as
that of religion, discloses a long series of blunders based
upon the assumption of finality for that which is partial
and temporary. There have been scientific as well as
religious orthodoxies, with their mistaken assumption of
authority, their suppression of dissent, their loan of
power to unprogressive institutions. Moreover, what
the sciences of today mean by science, just as what our

discussion has taken as religion, is no mere average of past performances. In both cases we understand ourselves, not by a mere summation of instances, but rather by noting a characteristic tendency. Such a tendency may be resisted; in a particular instance it may be suppressed. Science resists science just as religion resists religion. But each has its prophets who break through the resistance, and in doing so reveal the deeper nature of the enterprise. In neither case can it be said that we merely drift with a historical current; rather we press forward in an adventure, retrieving our own errors, and entering fresh territory.

The conclusion is that social valuation is of itself recognition of the real; that the evolution of social valuations is a progressive discovery of persons as reals; that intense valuation of persons, when it becomes reflective, tends to define itself in terms of a cosmic reality that has social character. What we have here is nothing less than a law of mental integration. Mind gets itself in hand—focalizing dispersed attention, organizing impulsive activities, and realizing a meaning in the whole—by a social process. This process is at once the valuation and the discovery of persons.[1]

[1] By an entirely different route, E. Murisier arrives at the conclusion that religion furnishes the chief organizing idea (*idée directrice*) for the evolution of personality. See *Les Maladies du sentiment religieux* (Paris, 1909), pp. 69–72.

CHAPTER XV

RELIGION AS SOCIAL IMMEDIACY

By all odds the most baffling item of experience is the fact that persons are present to one another and have experiences in common. It is baffling, that is, as soon as philosophy or science attempts to construe it, however luminous it may seem to be until such attempts begin. Metaphysics throughout its history has found the universal easier to handle than the particular, especially easier than the individual. Usually, too, the philosopher and his disciple converse together (by means of voice or print) concerning various objects of thought—unity and plurality, substance and attribute, time, space, matter, soul—without ever noting that philosophy is conversation, that every bit of philosophic thought is a mutual possession, and that such mutuality might conceivably be a qualifier of every particular philosophic doctrine.

Just so psychology, keeping its eyes upon states of mind and laws of mind, and assuming that there are individual minds to which these laws apply, has rarely taken into account the fact that these minds *converse with one another*. Psychology itself depends upon conversation between individuals; it *is* conversation. It assumes that psychologists can be mutually present to one another, and that an experimenter and his subject can be present to each other. No one, I think, has ventured to construe the "presence" of a laboratory subject in terms solely of inches apart; there is always

the additional fact of communication, or of having
meanings in common. Usually this having in common is
of the essence of the experiment, as in giving directions
to the subject, asking him questions, and having him
record what happens. But what is meant by or implied
in the notion of individual minds or persons who are
present to one another and have experience in common
is about the last thing that psychology inquires into.

There are good reasons for this reticence, such as
the danger of entanglement in metaphysical speculations
about the soul. There is, too, an abundance of other
problems that await solution. But underneath this
reticence lies also the sheer inapplicability of the methods
of structural analysis, which are the dominant methods.
Purely structural psychology construes experience regardless of experienc*ing* and of experienc*ers*. It knows
no Smith or Jones, but only idea-of-Smith and idea-of-
Jones. Nevertheless, in the concreteness of our experience as psychologists, *we* are not "ideas-of" this or that,
but Smiths and Joneses, experiencers. Our psychology,
being *ours*, is an experiencing, and since it is conversation
it is an experiencing in common.

A social presupposition—the real existence of a community of individual experiencers—is present in all
science, indeed, just as it is in the world of buying and
selling. And it remains a presupposition. It is not a
hypothesis that requires to be tested, but a pre-condition
of having any hypotheses at all and of testing them.
For a scientific hypothesis is (among other things) self-
restraint in view of a possible social judgment upon the
matter in question. The verification of a hypothesis is
the attainment of a proposition that can assert itself as

a social judgment. That which makes any proposition scientific, as opposed to mere opinion, is the rigor with which the conditions of social participation have been observed. These conditions include stimulus alike to individual self-expression and to a realization that some possible common meaning, precisely because it is common, expresses one's own most focalized self.[1]

To this extent science, as well as religion, is a social affair. Not seldom this phase of the scientific consciousness comes to the foreground, as when during the present war scientific men assert that they have a fellowship with one another that even the acid of national enmity cannot corrode. Here—in the social aspect of knowledge—is the chief clue to the reverence, the elevation, the obvious religiousness, that appear in so many of the greater men of science precisely in their devotion to science itself. "Science," said Huxley,

seems to me to teach in the highest and strongest manner the great truth which is embodied in the Christian conception of entire surrender to the will of God. Sit down before fact as a little child, be prepared to give up every preconceived notion, follow humbly wherever and to whatever abysses nature leads, or you shall learn nothing. I have only begun to learn content and peace of mind since I have resolved at all risks to do this.[2]

Further, just as in prophetic religion we find acute consciousness of human society bursting into consciousness of God, so the scientific consciousness occasionally prophesies. Huxley is an instance. He says:

In these moments of self-questioning, when one does not lie even to one's self, I feel that I can say that it is not so [that his intellectual work is done for honor from men]—that the real

[1] Cf. the description of deliberative religious groups, pp. 131 ff.

[2] *Life and Letters* (2 vols., New York, 1900), I, 235.

pleasure, the true sphere, lies in the feeling of self-development—in the sense of power and of growing oneness with the great spirit of abstract truth.[1]

Thus, immanent within all scientific reasons for things (mediated knowledge) there is social immediacy—the experience of a multiplicity that is also unity of individuals precisely where one's own individuality is focalized by the demand for critical judgments. The social immediacy of science is not an isolated thing. It is continuous with the ethical consciousness of being bound with others of one's own kind under a common law. Here, too, the individual, checked in his desires and compelled to scrutinize them, realizes that the ideal common will is his very own will; and just as the scientific mind now and then feels reverential awe toward the spirit of truth, so ethical law often becomes envisaged as a single will that is somehow also our own several wills. The same sort of movement appears in aesthetic experience. Social participation is a vital presumption of art, and the emancipation of the individual that is achieved in aesthetic contemplation is emancipation into a state much like communion.

All this social immediacy is continuous, too, with what we have found to be most remarkable in religion, namely, the resolution of strains and crises, which make self-consciousness acute, by spontaneous recognition of the experience as a shared one, a social experience. Religion is or includes so many things that only with caution should one venture to say that this or that is its chief distinction. Nevertheless, the perennial tendency of religion to anthropomorphize the world,

[1] *Op. cit.*, I, 75.

peopling it with spirits and gods; likewise its tendency to sum up and represent social organization, social
purpose, and social protest in such beings; finally,
the constant springing of faith in some large social
meaning within the lesser social meanings, and the
springing of this faith directly out of valuations without
waiting for rational verification—all this justifies the
theory that what keeps religion alive is this: that human
experience is an individuating process, a struggle to be
individual, unique, an "I"; but the experience of being
an individual is *per se* an experience of other individuals.
I say an "experience" of others for the same reason that
I speak of the "experience" of being an individual. Both
phases of experience simply arrive; they are not derived,
and they are as inexpugnable as any other data. Thus,
all our mediated knowledge rests upon—is made possible
and meaningful by—social immediacy, which is common
to science, art, morals, and religion.

Here is a root that lives on and on, ever germinating afresh when old usages and even sanctities are
cut to the ground. Religion repeatedly recalls attention from mediation that may seem to be self-sufficient
to its ground in social immediacy. This recall takes
many forms. The occasions of social excitement, such
as hunger and war, that yield the characteristic rites
of early religion have their focus in this question:
What is to become of *us?* Religion as an expression
of political unity means, Remember one another! On
the ethical-prophetic level, religion says, Value persons above all else. The repentant prodigal "comes
to himself." Reflective religion, striving to find some
wholeness in the fragments of experience (hence the

term *recollection* as used in devotional literature), culminates in its answer to the question, What is the meaning and value of life? That is, *cui bono—to whom is it good?* When men immerse themselves in a multiplicity of pleasures or in an accumulation of economic goods, religion asks, Have you found, or lost, yourself? If ever art, imagining itself to exist "for its own sake," invites us to enjoy regardless of consequences, religion asks whether anything can be beautiful that tends to a disorganized, ugly, or unsocial self. When science or philosophy offers as the truly objective world a system of merely mediated items, or mere content abstracted from experiencing, religion offsets the chill of such a world by the warmth and self-evidence of personal relations. After all, science is *our* reaction; the experience that makes science empirical is *our* experience; the objective world is *our* world, and there is no way to assert its objectivity without recognizing the multiplicity of persons who have it as their common world. This social immediacy within all mediation makes it forever impossible for science to supplant religion.

But we are not at the end of our problem when we have merely recognized social immediacy as the warp of our experience. There is a woof also. You and I are in process; we are parts of the very same system concerning which our illusions arise. We are born and we die, we come and we go, are present and absent. How many of "us" are there? Who knows? And how do we assure ourselves that a second or third or nth experiencer is at all, or of what sort he is? Nay, how am I, caught in the time-process, immediate even to myself?

Evidently we are mediated to one another as well as immediate, and each of us is both immediate and mediated to himself. I am self-conscious by an utterly original act, yet I find out only gradually and partially, by observation and inference, and with much self-deception, what this self of mine is. Just so, with equal originality, my self-consciousness is all one with consciousness of others like myself—my self-consciousness is social consciousness. Yet only by much putting of two and two together do I secure any working acquaintance with my *socii*. This intermingling of mediacy and immediacy, the presence of both at exactly the same point, may be paradoxical, but if so the paradox is in reality itself. If, then, we proceed to scrutinize a little more closely the psychology of social immediacy, our task will be, not to reduce one side of the paradox to the other, but only to indicate the main conditions under which the presence of another is realized, and the relation of these conditions to religion.

Let us begin with the self. Under what conditions do I experience myself as immediately present, and what help, if any, do our psychological categories give toward construing this "presence"? Are the conditions of introspection, for instance, favorable, and is the self an object of introspective perception? Professor Calkins has painstakingly pointed out that much experimental introspection expresses itself in such phrases as "I remember that I attended to the shape of the cube"; "I immediately experienced the feeling of familiar"; "I said to myself . . . . ."[1] But notice that the pur-

[1] M. W. Calkins, "The Self in Scientific Psychology," *American Journal of Psychology*, XXVI (1915), 495–524.

pose of the experiments would not be interfered with in the slightest if the phrases were changed to: "the shape of the cube was clearly seen to be so and so"; "A feeling of familiar occurred immediately"; "Verbal images so and so occurred." Notice, further, that the self of each introspector was in every instance presupposed in the experiment itself, presupposed by both the experimenter and his subject. When the subject uses "I" in the description of his introspections, he gives back this presupposition without addition or subtraction. Nobody's knowledge of personal selves as present was strengthened by the experiments, nor is it credible that Professor Calkins' certainty of these selves would be less than it is at present if no reference to a self had appeared in any of the introspective records. Finally, what is the attitude of the introspector if not that of postponing all self-assertion, of abstracting from the likes and dislikes, the approvals and condemnations, the co-operations and antagonisms—in fact, the whole social reference of the self, wherein lies the tang of selfhood?

This brings us to the heart of the matter. Whenever we try to fixate an individual as a mere particular, it mocks us for our pains. "Here you will find me," it promises, but it adds, "You found me before you commenced to hunt for me, and you didn't find a *mere me* but an *us*." The very first coming to myself "out of the deep" was a coming of loves and hates; considered as discovery, it was discovery of mutuality. The focalization into individuality is cross-focalization.

Society, consequently, whether it includes men only or men and God, is not an aggregate of individuals any more than the self is an aggregate of states. We do not obtain one another by adding together units that are originally separate or self-subsistent, but by progressive differentiation within what is *given* as mutual presence of individuals to one another. The ancient puzzle, "How do I know that other minds exist?" has led many a thinker into a trap by its assumption that one can know one's self without reference to other minds. No one ever did get his knowledge of the existence of his neighbors by first knowing his own existence and then finding a way outward. The *ego* phase and the *alter* phase of experience grow up together and reciprocally. Further, the differentiations of the at first indefinite *ego-alter* into a world of definitely-named persons are only secondarily inductive inferences. First comes love or hate, which focuses attention and provides the conditions for subsequent renewal of the interest that underlies every recognition of another's identity. Your identity is altogether dependent upon the loves and hates borne to you. Indeed, only the things that we can love and hate have any identity at all. An atom or an ion has no more identity than the letter A.

These remarks apply equally to my knowledge of my own existence. As we have already seen, I do not observe myself as merely there, like a museum specimen in a glass jar. Introspection fails to find me precisely because it is disinterested. It is only from an interested standpoint that the "mine" has meaning at all. I find myself by being a friend to myself.

Those who first assume that one can know one's self without any social reference are driven to guesses and paralogisms in order to make our belief in the existence

of others seem reasonable. Attempted proofs are bound
to fail because they refer each case—say, a body making
certain motions—to a presupposed class-notion "mind,"
whereas the question at issue is what right we have to
any such class notion at all. The crux of the matter is a
double experiencing of the same object, as in any case of
co-operation or of conflict. How can I from my experience of the object infer in another a coincident experience
of it ? Back of inferences as to the presence or absence of
other experiencers, there must be, obviously, some such
datum as mutuality or communion. There is no getting
behind the conviction that the experience of a particular
object may be a dual or multiple experience and may
include knowledge that it is multiple.[1]

[1] I have been able to collect eight kinds of answer to the question,
"How do I know that other minds exist ?" (1) "I touch, see, and hear
my fellows." To this a query is applicable: "Do you touch a second
experience of touching ?" (2) "I know other minds by analogy between
the motions of my own body, which I know to be associated with consciousness, and the observed motions of other like bodies." So F. H.
Bradley, *Appearance and Reality* (London 1893), p. 255. The position
of Leuba, as stated in "Religion and the Discovery of Truth," *Journal
of Philosophy*, IX (1912), 406–11, is as follows: "Human beings are
objects of sense to me: I touch, see, hear, them. They behave exactly
as I do and respond obviously to my presence. These beings meet
every scientific test of my belief that they think and feel as I do."
Here three different theories seem to be mixed together: (a) a naïve
theory of perception; (b) a theory of analogy; (c) a theory of verification
of a hypothesis by experiment. It would be interesting if Professor
Leuba would indicate the nature of the scientific evidence that he
himself thinks and feels, and then analyze the logic of the experiment
that seems to him to prove that others think and feel as he does. The
supposed analogy, which uses bodies as the bridge between minds,
breaks upon the fact that all the bodies in question, my own and the
others, are content of *my* experience and also content of *yours*. A body
could not be a bridge *between* these two experiences unless it were first
disengaged from both of them. In my knowledge of any other mind,

The differentiation of the primordial sociality of our experience into sharply focalized "I's" and "thou's" takes place primarily, I have said, by the way of loving and hating. An interesting side light upon this fact may be found in the parallel growth of the scientific movement and the social movement. Since the middle of the last century the natural and physical sciences have been successful as never before in constructing and applying the notion of an all-inclusive, impersonal nature. We ourselves have been made to appear as parts of a system that offers no shadow of justification for our partiality

then, there is no intermediate link that belongs to neither of the minds; I simply duplicate the experiencing of everything that could conceivably serve as a link. (3) My knowledge of the nervous system somehow brings me closer to the knowledge that another mind exists. So H. R. Marshall, *Consciousness* (New York, 1909), pp. 173 ff. Karl Pearson suggests that if I could connect your brain and mine by a commissure of nerve substance, I should then have a direct sense impression of your consciousness (*Grammar of Science*, 3d ed., Part I [London, 1911], pp. 48–50). But would I then know *you* as experiencing? If not how does Pearson's suggestion help? (4) The bridge between my mind and my neighbor's is not physical but spiritual. Through prior knowledge of God I have a category that I can use in the interpretation of sense data. So W. E. Hocking, *The Meaning of God*, etc. (New Haven, 1912), pp. 297–300. (5) My knowledge of the existence of other persons is a postulate of my life as a moral person (Fichte). (6) My knowledge of other minds is merely an instance of the universal method of the mind in outrunning the data of experience in the interest of subjective needs. So G. M. Stratton *Psychology of the Religious Life* (London, 1911), pp. 364 ff. (7) My knowledge of other minds is direct and intuitive; minds are continuous with one another; bodies do not come between. So J. E. Boodin, "Individual and Social Minds," *Journal of Philosophy*, X (1913), 169–80. (8) I know other minds by being in some degree or sense the very thing that I know: "Individuals may be included within other individuals" (J. Royce, *The World and the Individual*, II [New York, 1901], 238; see also pp. 168–74). Boodin (*op. cit.*, pp. 174 ff.) also holds that minds overlap.

for certain parts of nature as against others, and for certain natural processes, such as love, as against other natural processes, such as selfishness. The standpoint of the natural and physical sciences, taken by itself alone, implies, as an inclusive finality, the non-individual, the impersonal, the regardless. But precisely at the bloom period of these sciences the social movement, with its vast sensitiveness for humanity and for the individual, also arose with insistency and with no little power. What, now, is the relation between these parallel movements? The natural and physical sciences have not furnished fresh motives for loving, but they have opened fresh opportunity for it in the increase of human intercourse, and men have simply seized the opportunity. The fact seems to be that we love just because we can!

The immediacy of our social consciousness, that is to say, is not a static aspect of it, but dynamic. It is pressure toward further acquaintance, toward increasing recognition of myself in others and of others in myself. This dynamic principle of human nature appears in religion as follows: Its spirits and gods have been real to men because of the inner pressure to love and hate, but chiefly, as with human society, because of the inner pressure to idealize or love. These superior beings are differentiations of the immediate social consciousness by the ordinary method. Similarly, the decline of faith in any of them has followed the same law. As science never discovers an individual, so it never of itself dispels a social illusion. We outgrow the crude gods of our ancestors because we require greater scope for our loves and hates, particularly our loves. The prophets are

zealous to make the character of God appear admirable.
Xenophanes (about 500 B.C.) says:

Mortals fancy gods are born, and wear clothes, and have
voice and form like themselves. Yet if oxen and lions had hands,
and could paint with their hands, and fashion images as men do,
they would make the pictures and images of their gods in their
own likeness; horses would make them like horses, oxen like oxen.
Ethiopians make their gods black and snub-nosed; Thracians
give theirs blue eyes and red hair. Homer and Hesiod have
ascribed to the gods all deeds that are a shame and a disgrace
among men: thieving, adultery, fraud.

In opposition to all this, Xenophanes declares:

There is one god, supreme among gods and men; resembling
mortals neither in form nor in mind. The whole of him sees, the
whole of him thinks, the whole of him hears. Without toil he rules
all things by the power of his mind. And he stays always in the
same place, nor moves at all, for it is not seemly that he wander
about, now here, now there.[1]

Similarly, but with more fire, a Hebrew prophet describes
in most humorous fashion the attitudes and the incon-
sistencies of idol-worshipers:

The smith maketh an axe, and worketh in the coals, and
fashioneth it with hammers, and worketh it with his strong arm:
yea, he is hungry, and his strength faileth; he drinketh no water,
and is faint. The carpenter stretcheth out a line; he marketh
it out with a pencil; he shapeth it with planes and he marketh
it out with the compasses, and shapeth it after the figure of a
man, according to the beauty of a man, to dwell in a house. He
heweth him down cedars, and taketh the holm-tree and the oak,
and strengtheneth for himself one among the trees of the forest;
he planteth a fir-tree, and the rain doth nourish it. Then shall
it be for a man to burn; and he taketh thereof, and warmeth

[1] Bakewell's translation in his *Source Book in Ancient Philosophy*
(New York, 1907), pp. 8 f.

himself; yea, he kindleth it, and baketh bread; yea, he maketh a
god, and worshippeth it; he maketh it a graven image, and falleth
down thereto.   He burneth part thereof in the fire; with part
thereof he eateth flesh; he roasteth roast, and is satisfied; yea,
he warmeth himself, and saith, Aha, I am warm, I have seen the
fire: and the residue thereof he maketh a god, even his graven
image; he falleth down unto it and worshippeth, and prayeth
unto it, and saith, Deliver me; for thou art my god.   They
know not, neither do they consider: for he hath shut their eyes,
that they cannot see; and their hearts that they cannot understand.   And none calleth to mind, neither is there knowledge nor
understanding to say, I have burned part of it in the fire; yea,
also I have baked bread upon the coals thereof; I have roasted
flesh and eaten it; and shall I make the residue thereof an abom-
ination? shall I fall down to the stock of a tree? He feedeth on
ashes; a deceived heart hath turned him aside; and he cannot
deliver his soul, nor say, Is there not a lie in my right hand?[1]

It is the same immediate social dynamic that constitutes the basis of the Christian's experience of the God
of love.   Precisely as acquaintance between lovers is
idealization—yes, as all acquaintance is constituted by
the outward pressure of the social dynamic that constitutes us individuals—so a great love is the only conceivable mode of discovering the Christian God, or of being
discovered by him.   The Christian does not first find
God, and afterward love him.   Rather, repeated exercise
in loving one another and in overcoming hate and indifference (exercise that starts on the instinctive plane) at
last fixes attention upon the love motif itself, and we
take an approving attitude toward it, an attitude exactly
parallel with that which we take toward one another.
An ancient Christian writer says: "He that loveth not
his brother whom he hath seen cannot love God whom

[1] Isa. 44:12-20.

he hath not seen," and "No man hath beheld God at any time: if we love one another, God abideth in us"; and yet again, "Let us love one another: for love is of God; and everyone that loveth is begotten of God, and knoweth God. He that loveth not knoweth not God; for God is love." That is, the self-manifestation of God to us is precisely in this love that we experience toward one another, so that our communion with him lies in the attitude that we take toward the social motive itself.

To say that we fall in love with loving should not seem too paradoxical, especially in a world in which artists fall in love with beauty and thinkers fall in love with consistency. In any case, it is a fact. Jesus, gathering into one the intimate affection of Jewish family life, the prophetic appreciation of social righteousness, and sympathy for the needy life around him, found in this experience himself and the Father, and by his own steady living in this "love way" he helped his followers also to the unreserved love that is their experience of God.

To take as a personal presence this outgoing, social, or common will that is within us involves no process that is not already practiced in ordinary social intercourse.[1] My neighbor is present to me, not independent

[1] H. A. Overstreet ("God as the Common Will," *Hibbert Journal*, XIII, 155–74) thinks that religion is being transformed into devotion to the common will. He regards this will on grounds that are not specified as impersonal. Yet he makes it an object of affectionate devotion. He is on doubtful ground when he supposes that men do as a matter of fact devote themselves thus to such abstractions as "laws," "truth," or "the spirit of" something. Certainly the parallel that he gives—the transfer of political devotion from kings to democracy—hardly illustrates his point, since devotion to democracy is above all things a deeper recognition of personality as defining the sphere and ground of devotion.

of, but by virtue of, the love that I bear to him. My certainty of him is inseparable from my will-to-have-and-to-be-a-neighbor. This, of course, is not inference or proof in the case of either my neighbor or God, but the positing of a premise. Formal logic is at liberty to treat it as pure assumption. Nor is this anything strange or exceptional. "States of consciousness themselves," says James, "are not verifiable facts."[1] Because these matters are assumptions, they will never be verified, but only repeated. The Christian will never see God any more than he will see the neighbor. The beatific vision, if it should ever be realized, would be naught else than a society wholly controlled by love. God would still be, just as he is now, the common will in which each individual will realizes itself.

But the conditions for repeating the assumption of both neighbor and God may grow more or less favorable. In general, it is by indulging social impulses belonging to our original nature that acquaintance with others grows firm. Conversely, by suppressing these impulses, or by allowing them to atrophy through lack of exercise, we first stratify society, assuming that the many are not as we are, and then, having narrowed the range of our affection to our "set," we proceed to curb affection itself. It is perfectly possible for us thus to depersonalize our world. We can go on with such depersonalization until our fellows seem to be little more than things. On the other hand, by exercising social impulses, by forming, criticizing, and re-forming social purposes, by sharing in the joys and the woes of others, and by self-sacrifice for the neighbor, we can focalize and intensify our

[1] *Psychology* (Briefer Course), p. 467.

consciousness of social reals. We can intensify it until our real world is pre-eminently the world of persons. With the growth of intense devotion to the neighbor whom we have seen—one's own devotion, and the devotion of others—it becomes easier and easier to believe in God. Jesus' life of simple, unreserved neighborly love does, in truth, directly beget faith in a loving God, and this is the tendency of every similar life. Thus in and through the choice of others' good as our own, which may also be called the identification of our will with theirs, the real existence of a common will, and even the personality of it, become convictions. This conviction is the experience of an adequate object for love. It may take the form of adoration, or of friendship, or of rescue from a divided will, or of release from fears and strength to meet the ills of life. But whatever form it takes, what happens is the recognition of the common or social will as God in us, and this "recognition" is a getting acquainted that corresponds in process with the finding of any friend.

CHAPTER XVI

MYSTICISM

The social immediacy of which the last chapter treats is not to be forthwith identified with mystical experience or mystical theory. One obvious reason for caution is lack of preciseness in the term "mysticism." It is, in fact, used in so many senses that one might wish, in the interest of science and of religion alike, that it could be blotted out from memory, so that we might be compelled to devise different terms for different things. Here is a partial list of the ways in which it is used:

"Mysticism" means a great variety of religious experiences and practices. They range all the way from a savage's experience of "demon possession" to the trance state that Brahmanism represents as contentless absorption in the One.

"Mysticism" means the spontaneous or traditional interpretations put upon these experiences by the persons who have them. These interpretations always involve a psychological or quasi-psychological statement of what happens.

"Mysticism" means a doctrine of intuitive or immediate knowledge of God.

"Mysticism" means the metaphysical doctrine that only the One is real, and that we know reality only as we rid the mind of the phenomenal, the finite, and the individual, which are mere appearance or illusion.

"Mysticism" means religious internality of one sort or another (such as Christian love) as contrasted with ceremonialism, dogmatism, and external good works.

"Mysticism" means supernatural intervention in the natural order. The "mystical theology" of Catholic writers has this denotation.

"Mysticism" means what is popularly called superstition, that is, belief in spirits, or in magic, or in astrology, or in other hidden powers.

Without arguing for any exclusive use of this many-sided term, I shall first show that there is, as a matter of fact, a historically and psychologically coherent series of experiences to some or all of which the term "mystical" is commonly applied. I shall then examine from the structural standpoint the traditional accounts of mystical processes given by mystics themselves. The functional aspects of certain of these processes will then be noticed, and, finally, a question will be raised as to their relation to social immediacy.

The problem of mysticism, as far as psychology is concerned, arises from the fact that we partially, but only partially, foresee and control our bodily and mental changes. What we do that is habitual, familiar, or foreseen we call our own. But if my hand writes something that I have no recollection of intending to write, or possibly something that I have no recollection of having written, we call such writing automatic. So, also, we have automatic speech. Similarly, if I seem to hear the voice of a person who is not within hearing distance, or to see someone whose body is certainly far away, psychology calls the experience hallucination or mental automatism. The term "automatic" applies also to ideas or thought structures that unexpectedly dart into consciousness. The association of ideas is thus always at least partly automatic.

When primitive men experienced loss of self-control through drug intoxication or through any of the trance-inducing processes already described as the basis of shamanism, the only possible interpretation was "possession"—that somebody else was controlling the muscles and even the thoughts. When visions and auditions occurred the only possible view was that this was actual seeing and hearing. Out of such mental and bodily automatisms grew spiritistic practices—methods for securing visions, or for getting information by way of impressions, or for inducing spirits to do various kinds of work. Modern spiritism lives and moves in the same general sphere. Wherever it is not fraudulent, as it is in materializing séances, it has to do with such phenomena as automatic writing and speech, and with visions, auditions, and mental impressions which, whether they are veridical or not, fall under the general notion of the automatic. What distinguishes intelligent spiritism, such as exists among members of the Society for Psychic Research, is the view that the presence of spirits is evidenced, not in the automatic as such, however strange it may be, but rather in the critically sifted content of the automatic deliverances.

From spiritism, whether primitive or modern, to what the various religions have called inspirations, there is entire continuity in point of psychical process, and even in historical development. Saul consulting the medium at En-Dor; Saul meeting a band of raving prophets, and going into a trance; Saul troubled by an evil spirit which departed when David played the harp; the "hand of Jahwe" coming upon Elisha so that he prophesied when the minstrel played; the visions and overwhelming convictions of the great prophets—these are excerpts from a single historical series. If the term "inspiration" points to process as distinguished from content, then inspiration is common to spiritism and to prophetism. More than this: it exists in the Christian churches today as sense of guidance or of illumination, as assurance or witness of the Spirit, and as a sense of the presence of God or of Christ.

From inspirations to religious ecstasy also the passage is continuous. The man who is merely inspired keeps up more or less discriminative thought, but the saint who is "rapt" in God is supposed to let his thought activity cease in order that he may be filled with God only. Extreme mystics assert that a state is finally reached in which self-consciousness with its distinction of "I" and "thou" lapses, and God is all. This, which is ecstasy, is obviously just the maximum of "possession." Psychologically it is the automatic at its highest conceivable extreme. There is, then, psychological continuity between shamanism and the heights of mystical rapture. That there is historical continuity also will appear when we notice, in a subsequent paragraph, the peculiar relation of India to the whole mystical movement. The interrelations here involved between many sorts of experience, theory, and practice may be exhibited in the form of a tabular view, as shown on p. 267.

This, in very brief, is the genealogy of mysticism. The affinities here noted do not, however, exclude oppositions. Just as chemistry opposes the alchemy out of which it has sprung, so a mystic may abhor spiritism. The great prophets of Israel flouted the shamanistic prophets. Catholic writers of the present day condemn all dabbling with the "occult." Yet the great prophets did not deny actual inspiration to the shamanism that they condemned, and the Catholic condemnation of spiritistic practices rests on the precise ground that they bring one under the influence

A SURVEY OF THE MYSTICAL

Experience	Supposed Source	Deliberate Practice
The primitive root of the whole: Automatic experiences interpreted as possession		
Spiritism, ancient and modern:		*Attempts to control spirits or to communicate with them:*
Spirits seen, heard, "felt," etc.; spiritism proper shading into clairvoyance, premonitions, etc.	Spirits	Shamanism Mediumship of various kinds
Inspirations: The experience of the seer; sense of guidance or of illumination; assurance or witness of the Spirit; sense of divine communion; "sense of presence"; "anesthetic revelation"; "cosmic consciousness"	God or gods generally conceived as transcendent	*Attempts to realize the god on special occasions or for special ends:* Oracles Some forms of revivalism Holiness movements and allied practices Divine Healing Transsubstantiation
Form: Partial abeyance of self-control in mental functions; occasionally loss of muscular control also Content: somewhat specific ideas which seem to be self-evidently true		Method: surrender or quiescence of will, suggestion (largely social)
The supreme mystical state: Ecstasy Supposed form: complete absorption or loss of personality	God—tendency toward pantheistic conception	*Attempts to realize God as the All:* Yoga practices The Christian *via negativa* Christian Science and New Thought
Supposed content: either zero or infinity (These are only limiting notions)		Method: narrowing of attention and autosuggestion

of malign supernatural powers—"demons" in the evil sense.

Nor does this genealogy indicate of itself the possible value of mystical practices or the possible truth of mystical theology. An evolving order of any kind, as civil government or the natural sciences, is bound to contain in itself at the same time some things that we are moving toward and others that we are moving away from. Unmixed values and unclouded insight we never have; we never quite arrive; we never are altogether quit of our past. The question of values and of truth, therefore, always requires us to weigh various elements in relation to the movement both from and toward. Rejection of spiritism as illusory and injurious, consequently, would not of necessity carry with it condemnation of everything that has grown out of spiritism. Developed mysticism may be different in important respects from its own ancestors. We shall see, in fact, that the elements with which we have to deal, particularly in Christian mysticism, are complex and of varying values.

A structural account of mysticism requires consideration of the following items in reports that one or another mystic gives of his experiences:

1. Sense perception of objects not physically present, as Christ, the Virgin, heaven, and hell.

2. Systematized control (not mere isolated reflexes or associations), that seems not to be self-control, of muscles or of thought.

3. What James calls "noetic quality," and others call illumination. It seems to the one who has it to be direct certainty, in the more developed mysticism an intellectual "seeing" without the intellectual processes

of reasoning or proof. Other names for it are intuition and immediate knowledge. The objects of it are said to be God, or his loving disposition, or his attitude toward the mystic, or some doctrine, as the relation of Jesus to the Father. Now and then a Christian mystic is convinced that he has such immediate knowledge of each of the persons of the Trinity.

4. At the climax of mystical attainment, which is described as union with God so intimate that self-consciousness vanishes, the feeling tone is said to be utterly satisfying. This is ecstasy. Even the less extreme experiences are generally reported as bringing relief from the ills of ordinary existence. Yet some of the great mystics, particularly (perhaps exclusively) Christians, report states of terrible depression.

5. A remarkable feature of the situation is that, though mystics as a rule are fond of describing the mystical experience, and though they have produced a large literature of the inner life, they commonly declare that what they have experienced is indescribable. Visions and auditions, which are describable, they look upon as inferior. Indeed, beyond all apparent sense perception, even beyond all thought that moves in mental images, they find, they say, a higher, more illuminating experience. This they declare to be ineffable. Such declarations are so common that James makes ineffability one of his four marks of mysticism. From the declaration that something wonderful has happened, which cannot be described, some interesting consequences flow: (a) the mystic resorts to symbolic language; he uses terms of sense perception—sights, sounds, odors, touches—to express what he regards as

completely supersensible; (b) he employs the boldest paradoxes: God is a luminous darkness; the mystic's experience is a sweet pain, or a most active passivity; (c) the non-mystical investigator of mysticism is argued with, and yet assured that he cannot know because he lacks the experience out of which the mystic draws his certainty. Thus the mystic pleads his case in the court of discursive reason, yet denies the jurisdiction of the court. In order to remedy this inconsistency a tendency arises again and again to assert that mystical experience is universal, commonplace. At the present moment this attempt makes large use of the notion of the subconscious, and we are assured that what has heretofore treated science as an inferior instrument of the mind is itself becoming a matter of scientific knowledge.

6. Wherever mysticism is a systematic practice, the procedure contains certain common elements. The first is the withdrawal of attention from the activities and sense stimuli of the common life. The second is extraordinary concentration of attention upon some particular object. We have already seen how the shaman employs such processes. They reappear, in refined form, in the higher religions. The Buddhist, or Brahmin, or Christian mystic does not necessarily resort to any intoxicating, numbing, or fatiguing process, but he does systematize the fixation of attention technically called "contemplation." This term, as used in mystical literature, does not signify investigation, or discriminative thought that compares one thing with another. It is not analysis. It is not an effort to know anything new, but simply fixation of attention upon something already regarded as real and important. In Christian mysticism

the common objects of contemplation are God and Christ; in Brahmanism, the *pantheos* Brahma, in Buddhism, the extinction of desire. More or less elaborate directions are given to neophytes as to how to proceed, and the stages of the process are carefully set forth. In oriental mysticism there are directions as to how to sit, how to control the breath, how to exclude the distractions of sense, what to say to one's self. The various subjective phenomena that ensue are also described with minuteness and with sufficient objectivity to enable a psychologist to recognize connections and laws that are familiar to him.[1] In Christian mysticism less attention is given to mere psychological mechanics, and more attention to idea contents. Oriental mysticism as a whole is a mind-emptying process; Christian mysticism professes to be and in a large measure is, a mind-filling process. This is necessitated by the fact that the Christian God has a particular character, is assumed to have revealed himself in a particular way, and requires of the devotee active virtues. This distinction between oriental and Christian mysticism will occupy our attention later. At present it is sufficient to point out that the two are alike in the two points stated at the beginning of this paragraph.

7. What James calls the passivity of the mystic is a corollary of what has just been said. In the sense of bodily repose, and in the sense of unresponsiveness to ordinary incitements, passivity does mark the typical

[1] See, particularly, C. A. F. Rhys-Davids, *Buddhist Psychology* (London, 1914). This is not, as its title might lead one to suppose, a psychological analysis of Buddhist practices, but an exposition of the early Buddhist analysis of Buddhist mystical practices.

mystical technique. That is, the concentration of attention that it requires is a narrowing of attention, a retirement from enterprises and problems. But the control thus required has to be achieved by effort and practice, and the holding of the mind at just the right point is, in a sense, intense activity. Hence it comes to pass that both passivity and activity are attributed by mystical writers to the same mental state. This point is important for estimating the significance of the mystic's belief that his impressions are infused and that his whole being is possessed by God to the utter exclusion of self.

8. Wherever this general mystical technique is practiced, there mystical doctrines of a certain generic type are taught. The illusory character of sense experience; the exalted being of God (even beyond all predicates, as contrasted with a definite divine purpose); finite individuality a concealment rather than a revealment of the real, and attainment to reality, illumination, and bliss by absorption of the finite individual into God—these, with many variants, are the themes or the presuppositions of the mystical theory.

These are the facts and the items of testimony that require placement in our general scheme of mental elements and processes. The first of these facts falls under the general head of hallucination. As to the second fact—systematized automatic control—little need be said beyond what is contained in the chapter on "Religion and the Subconscious." The present application of what is there said is as follows: What seems to immediate consciousness to be the very opposite of self-control may be the product of self-control previously achieved, or of habitual acts previously performed. Now

and then the typewriting machine with which I am
writing these words seems to run itself; the control
seems not to be resident in my mind, but elsewhere—the
keys almost seem to attract my fingers. Yet this result
is strictly my achievement through practice. To determine the nature of the control in the case of a mystical
experience we must look, similarly, for possible traces
of former activities. A mere impression that one is not
the author of the ideas that stream into one's mind is
not sufficient evidence as to the fact. We must consider,
also, facts like these: poetic inspirations come, in anything like finished form, only to persons who have read
poetry, studied it, and attempted to produce it; mathematical inspirations come to mathematicians only;
musical inspirations come to musicians only. The
mystical insights of any religion are obviously colored
by the teaching that the mystic has already received—
every religion confirms itself through its mystics. The
Christian mystic feels that Christ or the Virgin Mary
is present; a Mohammedan mystic never. Each mystical religionist brings back from his contemplation the
sort of ideas that he took into it.

This is the general situation. It tends to refute the
theory that the mystic is ever released from the influence
of his own past, ever lifted out of the historical current
of religious life into a non-historical revelation. The
Brahmin enjoys communion with a single divine being
that has marks of India upon him; the orthodox Catholic
with plural divine beings that have the orthodox stamp.
Each mystic takes a socially produced idea as his
starting-point, and by contemplation makes it seem to
be something more than an idea, even a real presence.

Therefore his experience can never be exhaustively described in terms of a private relation to God.

The psychological process whereby the sense of real presence is produced is clearly marked in mystical literature. The management of attention in the manner already indicated under 6 above is precisely the process of suggestion, for a general description of which see p. 120. In the more extreme cases the mystic produces full self-hypnosis. He is then in what is called trance, a term without precise bounds, but indicative, when used of religious states, of a near approach to mono-ideism, or attention upon something without discrimination or change. If a mystic were *completely* absorbed into a divinity without attributes, subsequent memory would not enable him to say *into what* he had been absorbed. *Unio mystica* in the sense of consciousness of absolute oneness without duality is therefore only a limiting notion; it is not an experience. When it is testified to as actually occurring, what is offered us is an interpretation (by means of intellectual tools already at hand) of a gap in experience or (more probably) of an emotion that had slight objective reference of its own. In the latter case, the certainty, yet vagueness, of the *something there* is parallel to our occasional certainty upon awakening from sleep that we have had pleasant or unpleasant dreams, though we cannot say with what they were concerned.

From the generic agreements mentioned under 8 recent writers have drawn an argument for the truth or objectivity of mystical intuition. Just as all astronomers who are equipped with telescopes can see the rings of Saturn, so it is held that the mystics, the experts of all religions, perceive intuitively an all-encompassing spiritual world. Why this generic agreement exists will claim attention in a moment. But first let us avoid exaggerating the agreement. The mystic's certainty, which he regards as immediacy, covers the points at which he differs from his fellow-mystics, as well as the points that he holds in common with them. The differences in type are deeply significant. The Protestant mystic, to begin with, differs from the Catholic. For, whereas the latter accepts dogma as completed and all-sufficient, with nothing to be added, the former looks for fresh insights into the Bible and for particular guidance such as the church has never given. Nor does Protestantism encourage or often produce ecstasy or *unio mystica* in the classical or Catholic sense. Again, Christian mysticism as a whole is markedly different from that of India, as different as the Father and Christ are from Brahma. Now, when we consider that immediate knowledge is claimed by the mystics of each of these contradictory faiths, the supposed consensus of mysticism reduces itself to agreement in regard to a few picked items. Obviously, mystical intuition is not self-consistent, self-sustaining, nor self-correcting.

The generic similarities are found chiefly in the extreme mystics who employ the technique known as the *via negativa* already referred to under 6. The essentials are the negation of human interests, or the emptying of the mind, and the prolonged fixation of attention upon a single object or word. The resulting movement toward and into autohypnosis, which is indeed common to the mystics of different religions, can be shown with a high degree of probability to be the real source of the agreements in question. Let us begin with the sense of illumination or "noetic quality." Doubts disappear simply because attention is turned utterly away from the material by which doubt defines itself. Something parallel happens in the self-evident certainties of dreams. Similarly, one may experience illumination in yielding to the spell of a public speaker who employs suggestion skilfully. The illumination of the mystic's trance, in short, is the usual hypnotic self-identification with a situation that lacks shadows because attention has been directed away from them.

The mystic bliss has a similar explanation. Relaxation of muscles, and removal of mental inhibitions, both of which are involved in the "way," tend of themselves to yield satisfaction. The same comfort of relaxation sometimes accompanies, as we have seen, the use of narcotic drugs. Here also there arises a sense of freedom and of joy. Now, such drugs not only had a large place in the early development of mysticism, but they appear in the literature of today as adding evidence to the general argument for the validity of mysticism.[1] If we add to this general psychophysical condition the suggestive influence of the tradition of happiness attained through trance, we shall have all the explanation that the mystical rapture requires.

But a directly opposite phenomenon appears among the Christian mystics—periods of terrible depression, darkness, apparent abandonment by God. This, as far as I am able to discover, never occurs in Indian mysticism, nor do I know of any writer who has explained

[1] See pp. 158–61. See also James, *The Varieties of Religious Experience*, Index, *s.v.* "Drunkenness" and "Ether."

this remarkable disparity within the *via negativa*. Yet the explanation lies near the surface. The Indian mystic consistently seeks to empty his mind, for he looks for absorption into an absolute that is without predicates. But the Christian mystic inconsistently seeks both to empty his mind and to fill it; to lose himself in a divine abyss, and yet to apprehend God in the historical figure of Christ; to forget himself, and yet to remember that he is a sinner; to yield himself to passive bliss, and yet to obey the behests of active love; to enjoy individualistic spiritual luxury, and yet to follow the Christ who sacrificed and suffered. A tradition in which the supreme manifestation of the divine being is a crucifixion furnishes a background exceedingly different from that of the Indian mystic or the Mohammedan. The mental image of the crucifixion acts as a direct suggestion of distress. Further, the ethical elements in the Christian sense of sin, elements different emotionally from the Indian consciousness of finitude and multiplicity, tend to focus contrasts and oppositions which the Brahmin escapes by turning attention the other way. The Christian mystic, finally, has been taught to care for his own soul, to regard it as important even in the sight of God; so that here again attention turns to problems of moral status, to particular acts and dispositions, and even to emotional ups and downs.

Comparison of religious trances with our knowledge of suggestion yields still another explanatory item. Paul had an experience that led him to think that he might have been for a time "out of the body." Theosophists declare that they have direct experimental evidence that the soul can be separated from its fleshly habitation and return to it. Such statements undoubtedly spring from actually experienced changes in bodily sensibility. Functional anesthesia occurs again and again in hypnotic experiments. An arm or a hand may be to its possessor as if it were not, or it may seem strange, as, for example, without weight. Dental and other operations have now and then been performed under suggestive anesthesia so complete that the subject is unable afterward to recall any experience of pain. The basal fact here is a shifting or retractation of attention with respect to the mass of organic and other sensations upon which our habitual sense of the body rests. Such retractation underlies the remarkable anesthesias of hysterical patients also.[1] Still more profound alterations occur in other mental diseases, as when the body seems to be at some distance from the owner of it. Here, too, the basis is an interference with the usual mass of body sensations.[2]

With these general factors mingle, in many instances, influential circumstances of the individual's own psychophysical constitution or incidental condition. Nervous instability, whether inherited or induced, as we have already seen, favors automatisms. Or shall we say that when the automatic, which is omnipresent in all of us, is excessive in any individual, we call him unstable? Thus a close relation may be found to exist, in individual cases, between mystical religion on the one hand, and hysteria, or epilepsy, or delusional insanity on the other.

[1] Paul Janet, *The Major Symptoms of Hysteria*, Lecture VIII (New York, 1907).

[2] I have discussed some of these points still further in "The Sources of the Mystical Revelation," *Hibbert Journal* (January, 1908), pp. 359–72.

On the other hand, an incidental psychophysical condition may be a determining circumstance, as fatigue, hunger, or sexual longing. The general mechanism by which sexual longing influences religious states has been described in our discussion of adolescent conversions. It is now necessary to add that the extraordinarily frequent and circumstantial use of marriage as a symbol of the soul's relation to God or Christ can hardly be a mere accident of figurative language. Celibacy is undoubtedly a factor. Restless hearts have found in divine communion a companionship that serves as a substitute for that of husband and wife. Similarly, adoration of the mental image of the infant Jesus has furnished outlet for parental instinct that lacks the ordinary discharge. Therefore, in the analysis of mystical testimony three groups of factors must be taken into account: (1) The most general factor is the impressions produced by conditions that favor automatisms, and especially those that lead toward self-hypnosis. (2) Next comes the influence of the particular religion or sect in which the mystic has his setting. (3) Finally individual differences in original endowment or in induced psychophysical condition.

So much for the structure of experiences called mystical. The functional aspects must now be noticed. The matter is complicated because both the historical range of the facts and the individual variations are great. Nevertheless, functions can be discriminated, though they fuse with one another at the edges.

1. Taken as a whole, mystical experience focalizes in an individual some existing social idea or standard, and by thus focalizing it reimpresses it upon the group.

At first sight one would say that the highly individual and private character of mystical contemplation must produce variation and social dissent. On the other hand, one might infer that the surrender of self-control in favor of automatic control would lead toward the reinstatement of pre-moral, instinctive modes of behavior. In fact, neither of these results is prominent. Rather, the mystic, putting himself under the influence of tradition, reinforces its power. Except in occasional instances he is a scrupulous observer of conventional morality. As to intellectual variation, the most noteworthy fact is that the great Christian mystics are found in the church that exacts the strictest conformity.

2. On the other hand, the "Now I know for myself" is extremely satisfying to the individual who has it, even regardless of its particular content. In this respect mysticism is not at all peculiar. To accumulate, organize, and communicate experience is fundamental in the functions of the human mind. To behold what is beyond the mountains, to lift the veil of life's mystery, to see the invisible divinity—this of itself produces elation. Mysticism fascinates men partly because it produces, more largely because it promises, this exquisitely satisfying sense of individual selfhood.

3. The tradition of a mystical self-realization is most attractive to persons who suffer from a sense of "divided self." This term points to profound or recurrent strains like these: a struggle, that one cannot bring to a victorious conclusion, against sinful desires, with consequent deep sense of personal unworthiness and helplessness; profound distaste for the usual pleasures of life, with inability to find a substitute for them; restlessness and a

feeling of life's emptiness that arise from lack of exercise of the sexual and social instincts, or from lack of occupation adequate to one's intellectual or executive powers; changeability of mood, with self-criticism for inconstancy; persistent doubts, with insistent but vain protest against uncertainty. If we call all this "instability," we must understand by this term not only inherited nervous weakness, but also induced nervous depressions, and the sorts of habit that may make neurasthenic one who might be normal. All the mental strains just enumerated may find relief in mystical practices. The divided self may become unified, a commanding certainty displacing doubt, a focus for the emotional life being established, a central purpose being substituted for discordant impulses, and executive steadiness being achieved. These results are not uniform in kind or degree, of course, yet on the whole the tendency of mysticism is toward serenity, poise, and an organized will.[1] The mystic seems to himself to have sailed from a tempestuous sea into a sheltered harbor, or to have awakened from a troubled dream, or to have attained control of paralyzed organs. This result appears to depend comparatively little upon the specific content of the doctrine upon which the devotee fixes his contemplation. Hindu, Buddhist, Sufi, Catholic, Christian Scientist, nature-mystic—all show a generically similar unification of a divided self.

4. The inclusion of religious inspirations in our survey of the mystical, and the obvious similarity in point of process between these and other inspirations, as those of poets and artists, raise the question whether one

[1] On this point, see particularly Delacroix.

function of mysticism, after all, is not discovery. To say that mystics merely give back as personal experience the doctrines that they have received is surely not the whole truth, though it is a major part of it. Originality or mental invention appears in the prophets of Israel and in Gautama as surely as in Goethe, who was certain, as we have seen, of his own inspiration. Further, the characteristic mystical doctrines arose in the first place through experience, and not the experience through the doctrines. In one respect, namely, reduction of distractions and a moderate degree of muscular relaxation, mystical practices are favorable to thinking, just as quiet in an auditorium helps to make a symphony intelligible. It is rather surprising, in fact, that mysticism has not made more varied contributions to the world's thought. Still more notable is the fact that the most certainly original prophecy is that which contains the largest, not the smallest, amount of self-controlled discrimination (see p. 186); precisely as the more valuable poetic inspirations come to those who practice poetical composition with critical self-judgment. On the whole, it does not appear that mysticism has any special method of mental invention or any special tool of discovery. Its hold upon mankind lies rather in its practical efficiency in soothing troubled emotions, in steadying the will, and in conserving what has already been approved.

But it is said that the central claim of mysticism is direct acquaintance with God, and that the sort of immediacy thus claimed is involved also in all our acquaintance with one another. This identification of mystical doctrine with the doctrine of social immediacy is possible, however, only by ignoring certain sharp differences. It is not in India but within the Christian religion, which is fundamentally social, that this defense of mysticism arises. But the argument ignores certain basal elements in the Christian attitude, such as its appreciation of personality and its ascription of immeasurable worth to the individual. The love that is the fulfilling of the law individualizes both the lover and the loved. The unity that it requires is not the extinction of differences. It is rather a determination that what is other than myself and different from me shall have permanent validity for me. If *unio mystica* in the classical sense should really occur, it would involve the extinction of the reciprocity—whether between man and man or between man and God—that is of the essence of any social immediacy that the Christian religion can recognize.

The practice of the *via negativa* by the great Christian mystics, and their doctrine of union with God, contain as a matter of fact two unreconcilable elements. In the great prophets of Israel we behold a burst of emphasis upon the individual person. Jahwe is no longer represented as dealing with Israelites *en bloc*, but his commands and his condemnations for sin search out men one by one. Here is a movement, not toward, but away from absorption of the individual in the general. This individualizing of values reached its climax in Jesus, who taught that the Divine Father notices the fall of a sparrow, and numbers the very hairs of our heads. Compare this with *unio mystica*, in which supposably nothing in particular is noticed. Great is the contrast between the happiness of trusting a Father who thus values our individuality and the rapture of transcending all awareness of "I and thou."

In the Christian mystics called great the Indian denial of the value of the individual mingles inconsistently with the Christian doctrine of active love. Indian mysticism, with its doctrine of absorption, came into Christianity chiefly through neo-Platonism, and specifically through the writings of an unknown philosophical theologian of perhaps the fifth century who came to be mistakenly identified with Dionysius the Areopagite (hence the present name, Pseudo-Dionysius). These writings, translated into Latin by Johannes Scotus Erigena in the ninth century, exercised an important influence upon piety as well as upon speculation. They furnished a thread of doctrine, reaching through the generations, upon which mystical practices from both Christian and non-Christian sources could be strung. Hence the paradoxes of what is called Christian mysticism. Orthodox trinitarianism exists in the same mind side by side with a monism that is scarcely distinguishable from pantheism. Christian love is identified with an experience of "union" in which the distinction between lover and loved is supposed to be annihilated. Active regard for humanity is associated with the *via negativa*, which aims to get away from one's fellows into a purely individual bliss. That the practice of such mysticism did in many cases reinforce Christian love in the active, outgoing sense, is not due to the Indian element that was present, but to the persistence of standards that had come down from the prophets and from Jesus.

As far, then, as mysticism connotes the type of procedure that Christianity borrowed from India, mystical experience is not only not identical with social immediacy, but the two are diametrically opposed to each other. Social immediacy, the recognition of another as present, notices and fixates differences within a unity, and demands active attitudes with reference to the other. On the contrary, the negative way, at the moments when it is most completely represented, involves turning away from the neighbor whom one has seen, *away from the whole sphere in which love can act.*

CHAPTER XVII

THE FUTURE LIFE AS A PSYCHOLOGICAL PROBLEM

Belief in life beyond death is not a single belief based upon a single set of motives and considerations, but several different sorts of belief that arise in different ways. In the first place, instinctive avoidance of things that cause death is not at all the same as desire for the continuance of personal life. In the next place, the notion that one's double lingers around the place where one's body is interred arose before there was any clear notion of personal life—long before appreciation of the worth of personal-social experience could awaken longing for its continuance. The earliest spiritism, in fact, was an expression of fear rather than of hope. The dead man's shade was an object of avoidance, even of horror. In large areas and for long periods, as in Babylonia, India, Israel, and Greece, the land of shades was regarded, not as a place of fulfilment and of joy, but of feebleness and of darkness. Up to this point the basis of the belief in survival was: (1) Mental habit or association of ideas whereby further activities were expected where so many had already occurred. To early man life, with attitudes of "for and against," is the atmosphere of thought; it required no little experience before death could be thought of in antithesis to life. (2) Occasional experience of the apparently sensible presence of the dead—the sort of eye- and ear-witness that we classify as dream and hallucination. (3) Motor automatisms for which early man had no interpretation but possession. (4) The infusion of the whole with the *Einfühlung* of emotional thinking.

But by various stages and routes the picture of the future became ennobled to correspond with growing discrimination of the social values of this life. Such was the effect of embalming the body and securing magical control of the conditions of life in the other world, as in Egypt. The weighing of the soul against the feather of justice, and the ceremonial avowal of the soul that it has not committed this and that wrong, represent considerable carrying over of ethical values to the realm of the dead. The same is true of the Hindu doctrine of metempsychosis; the Jewish and Christian doctrine of resurrection; and the Zoroastrian and Christian doctrines of a future judgment. The doctrine of future rewards and punishments furnished some solace and strength to those who felt themselves the victims of injustice, and to the tempted at least a little restraint.

Yet even the notion of ethical continuity between this life and that which is to come does not unequivocally express appreciation for personality. For, though future rewards and punishments reproduce the standards of some group—the whole picture of trial and retribution being derived from human laws and courts—the individual is here represented as simply forced to submit to a power that imposes itself upon him. The valued thing in such a system is not the person and his capacities, but rather a body of laws conceived as somehow worth while on its own account, or, more generally, an arbitrary will that simply cannot be resisted successfully. This abstractedness of the future life from the experienced values of the personal-social life of the present appears with great clearness in the notion of a God who for his own glory imposes laws and administers penalties, and in the further notion that not by any possibility could a man deserve salvation.

A genuinely new approach to the whole question of the future life appears when men ask whether, after all, any life that we are capable of living is worth while, and if so under what conditions we might conceivably attain the worth that is potential in us. We have certainly accepted as valid the view that personal life as such is sacred. This is something different from taboo, though there is doubtless historical continuity between them. What we have in mind in "the sacredness of personality" is not some evil that will overtake us if we injure a member of a totem species, but rather the social possibilities that each individual must be allowed to live out simply because they are worth while in themselves. Though we are by no means faithful to this conviction in all spheres of social life, we acknowledge the validity of the principle, and we have incorporated various consequences of it into our laws and social customs.

This discovery of persons puts the notion of survival into an entirely new perspective. Death now appears to be an interrupter, if not destroyer, of what is most sacred. Consequently, directly out of the appreciation of personality, and without dependence upon antecedent spiritistic beliefs, or upon the doctrine of retribution, there arises a question whether or not death is simply defeat, as it seems to be, or whether it can somehow be fitted into the system of personal-social values.

In the presence of this question four types of reaction appear: (a) Some men persuade themselves that the life that now is, is good enough; or that, in view of the improbability of life after death, the part of wisdom is to make the most of the present, and meantime to cultivate indifference to the future; or that they really do not care to live after death. (b) Some attach their thought of the worth of life to the notion of a social or otherwise admirable process that shall go on indefinitely, even though the individuals who compose society perish. (c) Some, holding that survival is desirable, turn to the ancient phenomena of spiritism, or to fresh methods of evoking spiritistic phenomena, in the hope of establishing survival as a scientific certainty. (d) Some translate the ancient faith in heaven, the bright abode of divinity, and in hell, the portion of the wicked, into an entirely different faith, namely, in the continuity of personal-social values. In the new faith this means scope for carrying forward such social enterprises of ultimate worth as the discovery and control of the conditions of existence and the creation of art.

Three questions arise here that may be considered, without too much stretching, as the concern of psychology: (1) the scientific character and the results of researches into spiritism fostered by the societies for psychical research; (2) the function of the future in present personal-social life; a preliminary formulation of this question being, Do men desire to survive death, and if so, why? (3) what effect, if any, such desire may have upon the further evolution of mind.

Psychic research has had scant recognition from orthodox psychology. Some little advantage has been taken, it is true, of data that concern the subconscious and processes of both intentional and unintentional deception, but the enterprise as such stands outside of recognized science. Why? Partly because the motive of psychical research is supposed to contain a large emotional element—longing for communion with the dead; partly because of a conviction that the facts, whatever they are, are imbedded in such a mass of trickery as to require the methods of the detective rather than of the psychologist; partly, one may fairly surmise, because of a certain disrespect for mediums, psychics, and the whole tangle of delusions that certainly envelops the history of spiritism; finally, partly because many men are simply not interested enough in the question of a future life to warm up to the hard work involved in an investigation concerning it. This is as much as to say that orthodox psychologists as well as psychical researchers are to some extent emotionally guided—the emotions are different, that is all.

But there remains one distinction that is not emotional, a distinction of method. The attempt to establish the existence or non-existence of a person is utterly different from anything that occurs in the laboratory. Here, as I have already shown, all the persons involved are fully recognized as such in advance of experiment. Moreover, the mental processes that laboratory experiment isolates and controls for purposes of study are only fragments of an individual's experience; and what experiment does is to relate one such fragment, not to the integral self-realization of the subject, but to another fragment, or to some particular circumstance (as a drug, an hour of the day, or the passage of time). As far as I know, no one ever became convinced of the existence of a mundane person by analyzing a set of phenomena to see whether they require the hypothesis of an individual consciousness.[1]

Hyslop's conception of the method whereby psychical research might conceivably establish survival is based squarely upon the assumption that one's only knowledge of one's neighbor's existence is inferential, specifically a causal inference.[2] That this is not the actual method whereby we have become acquainted with one another, and that it is in any case illogical, I have already shown in chap. xv. I see no ground for expectation, therefore, that a crucial experiment or set of experiments will ever be devised that will demonstrate whether or not there is a personal presence in given phenomena. In the recognition of persons as present we are moving in the realm of ultimate assumptions, that is, a realm of selection rather than of inference.

In spite of the suspicion on the part of critics that psychic research is emotionally controlled, it has made a remarkable attempt to eliminate the heart from its labors. It has undertaken to deal with actual or hypothetical trans-mundane persons as if they could be mere cold facts. It therefore challenges all comers to construct if they can a hypothetical causal explanation for certain phenomena without employing the notion of personality. In the nature of causal explanation such a challenge can

[1] Two recent presidential addresses before the English Society for Psychical Research go far toward a resetting of the whole problem. See Bergson's address in *Proceedings of the Society for Psychical Research*, XXVII (1913), 157–75, and Schiller's address, *ibid*, XXVII, 191–220.

[2] J. H. Hyslop, *Psychical Research and Survival* (London, 1913), pp. 64 ff.

always be met. The facts can be fitted into our current notions of psychic mechanisms irrespective of the presence or absence of persons other than those whose existence is already assumed (never proved) by those who make and those who answer the challenge. At the present moment telepathy in a very extended sense is the resort of those who engage in psychical research but whose hearts do not warm up to the alleged communicators.[1] This is exactly parallel, in respect to method, to the avoidance of personal selves altogether by such psychologists—structuralists and behaviorists— as are not interested in the full concreteness of human experience. Whether a psychical researcher shall continue to develop hypotheses of the abstract, quasi-mechanical sort, or shall let go and recognize a discarnate spirit, involves something more, in every case, than the adequacy of a given hypothesis or the amount of evidence for it. It involves transferring himself from a purely structural to a functional point of view, and it requires specifically *Einfühlung* or so-called self-projection, with its attitudes of sympathy, liking and disliking, or co-operation and antagonism.

It appears, then, that the problem of survival, if it is to be worked out at all, will have its seat just where the general problem of being a person meets us in the present existence, namely, in social enterprise with its give and take, its self-seeking and self-sacrifice. Here we do not discover one another as already there in some merely factual sense; rather, we mutually *become* persons. We do it, not by adapting ourselves to proved

[1] See, for example, Podmore's *The Newer Spiritualism;* cf. Hyslop's criticism in *Psychical Research and Survival.*

facts, but by reaching out for unprecedented values, and by imposing upon ourselves the cost of seeking them even against some of our natural impulses and in the absence of certainty as to the outcome.

We are thrown back, therefore, into the process of social evolution as such. We cannot isolate the question of survival from that of the issues that we are fighting out in mundane society. Here we encounter some significant considerations. Where once the world was impersonal and loveless, it has already blossomed into family affection, and friendship, and the beginnings of justice. Star-dust and protoplasm, judged by their actual performances, gave no promise whatever of a personal world. Even when mind in the form of instinct arrived, still there was no clear promise. Who could have foreseen the coming of self-control, self-discipline, and the organization of good-will by mutual consent? That in such an originally unpromising situation personal-social life should arise at all involves at least as great a contrast as would be implied if our present personal-social integrations should finally become too firm to be dissolved.

But it will be said, and justly, that rudimentary psychic attraction and repulsion have been able to develop into a society of integrated persons because there has always been objective sense-material, persistent and organically integrated as the human body, to which these attractions and repulsions could attach themselves and find support. It is bodied, not disembodied love and hate that have produced society. Love, whether parental or conjugal, is not easily disentangled from touch and other sensations that stimulate it. Moreover, the discovery of persons has been bound up with co-operative and antagonistic activities upon sense-material, such as food, land, and money, and it has been immensely assisted by language. The question is a fair one, therefore, whether the rise of personal life under these conditions can have any bearing upon what may happen with the dead, whose environment we know nothing about, and in which we may possibly have no share. Even if we were not on other grounds distrustful toward mediumistic accounts of what the other world is like, is it certain that much could be gained from them? What is needed to create a personal-social situation between us and the dead, as between us and the living, is objective material upon which *common work* can be done. There is, therefore, good psychological ground for holding that, if any social relations actually exist between the dead and the living, they will be realized by the living only in and through social enterprises in which our own world of sense is being made instrumental to social purposes. The problem of the future life, consequently, is most likely to center in such parts of our experience as the struggle for social welfare and righteousness rather than in mediumistic phenomena, though these may well contribute something thereto.[1]

This brings us to our second question, namely, whether within our recognized social experience there

[1] The persistence with which so many able men and women have pursued psychical researches against many odds seems to me altogether admirable. Whether the primary interest is in communion with the dead or not, and whether the results establish the fact of such communion or not, mediumship requires investigation, and so do the reactions of men toward mediumistic phenomena.

is springing up any desire for survival of bodily death. Are the motives of the social struggle such as to require survival for their full expression and effect? The question, let it be noted, is not whether we ought to engage in enterprises of so great pith and moment, but whether the valuations that move us in our present enterprises actually have this scope, or tend to acquire it. It is certain that we attach values to the future, often to that which we recognize as having no precedent. The future, therefore, has present functions. As, however, the future is only relative, and is always becoming the past, we are dealing here with present functions of the past also, and the question whether desire for survival is growing up is inseparable from the further question whether historical characters are playing in our social struggle any such part as involves us in an attitude of fellowship toward them.

The question, Do men desire immortality? is ambiguous. It may mean, Do I desire an extension of consciousness merely as mine? or, Do I desire to be a permanent part of a permanent society? One who answers emphatically Yes! to the latter question may well say No! to the former. Now, the whole conduct of men shows that the personal-social relationships that they most value they do desire to continue. One does not willingly lose friend A, even if one is convinced that an equally good friend, B, is ready to take A's place. Love individualizes the object to which it attaches itself, so that something of the value is lost if the individual perishes. Moreover, immortality, or something like it, is desired for the great souls who have made the social struggle their own—souls like Lincoln, for example.

Nobody is willing to have such a person dissolved.   If we assent to the dissolution it is because we feel helpless to prevent it.   But even then we commemorate our friend and hero in anniversaries that re-awaken or freshly create a sense of fellowship, as in the cause of liberty.   More than this, by these processes we incorporate him into our communal life as a permanent force. This does not of itself imply that we believe him immortal, or that we are trying exactly to bestow some sort of immortality upon him, but rather that fellowship with him is so precious that every trace of it is as far as possible preserved—we would have him live if we could, and we would stay in his society if we could.   This process is carried only a step farther, if even a step, in the faith of several religions that their founder remains after his death as the actual, living leader of his people. When Christians cling passionately, as many do, to "the living Christ," they bear witness to this at least, that Jesus is to them so satisfying a personality that he deserves to live forevermore.

There is little evidence that many men desire immortality for themselves as mere individuals.[1]   Nor does such desire, as far as it is mere self-assertion, command particular respect when it does exist.   It is this consideration, apparently, that leads Höffding to

[1] See F. C. S. Schiller, "The Desire for Immortality," chap. xiii of *Humanism* [London, 1903].   See also his "Answers to the American Branch's Questionnaire Regarding Human Sentiment as to a Future Life," *Proceedings of the Society for Psychical Research*, XVIII (1903–4), 416–53; cf. G. Lowes Dickinson, *Is Immortality Desirable?* Boston, 1909.   A number of articles and books that deal with attitudes toward death and survival is listed by R. S. Ellis, "The Attitude toward Death and the Types of Belief in Immortality," *Journal of Religious Psychology*, VII (1915), 466–510.

deny that conservation of values has any relation to conservation of persons.[1]   But the case is distinctly not the same when society perceives that a social ideal is realized in an individual.   In this case the finality of social values inheres in the individual who incarnates them.   Life continued indefinitely is desired *for him*, and for *social* reasons.

Men who are unconvinced of individual survival often devise a surrogate to which to attach a feeling of the finality of social value and a desire for its continuity. The succession of the generations, stretching on and on through indefinite centuries, particularly when the notion of social amelioration is added, is to many persons so appealing as to be an object of love, though every individual in the whole procession is thought to perish utterly.   Men of good will are as eager as this to have an object of love to which some sort of immortality can be attributed!   Even when the probable extinction of the race is taken into account, affection turns now and then to the cosmic order, glad that *it* is forever to go on its orderly way.   In all these cases *Einfühlung* reads into a series or a law some of one's own gladness in individual self-realization in society.

These facts justify the judgment that when men reach a high level of social regard they tend to desire immortality, if not directly for themselves, then for others who better deserve it.   But if so, a psychical situation is in process of formation that may well have important consequences.   In the first place, as Schiller has pointed out, in some cases the possibility of finding out what is true depends upon the awakening of an

[1] *Philosophy of Religion*, p. 259.

interest that makes investigation seem worth while.[1] It may be that one factor in our ignorance with respect to the conservation of personality is fitfulness and lack of whole-heartedness in present, mundane social justice. Certain it is that social discovery is not independent of social devotion. Our age is called, for example, the century of the child, because childhood has been, in a real sense, just discovered. Now, this line of discovery took its start precisely in devotion to child-welfare, especially in education. Even if, therefore, the old interest in survival, which supported and was supported by automatic phenomena, should continue to fade away, it by no means follows that the problem of survival will grow cold, or that the possibilities of discovery are being closed.

But not only may the growth of devotion to social justice in mundane affairs, with its upspringing desire for the unending life of the socially worthy, ultimately open our eyes to what we do not now see for lack of interest, but it may also be a factor in a process whereby immortality, in the literal sense of indissoluble fellowship between persons, is being achieved. Here it would be easy for this discussion to go over into speculation or guesswork, or into glorification of the larger hope. Instead, let us close this sketch of the problem by a final glance at the actual relation of developing mental functions to the structural facts that partly condition them.

In the first place, then, between the development of structure and that of function no exact parallel exists. Function is not related to structure as the inner side of a

---

[1] See article referred to above in *Proceedings of the Society for Psychical Research*, XVIII (1903–4), 416–53.

curve to its outer side. This is already implied in our discussion of the question whether human nature remains the same or whether desires actually evolve. It is demonstrable that fresh self-criticism has developed and become a part of social standards within a period in which no corresponding evolution of the human body is believed to have occurred.

Moreover, the integration into personality and into mutual regard for one another is different in kind from the evolution of structure. The latter consists altogether in recombinations of unchanging elements—this is the whole point of view. Structures compared with one another are more or less complex, more or less resistant and persistent, but no one is better or worse than any other. But the evolution of desires, as we have seen, brings forth, not mere recombination of old rudiments of instinct, but criticism thereof and even desire to have desires. Here is an integration that has no parallel in chemical or neural structure, a kind of unity that is not mere combination of antecedent and persistent elements. When a distraught mind "gathers itself together" it does not merely heap up what is already there, which would yield no greater unity than was there before, but takes a new interest, forms a new purpose, uses its organs differently.

So also social integration through mutual regard does not merely bring into propinquity certain organisms; it is no mere aggregating of pre-existing elements. If we could suppose that parental instinct is nothing but the obverse of prolonged physiological infancy, even then there would remain the fact that this instinct has grown into affection, and that this sort of regard has spread out over other relations than that of parent and child. Thus, to some extent at least, functions go their own way. There is nothing to show that a society of mutual regard is a biological necessity or that men are merely squeezed together. No; in such a society the cohesive principle is new values, which must be seen from their own point of view or they will never be understood at all.

Finally, functions develop themselves by using the structures upon which we are accustomed to say that they are dependent. Thus, parental affection, though it is in a sense dependent upon brain development, uses brain to build homes, secure food, build schools, make protective laws; and in doing so parental affection is itself enlarged and purified. Parallel experiences occur in every line of endeavor in the interest of simple good-will.

In short, there is at work, on the functional side, a principle of personal-social integration that is no appendage of the physical conditions of life, but a user of these conditions for purposes of its own. In this use of conditions the nature of the conditions is in part discovered. And the overplus of desire whereby it outruns instinct and recurrently reconstructs itself has again and again anticipated knowledge of what is possible. Parental yearning that goes a little beyond the instincts of physical welfare has led on, for example, to actual social integration and to the use of material resources and conditions in the interest thereof to a degree that could not have been known as possible, except through the yearning and the acts to which it led. How far this sort of personal-social integration can go, and how far physical conditions can be brought into this relation of use, cannot be said with certainty from what has already occurred. But in view of the past one would take a hazardous position who should assert that society as we now know it is the concluding stage. If, as appears to be the case, desire for still further integration, which shall use death as a resource rather than submit to it as a defect of life—if such desire is now arising, there is nothing in the nature of the case that can justly rebuke it.

CHAPTER XVIII

PRAYER

A history and psychology of prayer would be almost equivalent to a history and psychology of religion. For religion concerns the focusing of life's values, and prayer is the vocal expression, or at least bringing to mind, of the value focus. Because the focus tends to take personal form, prayer is, typically, talking to or with a god. But from talking to a god the facts shade off in every direction. On the side of classical mysticism, prayer, sometimes called "interior prayer," becomes contemplation or mere fixation of attention without speech, and even without word images. In the opposite direction, that of ritualism, vocal formulae are exactly repeated, as in connection with the sacrifice, under an impression that the formula has some sort of efficacy in itself. The sacred literature of Hinduism, of Zoroastrianism, and of Egypt is made up to a considerable extent of such efficacious words. Effects are sometimes supposed to be accumulated or rendered more certain by mere repetition, as by the reiteration of the name of Allah by dervishes, by the use of the prayer wheel in India, and by the saying of many masses for the dead. A touch of the same thing is in the minds of some Protestants, who do not feel that a prayer is quite right unless it ends with an "amen" preceded by some such formula as "through Jesus Christ our Lord." If we go a step farther we come upon magical spells (however magic be defined) and upon dealings with spirits by means of speech.

Between these diverse facts there is not merely some external similarity of process, but also the unity of a single lineage. Wherever prayer in the "proper" sense begins—say, with the appearance of gods in the strict sense—it springs, as the gods themselves do, out of earlier anthropomorphisms. We may think of the beginnings as mere exclamations expressive of naïve emotions that involve a sense of friendliness or of unfriendliness in any extra-human object that is felt to be important. Neither here nor later is the language exclusively that of supplication. Any recognition of the "other" may be found in prayer—as praise and flattery; thanksgiving; expressions of fellowship or of common interests; attempts to help the god in some vicissitude of his career; faultfinding; compulsion of the god by the magic use of his name; submission to the wisdom or to the ethically superior will of the divinity; finally, enlistment with the divinity in a social enterprise.

If from this wide range of facts we separate for special study those that involve recognition of a god like one's self, leaving aside both the mystic's sense of the divine as an impersonal or supra-personal abyss, and the mechanical use of speech forms, two types of problem will confront us: On the one hand we shall have the problem of the structure of prayer—how, within one's own mind, one experiences this apparent duality of self and god. On the other hand, we shall need to inquire into the functions of prayer—what has moved men so persistently to pray, and what advantages have accrued therefrom.

In its earlier stages there is nothing to distinguish prayer structurally from any other conversation, except that the divinity is ordinarily invisible and inaudible. He is supposed to have body and bodily senses; to hear with literal ears; to smell the sweet savor of the sacrifice, and even to taste it and be strengthened by it. Speech *to* him therefore moves in the ordinary channels. As yet no question arises as to whether the worshiper be not talking to vacancy or addressing a mere wish-being, an ideational construct of his own. There is as yet no doubt that prayer has two termini.

Nevertheless, communication *from* the god does not flow as easily as communication to him. The god can, indeed, make himself visible and audible, and he does so upon occasion. But dreams, visions, and auditions are too occasional to meet the constantly recurring wants of the worshiper. Therefore other signs are looked for; rather, the worshiper's anxious interest endows with the meaning of response any unusual or attention-compelling phenomenon. Thunder and lightning, a stormy sea, sudden sickness, a rainbow, certain states of the entrails of animals—all have been taken as divine language. Casting the lot, too, has been a widespread method of, so to speak, putting words into the god's mouth. Just so, some Christians have practiced opening the Bible and placing a finger upon a text at random in the firm belief that in the text thus indicated a divine message will be found specifically intended for the individual concerned. This devising of language for the god went so far that systems of augury, with rules for interpreting what we regard as ordinary phenomena, were employed by the state for consulting the

gods, as at Rome, before important enterprises were begun.

By a parallel process, tangible objects of many sorts became the abode of divinities, so that the gods lived among men, even if dumbly. It is not to be supposed, of course, that early men, realizing a need for sensible support for their thought of the divine, deliberately constructed pictures and images as reminders, as we seek to possess photographic portraits of our friends. Rather, first of all, savages who came upon some object which, by reason of its association with some emotional experience, could be taken as possessing the powers that ultimately constituted the attributes of divinity, treasured it carefully, sometimes as the very center of the tribal life. If the object was similar in form to the human figure, so much the better. Natural objects that resemble the phallus, for example, have been widely preserved and reverenced. But emotional associations have endowed almost all sorts of things with some of the qualities of a present divinity. For example, in Australia, and in other parts of the world, a stick of a certain shape which when whirled in the air upon a cord makes a whirring sound (hence called the bull-roarer) is treasured among the sacred and secret objects. That the men's society, which uses it in the annual initiations to awe the neophytes, does not now regard it as possessing in itself any extraordinary virtue does not detract from the significance of the fact that other members of the tribe do so regard it, or from the probability that it acquired its importance in the first place through the unaffected emotion that it awakened.

Under the primitive theory that the qualities of a thing inhere in any representation of it, whether a picture, an image, or even a name, further channels were found for expression from the god to the worshiper. The earliest drawings of animals were probably intended as a means of control or influence, as in the chase. But some early art involved more than the notion of success in hunting or fishing. The savage wanted also some of the *mana* that the swift, or powerful, or courageous, or cunning animal possessed. *Mana* was obtained in part by eating this animal. But a pictured or carved representation of it, particularly the totem animal, also partook of its *mana* and became a sacred object. Hence the regard for the totem pole, and the indignation that arises when sacrilegious whites hew it down and carry it away to a museum. The essential anthropomorphism in this whole procedure came to clearer expression in images and idols that took on more distinctly the human form. Before them sacrifices were offered, and supplications made, as to a present divinity.

But the visible object, which was at first supposed to have inherent divine attributes, came to be merely a residence of an invisible god, and at last only a symbol for him rather than a residence. The Catholic of today prays *before* the crucifix, not to it, and he uses pictures of saints and of the stages of the cross, theoretically at least, merely as helps to concentration of mind. Nevertheless, the sacredness that attaches to what is theoretically only a symbol, a sacredness that extends even to the building in which the symbols are kept and used, bears witness to continuity with times when a temple was in a literal sense the house or dwelling-place of the god, where his people could talk to him and feel his

nearness as a sort of response. The especial sanctity of the altar and of its utensils in many Christian churches traces its lineage back to the holy of holies in ancient temples like that at Jerusalem. The sacrosanct character of this particular part of the Jewish temple was due to the presence there of an "ark" or chest that contained, it is believed, one or more small images, or even more primitive, uncarved objects, in which the divinity himself was supposed to be present. The continuity has been maintained even more completely in the mass than in the altar, for here, by the miracle of transubstantiation, bread and wine become the flesh and blood of the god himself, before whom the congregation prostrates itself. The consuming of this bread and wine reproduces in an attenuated form the totemic eating of the god.

All these may be taken as modes of divine approach to man or as divine responses to man's approach. Further responses are found in the good and evil fortunes that befall men. Here men read specific meanings, or divine ideas, related to human conduct or to prayers. At the lower end of the scale we have, even among ourselves, the reading of omens; at the other end, the notion of rewards and punishments, divine discipline, or divine self-revelation. To the question why this calamity has come upon me, the answer is given that it is sent as correction for a fault, or as training in such virtues as patience and perseverance. Prosperity is now and then frankly taken as a divine reward for goodness.[1]

---

[1] A Mormon lady related to me that one night a destructive frost visited the region of her residence, but extended only to the edge of the farm occupied by herself and her husband. She was firmly of the opinion that they had been spared the frost in recompense for care bestowed upon the husband's aged parents.

As all Europe up to recent times saw in comets a mode of divine speech, so when the present war started some persons felt constrained to seek for the specific ground of the divine displeasure that was thus made manifest.

When events turn out in accord with the specific desires expressed in a prayer, the notion often prevails that the event is a direct answer to the prayer. If rain promptly follows a petition for rain, it is taken as a divine response; but if rain does not follow, people say, "God knows better than we do what is good for us," whereupon events, whatever they are, are scrutinized and sorted in such a way that a divine purpose may be read in them. In this manner any section of the natural order, or the whole of it, may acquire the character of divine speech in reply to prayer.

All these methods of ascertaining the thoughts of the god, with the exception of dreams, visions and auditions, involve the use of something intermediate between the worshiper and his god, and lead to a requirement of skill of one sort or another. Just as the primary requirement of shamanism is greater facility in automatisms than the ordinary man possesses, so, when natural objects are taken as signs of divine presence or meaning, they have to be selected. When events are studied with the same intent, there has to be some sort of rule for scrutinizing and judging. When images of the god are to be made, it is, of course, important that they be made just right. Here is added opportunity for priestly skill. Just as priests came to possess the ritualistic keys to the right approach to the gods through sacrifice, so they became also the holders of the keys whereby the divine responses were made. They spoke both to the divinity and for him, confessing the people's sins, for example, and also pronouncing absolution. Even the sacred scriptures, which are supposed to contain human language as a vehicle of divine thoughts, and are treated as revelation, need to be officially interpreted. Thus fully do both worshiper and worshiped, in sacerdotal systems, become dependent upon the priest or upon the doctors of the law.

One mode of apprehending the divine response remains, however, that does not require any external intermediary, though it often includes considerable interpretation. For it is possible to take the movement of one's own thoughts, emotions, and purposes, even apart from dreams, visions, and auditions, as an immediate communication from another being. Zoroastrianism held that the mind of man is a scene of conflict between Ormuzd and Ahriman. A similar view has been characteristic of Christianity. Evil impulses were for a long time attributed to an inner solicitation from Satan, and good impulses to a corresponding solicitation from the Holy Spirit. There even arose a doctrine that without directly imparted divine impulsions man is utterly incapable of having a holy desire. Here, then, is a basis for a rich development of supposably divine language. As before, the scale is a long one. We have already noted the growth of prophecy from shamanistic automatisms (under which head should be included tongue-speaking) to ethical convictions taken as the divine will. Since ethical convictions can be a possession of common men, all are potentially prophets. When this point of view is reached, the everyday sense of obligation becomes a commanding "voice of God"; self-condemnation becomes "conviction of sin"; the answer of a good conscience becomes a "witness of the Spirit"; a firm conviction as to what is right and what wrong becomes "guidance"; and the steady organization of the emotional life around this divine ethical center becomes the "peace of God."

Here at last prayer can take wholly the form of internal conversation. The worshiper's words may be vocal or only mentally spoken, and they may or may not follow a fixed form; in any case the direction of thought and desire Godward is what makes the act a prayer. That is, the present meaning of something to the worshiper, or his valuation of it, is his prayer, and the resulting changed or confirmed meaning of the same thing is the divine response. The point is not that the worshiper experiences something strange for which he figures out a cause. His mind is not now engaged in looking for causes, nor does he necessarily think of God as the cause of the upspringing ethical convictions. Just as, in conversation with a friend, I deal with meanings directly as mine and his without stopping to think of him as producing certain of my sensations and chains of ideas, so it is in the type of prayer now under consideration.

The causal question might, of course, arise in either case. That is, by abstracting events from persons, and fixing attention upon events simply as occurring, one might ask what particular sort of event is the uniform antecedent of the event in question. If the religionist should ask, "What but God could cause such a change in my ideas, emotions, and purposes?" and the friend should say, "What but my friend could cause the auditory sensations that I experience?" the structural psychologist not only might but also should reply in terms of my physiological conditions, neural processes and dispositions, instinctive tendencies to action, and the ordinary laws of ideation, emotion, and so on. No remainder that is God will be found in the one case, and no remainder that is my friend will be discovered in the other. All this can be said in advance of analysis as well as afterward, for it is involved in the structural method itself. Persons are not simply residual causes.

The specific and characteristic process by which the worshiper's valuations are reorganized or confirmed and taken as a divine response is that of suggestion. He who prays begins his prayer with some idea of God, generally one that he has received from instruction or from current traditions. He commonly retires to a quiet place, or to a place having mental associations of a religious cast, in order to "shut out the world." This beginning of concentration is followed by closing the eyes, which excludes a mass of irrelevant impressions. The body bows, kneels, or assumes some other posture that requires little muscular tension and that may favor extensive relaxation. Memory now provides the language of prayer or of hallowed scripture, or makes vivid some earlier experiences of one's own. The worshiper represents to himself his needs, or the interests (some of them happy ones) that seem most important, and he brings them into relation to God by thinking how God regards them. The presupposition of the whole procedure is that God's way of looking at the matters in question is the true and important one. Around God, then, the interests of the individual are now freshly organized. Certain ones that looked large before the prayer began now look small because of their relation to the organizing idea upon which attention has focused. On the other hand, interests that express this organizing idea gain emotional quality by this release from competing, inhibiting considerations. To say that the will now becomes organized toward unity and that it acquires fresh power thereby is simply to name another aspect of the one movement. This movement is ideational, emotional, and volitional concentration, all in one, achieved by fixation of attention upon the idea of God. This, as far as structure is concerned, is simply autosuggestion. It is directly in line with autosuggestion of health, and it is just the reverse of the autosuggestion of weakness, which leads toward sin, and of the autosuggestion of sickness, that disarranges various physiological functions.

It is sometimes said that faith is a prerequisite for success, whether in prayer or in autosuggestion of health. Therefore, when success occurs where there is contrary suggestion or lack of confidence, the inference is drawn that here a foreign cause, not autosuggestion, is the explanation. But the supposition that faith is prerequisite is faulty at the best. Many a person, skeptical of the powers of a hypnotizer, has submitted himself as a subject in the expectation of utterly "resisting the influence," but has been astounded to find himself a follower of the operator's suggestions just like credulous subjects. Faith-healing and mental-healing cults often win adherents by producing physical relief in the as yet unconvinced. At revival meetings scoffers are sometimes brought to their knees in spite of their unfaith.

Just so, surprising reversals sometimes take place in prayer, faith being there born or reborn, instead of being merely exercised. What is prerequisite in all these cases is not a particular expectation, but a particular direction of attention. Merely repeating certain sentences with attention to their meaning, but regardless of their truth or falsity, will sometimes result in marked control of further mental processes. Persons who have been troubled with insomnia, or wakefulness, or disturbing dreams, have been enabled to secure sound sleep by merely relaxing the muscles and repeating mechanically, without effort at anything more, some formula descriptive of what is desired. The main point is that attention should fix upon the appropriate organizing idea. When this happens in a revival meeting one may find one's self unexpectedly converted. When it happens in prayer one may be surprised to find one's whole mood changed from discouragement to courage, from liking something to hating it (as in the case of alcoholic drinks, or tobacco), or from loneliness to the feeling of companionship with God.

Now and then a student imagines that by sufficiently careful introspection of his own prayers he will be enabled to determine once and for all whether or not God is there. Apart from the tendency of introspection to prevent the real spirit of prayer, there is the further difficulty that, in any case—that is, whether God is there or not—what one introspects in praying is mental content of one's own that one is purposely manipulating at the time. What introspection reveals, therefore, is not God but one's own idea of God, and the only causal sequences that one gets trace of by this method are sequences between particular events, not between different persons.[1]

On the other hand, as Strong has pointed out,[2] the internal conversation that constitutes prayer is not an isolated thing, but a specific instance of a general form of mental procedure. Thinking as a whole has the same form. Not merely does rudimentary thinking, which is impulsive and emotional, involve the assumption of reciprocal attitudes between the thinker and his objects, but even the more cautious and controlled sort that weighs considerations, and advances from position to position, moves on in the form of question and answer, proposal and counter proposal, internal debate, and final agreement of the debaters. More than this; considered from the standpoint of mental structure only, my intercourse with my fellows also is internal conversation, a give and take, both sides of which are in a way accessible to my own introspection.

The tendency of these considerations is not necessarily toward skeptical subjectivism or solipsism unless one first assumes that the whole reality of the I-and-thou relation can be set forth in the structural terms of particular states succeeding one another. If the essence of a conversation lies not in a particular succession of sounds or even in a particular succession of ideas, but in meanings for selves, then a particular movement of

[1] A skeptical student was advised to determine for himself whether or not there be a God by the experiment of praying. Being of a scientific turn of mind, he decided to vary only one circumstance at a time. So he offered the same prayer first to the Christian God and then to the Buddha. His introspective account of the effects showed that in each case he got the same results, such as peace and feeling of elevation.

[2] A. L. Strong, The Psychology of Prayer (Chicago, 1909).

my own states might have meaning for two selves. The
second self for which the situation has meaning is never
found as an additional item in the succession of states,
any more than I myself can discover myself as one of my
own states. The fact that prayer is a conversation both
sides of which, structurally considered, are mental states
of the one who prays, has no particular bearing upon
the question whether prayer is a mutual relation between
the worshiper and God.

This analysis of the structure of prayer has already
touched upon some of its functions. It is a way of getting
one's self together, of mobilizing and concentrating one's
dispersed capacities, of begetting the confidence that
tends toward victory over difficulties. It produces in a
distracted mind the repose that is power. It freshens a
mind deadened by routine. It reveals new truth, because
the mind is made more elastic and more capable of sustained attention. Thus does it remove mountains in the
individual, and through him in the world beyond.

Prayer fulfils this function of self-renewal largely by
making one's experience consciously social, that is,
by producing a realization that even what is private to
me is shared by another. Burdens are lightened by the
thought that they are burdens to another also, through
his sympathy with me. This would be a gain even if I
were not sure that this friend would remove the burden
from my shoulders. The values of prayer in sickness,
distress, and doubt are by no means measurable by the
degree to which the primary causes thereof are made to
disappear. There is a real conquest of trouble even while
trouble remains. Now and then the conquest is so
precious that one rejoices in the tribulation itself as a

friendly visitation.[1] It is sometimes a great source of strength, also, merely to realize that one is fully understood. The value of having some friend or helper from whom I reserve no secrets has been rendered more impressive than ever by the Freud-Jung methods of relieving mental disorders through (in part) a sort of mental housecleaning, or bringing into the open the patient's hidden distresses and even his most intimate and reticent desires. Into the psychology of the healings that are brought about by this psycho-analysis we need not go, except to note that one constant factor appears to be the turning of a private possession into a social possession, and particularly the consciousness that another understands. I surmise that we shall not be far from the truth here if we hold that, as normal experience has the *ego-alter* form, so the continuing possession of one's self in one's developing experience requires development of this relation. We may, perhaps, go as far as to believe that the bottling up of any experience as merely private is morbid. But, however this may be, there are plenty of occasions when the road to poise, freedom, and joy is that of social sharing. Hence the prayer of confession,

[1] The greatest sufferer from physical causes whom I have ever known, the late Byron Palmer, of Ashtabula, Ohio, was not only one of the serenest of spirits, but also one of the most convinced that God is wholly good. During years of unrelieved pain he occupied himself, when writing was possible, by producing tracts, letters, and finally a book, *God's White Throne*, to enable other sufferers to realize, as he did, that there is not a speck of injustice in God's government of the world. I mention this case, not at all in order to suggest that there is logical justification for his attitude, but only as an example of the remarkable function that communion with God may have in the deepest distress. The prayer-life may be said to be, in cases like this, the organization into the self of the very things that threaten to disorganize it.

not only because it helps us to see ourselves as we are, but also because it shares our secrets with another, has great value for organizing the self. In this way we get relief from the misjudgments of others, also, and from the mystery that we are to ourselves, for we lay our case, as it were, before a judge who does not err. Thus prayer has value in that it develops the essentially social form of personal self-realization.

Moreover, where the idea of God has reached high ethical elevation, prayer is a mode of self-assurance of the triumph of the good, with all the reinforcement that comes from such assurance. Confidence in ultimate goodness may support itself upon various thought structures. Many Christians attach their thought of God and of a meaningful world to Jesus as the revealer and worker-out of the divine plan. With him as leader they feel that they cannot fail. Others attach their ethical aspirations directly to God, who may then be thought of as present with the worshiper in these very aspirations. Others think the world-purpose in less sharply personal terms, as the evolution of the cosmos toward a moral life that was not, and now is only beginning to be, but is nevertheless the inmost law of the system. In the last case prayer shades off from conversation toward mere contemplation, yet without failing to identify the individual's own purpose with a world-purpose that is moving toward sure fulfilment. In all these types of self-assurance the individual may do little more than apply to himself by suggestion an idea that is current in the cult with which he is familiar. Yet the idea that is thus applied grows in the process of appropriating it to one's self. It has, in fact, been generated in men in and through prayer. That is to say, prayer is a process in which faith is generated. It is a mistake to suppose that men assure themselves of the existence and of the character of God by some prayerless method, and then merely exercise this ready-made faith in the act of praying. No, prayer has greater originality than this. Alongside of much traditionalism and vain repetition there is also some launching forth upon voyages of exploration and some discovery of lands firm enough to support men when they carry their heaviest burdens.

To complete this functional view of prayer we must not fail to secure the evolutionary perspective. If we glance at the remote beginnings, and then at the hither end, of the evolution of prayer, we discover that an immense change has taken place. It is a correlate of the transformed character of the gods, and of the parallel disciplining of men's valuations. In the words of Fosdick, prayer may be considered as dominant desire.[1] But it is also a way of securing domination over desire. It is indeed self-assertion; sometimes it is the making of one's supreme claim, as when life reaches its most tragic crisis; yet it is, even in the same act, submission to an overself. Here, then, is our greater problem as to the function of prayer. It starts as the assertion of any desire; it ends as *the organization of one's own desires into a system of desires recognized as superior and then made one's own.*

At the beginning the attitude is little more than that of using the gods for men's ends; at the culmination prayer puts men at the service of God for the correction of human ends, and for the attainment of these corrected ends

[1] H. E. Fosdick, *The Meaning of Prayer* (New York, 1915).

rather than the initial ones. Like everything else in religion, prayer has several lines of development. Every religion has its own characteristic ways of approaching its divinity or divinities, and its own characteristic valuations are expressed thereby. All, however, as we may be sure from our whole study of religious evolution, reflect the notion of society then and there prevailing. In the Christian religion, with its central emphasis upon love, prayer tends to become, wherever the constructive significance of love has not been submerged by ritualism or dogmatism, the affirmation of what may be called social universalism of essentially democratic tendency. On the one hand, the act of praying now becomes highly individual. To be prayed for by a priest is not enough, nor does mechanical participation in common prayer suffice. Whether one prays with others or alone, one is required to pray in one's own spirit, and to do it sincerely. Paradoxical as it may seem, this throwing of the individual back upon himself, with insistence that he here and now express his very self, produces, not individualistic desire, but criticism of desires from a social point of view. Here self-assertion becomes self-overcoming in and through acceptance of the loving will of the Father as one's own. Now, because the Father values so highly every child of his, in prayer to him I must adopt his point of view with respect to my fellows, desiring for each of them full and joyous self-realization. This sort of submission—to a God who values each individual—tends therefore toward the deference for each individual that is the foundation of democracy. Here the function of prayer is that of training men in the attitudes of mind that are fundamental to democratic society.

Finally, prayer has the function of extending one's acquaintance with agreeable persons. Here and there, at least, men enjoy God's companionship just because of what he is, without reference to benefits that he may bestow. This pure friendship sometimes includes the joy of helping the Great Friend. It is true that when philosophy identifies God with some abstract absolute the notion of helping him is ruled out. But religion is different from philosophy. As a rule the gods of religion—and not less the God of Christianity—stand to their worshipers in a relation of mutual give and take. As a primitive group feeds its god in order to make him strong, and rejoices and feasts with him as an invisible guest, so in Christianity God and men stand in mutual need of each other. This must be so if God is love. Men are saved by grace alone, but there is joy in heaven over one sinner who repents; men are called into the family of God, yet only as men fulfil fraternal relations with one another can God have the satisfactions that belong to a father. Thus it is that Christian prayer has to be reciprocal as between God and the worshiper. There is an ancient doctrine that our prayers are inspired in us by God himself, so that he also prays in our prayers. That is to say, at this point each of the two, God and the worshiper, finds himself by identifying his own desire with that of the other.

This is the culmination of the self-and-*socius* consciousness that makes us persons. The function of prayer at this level, then, is to produce (or, as the case may be, sustain) personal life, which is also social life, as something of ultimate worth.

CHAPTER XIX

THE RELIGIOUS NATURE OF MAN

There is a traditional opinion that man is naturally or "incurably" religious. The sense in which this is true, if it be true at all, may well be the closing problem of this long discussion of the naturalness of religion. That religion lies wholly within the natural psychological order, just as regard for one's family, or seeking to buy at the lowest price, needs no further affirmation. What we still need to consider, however, is the relation of fundamental to accessory. In the natural order some things are merely incidental workings out of something that lies deeper. Affection for offspring is fundamental; the fashions that parents adopt for children's clothing are superficial, but both are natural. Is religion one of the deep and permanent springs of human life, like parental affection, or is it an incidental expression of a nature that can satisfy itself in other ways also?

Before answering this question, two or three other distinctions must be noted. "Man" might be taken to mean either one of three things: each particular man, or the species as a whole, or a type toward which the species is moving. Non-religious individuals here and there might be members of a religious race, just as there are non-musical persons, the peculiarity in each case being due to a particular congenital lack. Again, there could be periods of arrested religiosity in a race the general movement of which is toward rather than away from religion.

The term "nature" of man likewise requires scrutiny. A religious nature has been attributed to man in each of the following senses: That a religious intuition, as of God, or of infinity, or of immortality, exists; that there is a religious instinct; and that religion belongs to man's nature as a specific longing, restlessness, or discontent that assuages itself by evoking out of itself faith in some divine being. There is a fourth possibility: that, even in the absence of any such special emotion, instinct, or intuition, there might be a spontaneous, typical mode of organizing experience. Here we come upon the ever-necessary distinction between structure and function. If by "nature" we mean structure only, and if by structure we mean merely the elements into which a whole can be decomposed, it might well happen that nothing religious could be found in human nature although the most characteristic way of organizing the elements were religious. A bit of canvas and some tubes of pigment are scarcely aesthetic in their nature, yet they may be organized into an aesthetic masterpiece.[1]

[1] Here an ancient problem, which is likewise one of the freshest, confronts us if we wish to think our question through. Can we pack into our "elements" enough specific qualities to account for all that the elements do, and for all the relations that they ever bear to one another? Or, must we have also an "entelechy," or a "form," or "self-guidance"? The question is two-edged. As I have indicated in one of the early chapters, our problem as psychologists is not whether we shall recognize a self *in addition to mental elements*. As well might we ask whether we shall recognize mental elements in addition to the personal selves who are carrying on the present discussion. The notion of elements seems to me hopelessly abstract as long as no account is taken of that which makes the elements amount to something.

The general course of our investigation leads toward the following negative conclusions as to the supposed religious nature of man: (1) There is no evidence that a religious intuition ever occurs. I use the term intuition in the sense of insight (or, if one prefers, conviction) arrived at by an individual without dependence upon his own accumulated experience, and without dependence upon the history of his people. (2) There is no religious instinct. That is, no object or set of objects can be named that has any peculiar power, apart from previous experience thereof, to call out a specifically religious reaction. (3) There is no adequate evidence that all individuals experience the particular longing, restlessness, or discontent that has just been mentioned. On the contrary, men can be absorbed by almost any interest, from love to business, and from research to golf. Nor is it clear that the longing here referred to— the sense of a vague but great beyond, and of vast capacities within one's self that are as yet unfilled—has any better title to be called religious, or to be taken as the focus of man's religious nature, than various other emotions and active states. (4) No specific attitude toward the divine or the human can be attributed to all individuals. Attitudes grow; they are not given ready-made. And they grow in all directions, out of every sort of instinct, under the influence of particular situations, with their respective satisfactions and annoyances.

On the other hand, two positive conclusions as to a religious nature grow out of our entire study: In the first place, there are human modes of organizing experience, so that there is in experience, as ours, a kind of predetermination other than that of the instincts taken one by one. So much has already been said of the passage of instinctive attachments into discriminated values, with scales of preference, and with efforts at unification and completeness, that it will be sufficient at this point to emphasize the fact that this is, indeed, a distinctive mode of human mental organization. Any individual who fails to meet the conditions of life in this way we classify as imbecile. It is true that we have here no stereotyped thing. The range or sweep as well as the firmness of organization varies from individual to individual, and the scales of preference vary qualitatively. Nevertheless, it is of the utmost significance that, whenever one takes an absorbing interest in any particular thing or enterprise, one idealizes it, organizes other interests about it, and thus finds one's real world partly by having a share in making it real. This way of organizing experience in terms of ideal values is a first item in the religious nature of man. It is present in all normal individuals, and it is a type toward which freedom, popular education, and democracy tend.

A second conclusion is that nature has not placed all the possible centers for this organization upon the same level. It is true that any instinctive interest may become controlling. Yet the social instincts have a preeminence that is unmistakable. Ethical control, ethical standards, and ethical ideals, all springing from social instincts primarily, but having as their sphere of operation all the instinctive and impulsive tendencies, have unique significance as determinants of what constitutes specifically human nature. Here, of course, we take "man" in the racial rather than the individual sense. There is, indeed, nothing in human nature that guarantees how hearty or complete shall be one's social response.[1] But we know that social pressure upon individuals will keep up. That is, the race has a character, or is forming one, on the basis of regard for one another. Hence, even though an individual act intensely and ideally, he may nevertheless be convicted of insufficient religiousness if his ideals have an individualistic rather than social focus.

These two are the main roots of the more obvious facts of religion—its dealing with affairs that are sacred, that concern some important group interest, and that have their culminating expression in fellowship with a divine being. To say that these roots will live on forever, or that as long as they do live they will nourish religious beliefs and organizations like those of the past, is more than any accessible data can more than approximately justify. For, after all, to describe the nature of an evolving species is to say how it *has* moved, not how it must hereafter move. There is, nevertheless, one ray of light upon the direction of future movements of humanity. The forming of scales of value, and especially our social criteria, have become matters of deliberate reflection and choice, and a beginning has been made of systematic measures for perpetuating them, particularly

[1] Hence, if we should determine the degree of sociality that entitles one to be called religious, we could then set off certain classes in the community, as Ames has done, as made up of non-religious persons. As far as I can see, however, Ames has not determined, or given any principle for determining, the religious threshold that he employs. One might question, also, whether we have as yet any secure way of determining degrees of sociality. Certainly many who are regarded by society as its enemies have been made enemies precisely by society's unsocial ways, and not seldom it is the exercise of social qualities that first brings on a collision with organized society.

through educational procedures. It is, of course, possible that, in spite of all that education can do, or even through perverted education, the race will revert to barbarism, or end humanity's career in a welter of mere instinct. But eyes open to the problem of relative values, and seeking the permanent organization of valuational processes, give hope for better things. Our study justifies the prediction that human nature will go on building its ideal personal-social worlds, finding in them its life and its home. This process will continue to be carried out toward ideal completeness as faith in a divine order in which our life shares. The thought of God may, indeed, undergo yet many transformations, but in one form or another it will be continually renewed as an expression of the depth and the height of social experience and social aspiration.

ALPHABETICAL BIBLIOGRAPHY

NOTE.—This bibliography makes no pretense to any sort of completeness. In particular, it contains comparatively few titles that concern anthropology on the one hand, and systematic theology on the other. But the reader can easily fill these gaps by consulting the list of bibliographies given in the "Topical Bibliography." On the other hand, I have attempted, in accordance with my conviction that the psychology of religion is properly nothing more than an expansion of general psychology in certain directions, to present fairly abundant references to the particular psychological discussions that deal with the principles and the topics that appear in the main body of the work.

Those whom I have had chiefly in mind as probable users of the bibliography are American students. In order that they may be saved from desultoriness, and may get promptly into the various specific problems, I have added a set of topical lists that refer back, for the most part but not exclusively, to the titles here given in alphabetical order.

I am under obligation to certain American writers who have published extensively in this field—Ames, Leuba, Pratt, and Starbuck—for complete lists of their writings in the psychology of religion.

In a few cases I have permitted myself to include works to which I have not yet had access.

Abelson, J., *Jewish Mysticism*, London, 1913.

Adams, George P., "The Interpretation of Religion in Royce and Durkheim," *Philosophical Review*, XXV (1916), 297–304.

Allones, G. R. de, *Psychologie d'une religion*, Paris, 1908.

Ames, Edward Scribner, (1) "Theology from the Standpoint of Functional Psychology," *American Journal of Theology*, X (1906), 219–32.

———, (2) "Religion and the Psychical Life," *International Journal of Ethics*, XX (1909), 48–62.

———, (3) "Non-religious Persons," *American Journal of Theology*, XIII (1909), 541–54.

———, (4) "The Psychological Basis of Religion," *The Monist*, XX (1910), 242–62.

Ames, Edward Scribner, (5) *The Psychology of Religious Experience*, Boston, 1910 (pp. xii+428). Reviewed by Coe, G. A., in *American Journal of Theology*, April, 1911.

————, (6) "Social Consciousness and Its Object," *Psychological Bulletin*, VIII (1911), 407–16.

————, (7) "Psychology of Religion," in Monroe's *Cyclopedia of Education*, V (1913), 143–44.

————, (8) "The Survival of Asceticism in Education," *American Physical Education Review*, XIX (1914), 10–18.

————, (9) "Prayer," in *University of Chicago Sermons*, Chicago, 1915.

————, (10) "Mystic Knowledge," *American Journal of Theology*, XIX (1915), 250–67.

Angell, J. R., "The Relation of Structural and Functional Psychology to Philosophy," *Philosophical Review*, XII (1903), 243–71; also in *Decennial Publications of the University of Chicago*, 1903.

Aschkenasy, H., "Grundlinien zu einer Phänomenologie der Mystik," *Zeitschrift für Philosophie und philosophische Kritik*, CXLII (1911), 145–64; CXLIV (1911), 146–64.

Aston, W. G., "Fetishism," in *Encyclopedia of Religion and Ethics*.

Baldwin, J. M., *Social and Ethical Interpretations in Mental Development*, New York, 1897; see especially pp. 394 ff., 434 ff.

Le Baron, A., "A Case of Psychic Automatism including Speaking with Tongues," *Proceedings Society for Psychical Research*, XII, 277–97.

Bergson, H., (1) see Miller, L. H.

————, (2) Presidential Address before the English Society for Psychical Research, *Proceedings*, XXVII (1913), 157–75.

Berguer, G., *Psychologie religieuse: Revue et Bibliographie générales*, Genève, 1914.

Billia, L. M., "On the Problem and Method of Psychology of Religion: Psychology More than a Science," *The Monist*, XX (1910), 135–39.

Bois, H., *Le Reveil au pays de Galles*, Toulouse, Fischbacker, 1906.

Le Bon, G., *The Crowd*, London, 1896, Book I, chap. iv, "A Religious Shape Assumed by All the Convictions of Crowds."

Boodin, J. E., (1) "The Existence of Social Minds," *American Journal of Sociology*, XIX (1913), 1–47.

——, (2) "Individual and Social Minds," *Journal of Philosophy*, X (1913), 169–81.

Boutroux, E., *The Beyond That Is Within*, London, 1912.

Bradley, F. H., *Essays on Truth and Reality*, Oxford, 1914, chap. xiv, "What Is the Real Julius Caesar?"; chap. xv, "On God and the Absolute"; see also, on the reality and the personality of God, pp. 448–51; on immortality, pp. 438 ff., 451 ff., 467 f.

Buckham, J. W., (1) *Personality and the Christian Ideal*, Boston, 1909.

——, (2) *Mysticism and Modern Life*, New York, 1915.

Burr, A. R., *Religious Confessions and Confessants*, Boston, 1914.

Caldecott, A., "The Religious Sentiment: An Inductive Inquiry," *Proceedings of the Aristotelian Society*, N.S., VIII, 78–94, London, Williams & Norgate, 1908. Also separately printed.

Calkins, M. W., (1) "Psychology as Science of Selves," *Philosophical Review*, IX (1900), 490–501.

——, (2) *Introduction to Psychology*, New York, 1901, especially chap. xxii.

——, (3) "Reconciliation between Structural and Functional Psychology," *Psychological Review*, XIII (1906), 61–80.

——, (4) "Psychology as Science of Self": I. "Is the Self Body or Has It Body?" *Journal of Philosophy*, V (1908), 12–20; II. "The Nature of the Self," *ibid.*, V (1908), 64–68; III. "The Description of Consciousness," *ibid.*, V (1908), 113–22.

——, (5) "Ultimate Hypotheses in Psychology," *ibid.*, V (1908), 634–36.

——, (6) "The Nature of Prayer," *Harvard Theological Review*, IV (1911), 489–500.

——, (7) "Defective Logic in the Discussion of Religious Experience," *Journal of Philosophy*, VIII (1911), 606–8.

——, (8) "The Self in Scientific Psychology," *American Journal of Psychology*, XXVI (1915), 495–524.

Coe, George A., (1) *The Spiritual Life*, New York, 1900.

——, (2) *The Religion of a Mature Mind*, New York, 1902.

Coe, George A., (3) "Sources of the Mystical Revelation," *Hibbert Journal*, VI (1908), 359–72.

———, (4) "Religious Value," *Journal of Philosophy*, V (1908), 253–56.

———, (5) "What Does Modern Psychology Permit Us to Believe in Respect to Regeneration?" *American Journal of Theology*, XII (1908), 353–68.

———, (6) "The Mystical as a Psychological Concept," *Journal of Philosophy*, VI (1909), 197–202.

———, (7) "Religion and the Subconscious," *American Journal of Theology*, XIII (1909), 337–40.

———, (8) "The Origin and Nature of Children's Faith in God," *ibid.*, XVIII (1914), 169–90.

———, (9) "On Having Friends: A Study of Social Values," *Journal of Philosophy*, XII (1915), 155–61.

———, (10) "A Proposed Classification of Mental Functions," *Psychological Review*, XXII (1915), 87–98.

———, (11) Articles "Adolescence," "Childhood," "Growth," "Infancy," "Morbidness," in Hastings' *Encyclopedia of Religion and Ethics*.

———, (12) "Recent Publications on Mysticism," *Psychological Bulletin*, XII (1915), 459–62.

Colvin, S. S., "The Psychological Necessity for Religion," *American Journal of Psychology*, XII (1902), 80–87.

Conybeare, F. C., "Purification," *Encyclopaedia Britannica*.

Cooley, G. H., *Human Nature and the Social Order*, 1902.

Creighton, J. E., "The Standpoint of Psychology," *Philosophical Review*, XXIII (1914), 159–75.

Cutten, G. B., (1) *The Psychological Phenomena of Christianity*, New York, 1908.

———, (2) *Three Thousand Years of Mental Healing*, New York, 1911.

Dallenbach, K. M., "History of the Term Function," *American Journal of Psychology*, October, 1915.

Davenport, F. M., *Primitive Traits in Religious Revivals*, New York, 1905.

Davies, A. E., "The Genesis of Ideals," *Journal of Philosophy*, III (1906).

Dawson, G. E., "Suggestions towards an Inductive Study of the Religious Consciousness," *American Journal of Religious Psychology*, VI (1913), 50–59.

Delacroix, H., *Études d'histoire et de psychologie du mysticisme*, Paris, 1908.

Dewey, John, *Influence of Darwin on Philosophy*, New York, 1910; see chapter on "Beliefs and Existences."

Dike, S. W., "A Study of New England Revivals," *American Journal of Sociology*, XV (1909), 361–78.

Draghicesco, D., "Essai sur l'interprétation sociologique des phénomènes conscients," *Revue philosophique*, 1914, pp. 225–50 and 305–44.

Dumas, G., *Psychologie de deux messies positivistes: Saint Simon et Auguste Comte*, Paris, Alcan, 1905.

Dunlap, K., "Psychic Research and Immortality," *American Journal of Religious Psychology*, V (1912), 195–201.

Durkheim, E., *Les Formes élémentaires de la vie religieuse*, Paris, 1912; English tr. by Swain, J. W., *The Elementary Forms of the Religious Life*, London, 1915. Reviews: King, *Philosophical Review*, July, 1913; Lalande, A., *ibid.*, July, 1913, pp. 357–74; Leuba, J. H., *Revue philosophique* (1913), pp. 337–57; Wallis, W. D., *Journal of Religious Psychology*, VII (1914), 252–67; Adams, G. P., *Philosophical Review*, XXV (1916), 297–304.

Ellwood, C. A., "The Social Function of Religion," *American Journal of Sociology*, XIX (1913), 289–308.

Everett, Charles C., *The Psychological Elements of Religious Faith*, New York, 1902.

Ewer, B. C., "Veridical Aspects of Mystical Experience," *American Journal of Theology*, October, 1909.

Faber, Hermann, *Das Wesen der Religionspsychologie und ihre Bedeutung für die Dogmatik*, Tübingen, 1913.

Farnell, F. R., *Evolution of Religion*, New York, 1905.

Féré, Ch., *La Pathologie des émotions*, Paris, 1892.

Fite, W., "The Motive of Individualism in Religion," *Harvard Theological Review*, VII (1914), 478–96.

Fleming, W. K., *Mysticism in Christianity*, New York, 1913.

Fletcher, M. S., *The Psychology of the New Testament*, London, 1912.

Flournoy, Th., (1) *Le Génie religieux*, Association Chrétienne Suisse d'Étudiants, 1910 (pamphlet).

——, (2) "Les Principes de la psychologie religieuse," *Archiv de Psychologie*, II (1903), 37–41.

——, (3) "Observations de psychologie religieuse," *ibid.*, II (1903), 327–66.

Fosdick, H. E., *The Meaning of Prayer*, New York, 1915.

Fryer, A. T., "Psychological Aspects of the Welsh Revival," *Proceedings of the Society for Psychical Research*, XIX, 80–161.

Fursac, J. Rogues de, (1) "Notes de psychologie religieuse: les conversions," *Revue de Philosophie*, XXXII (1907).

——, (2) *Un Mouvement mystique contemporain: le reveil religieux du pays de Galles*, Paris, Alcan, 1907.

Galloway, G., *Principles of Religious Development*, London, 1909.

Gardner, C. S., "Assemblies," *American Journal of Sociology*, XIX (1914), 531–55.

Gutberlet, C., "Religionspsychologie," *Philosophische Jahrbücher*, XXIV (1911), 147–76.

Hall, G. S., (1) *Adolescence*, 2 vols., New York, 1904.

——, (2) "Thanatophobia and Immortality," *American Journal of Psychology*, XXVI (1915), 550–613.

Hamilton, Mary, *Incubation, or the Cure of Disease in Pagan Temples and Christian Churches*, St. Andrews, Scotland, 1906.

Harrison, Jane Ellen, *Themis: A Study of the Social Origins of Greek Religion*, Cambridge, 1912.

Hartshorne, H., *Worship in the Sunday School*, New York, 1913.

Haw, G., "The Religious Revival in the Labour Movement," *Hibbert Journal*, XIII (1915), 382–99.

Hayes, D. A., *The Gift of Tongues*, New York, 1913.

Haynes, Rowland, "Case-taking in the Psychology of Religious Experience," *Psychological Bulletin*, VIII (1911), 50–51.

Heidel, W. A., "Die Bekehrung im klassischen Alterthum mit besonderer Berücksichtigung des Lucretius," *Zeitschrift für Religionspsychologie*, III (1910), 377–402.

Henke, F. G., (1) "Gift of Tongues," *American Journal of Theology*, XIII (1909), 193–206.

——, (2) *A Study in the Psychology of Ritualism*, Chicago, 1910.

Hocking, W., *The Meaning of God in Human Experience*, New Haven, 1912. Reviewed by Coe, G. A., *Psychological Bulletin*, May, 1913.

Höffding, H., (1) *Philosophy of Religion*, London, 1906.

———, (2) *Problems of Philosophy*, New York, 1905.

———, (3) "Problème et méthode de la psychologie de la religion," *Rapports du VI. Congrès International de Psychologie*, Genève, Kündig, 1910, pp. 106–18.

Howard, G. E., *Social Psychology: A Syllabus and a Bibliography*, Lincoln, Nebraska, 1910.

Howison, G. H., *The Limits of Evolution*, New York, 1901.

Hügel, F. von, *The Mystical Element of Religion*, 2 vols., London, 1908.

Hylan, J. B., *Public Worship*, Chicago, 1901.

Hyslop, J. H., (1) *Psychical Research and the Resurrection*, Boston, 1908.

———, (2) *Psychical Research and Survival*, London, 1913.

Inge, W. R., (1) *Christian Mysticism*, London, 1899.

———, (2) *Studies of English Mystics*, London, 1906: Juliana of Norwich, Hylton, Law, Wordsworth, and Browning.

James, William, (1) "A List of the Published Writings of William James," *Psychological Review*, XVIII (1911), 157–65.

———, (2) *The Varieties of Religious Experience*, London, 1902. Reviewed by: Leuba, J. H., *International Journal of Ethics*, 1904, pp. 322–39; Coe, G. A., *Philosophical Review*, January, 1903; Crook, E. B., *The Monist*, 1903, pp. 122–30; Flournoy, Th., *Revue philosophique*, 1902; Delacroix, M., *Revue de métaphysique et de morale*, XI (1903), 642–69; Boutroux, E., *William James*, New York, 1912; Wundt, W., *Probleme der Völkerpsychologie*, Leipzig, 1911, pp. 93 ff.; Faber, H., *Das Wesen der Religionspsychologie*, Tübingen, 1913, pp. 25–32; Wobbermin, G., *Die religionspsychologische Methode*, etc., chap. xvi.

———, (3) "The Experience of Activity," *Psychological Review*, XII (1905), 1–17.

———, (4) "The Energies of Men," *Philosophical Review*, XVII (1907), 1–20.

James, William, (5) "The Confidences of a 'Psychical Researcher,'" *American Magazine*, October, 1909. Cf. Leuba, J. H., "William James and Immortality," *Journal of Philosophy*, XII (1915), 409–16.

———, (6) "A Suggestion about Mysticism," *Journal of Philosophy*, VII (1910), 85–92.

Jastrow, Joseph, (1) *Fact and Fable in Psychology*, Boston, 1900.

———, (2) *The Subconscious*, Boston, 1906.

Jevons, F. B., *The Idea of God in Early Religions*, Cambridge, 1910.

Jones, R. M., (1) *Studies in Mystical Religion*, London, 1909.

———, (2) *Spiritual Reformers in the Sixteenth and Seventeenth Centuries*, London, 1914.

———, (3) "Mysticism in Present-Day Religion," *Harvard Theological Review*, VIII (1915), 155–65.

Judd, C. H., (1) "The Doctrine of Attitudes," *Journal of Philosophy*, V (1908), 676–84.

———, (2) "Motor Processes and Consciousness," *ibid.*, VI (1909), 85–91. Cf. Baldwin, *ibid.*, p. 182.

———, (3) "Evolution and Consciousness," *Psychological Review*, XVII (1910), 77–97.

King, Irving, (1) *Psychology of Child Development*, Chicago, 1903.

———, (2) *The Differentiation of the Religious Consciousness*, Monograph Supplement of the *Psychological Review*, VI (1904), No. 4.

———, (3) "The Pragmatic Interpretation of Christian Dogmas," *The Monist*, April, 1905.

———, (4) "The Real and the Pseudo-Psychology of Religion," *Journal of Philosophy*, II (1905), 622.

———, (5) "The Problem of the Subconscious," *Psychological Review*, XIII (1906), 35.

———, (6) "Notes on the Evolution of Religion," *Philosophical Review*, XVIII (1909), 38.

———, (7) "The Evolution of Religion from the Psychological Point of View," *American Journal of Sociology*, XIV (1909), 433.

———, (8) "Australian Morality," *Popular Science Monthly*, February, 1910.

King, Irving, (9) *The Development of Religion*, New York, 1910. Reviewed by Coe, G. A., *Harvard Theological Review*, July, 1910.

――, (10) "The Religious Significance of the Psycho-therapeutic Movement," *American Journal of Theology*, XIV (1910), 533.

――, (11) "Some Problems in the Science of Religion," *Harvard Theological Review*, November, 1910.

――, (12) "The Psychology of the Prophet," *Biblical World*, June and July, 1911.

――, (13) "The Question of an Ultimate Religious Element in Human Nature," *Psychological Bulletin*, February, 1911.

Lang, Andrew, (1) "Mythology," in *Encyclopaedia Britannica*.

――, (2) "Totemism," *ibid.*

Leuba, J. H., (1) "Studies in the Psychology of Religious Phenomena" (on conversion), *American Journal of Psychology*, VII (1896), 309–85.

――, (2) "The Psycho-Physiology of the Categorical Imperative; a Chapter in the Psycho-Physiology of Ethics," *ibid.*, VIII (1897), 528–59.

――, (3) "Introduction to a Psychological Study of Religion," *The Monist*, II (1901), 195–225.

――, (4) "The Contents of Religious Consciousness," *ibid.*, pp. 536–73.

――, (5) "Religion, Its Impulses and Its Ends," *Bibliotheca Sacra*, LVIII (1901), 751–73.

――, (6) "Les Tendances fondamentales des mystiques chrétiens," *Revue philosophique*, LIV (1902), 1–36, 441–87.

――, (7) "The State of Mystical Death; an Instance of Internal Adaptation," *American Journal of Psychology*, Commemorative Number, XIV (1903), 133–46.

――, (8) "Empirical Data on Immortality," *International Journal of Ethics*, XIV (1903), 90–105.

――, (9) "Professor William James's Interpretation of Religious Experience," *ibid.* (1904), pp. 323–39.

――, (10) "Faith," *American Journal of Religious Psychology and Education*, I (1904), 65–82.

――, (11) "The Field and the Problems of the Psychology of Religion," *American Journal of Religious Psychology*, I (1904), 155–67.

Leuba, J. H., (12) "On the Psychology of a Group of Christian Mystics," *Mind*, N.S., XIV (1905), 15–27.

———, (13) "Fear, Awe, and the Sublime," *American Journal of Religious Psychology*, II (1906), 1–23.

———, (14) "Revue générale de psychologie religieuse," *Année psychologique*, XI (1905), 482–93.

———, (15) *Ibid.*, XII (1906), 550–69.

———, (16) "Religion as a Factor in the Struggle for Life," *American Journal of Religious Psychology*, II (1907), 307–43.

———, (17) "The Psychological Origin of Religion," *The Monist*, XIX (1909), 27–35.

———, (18) "Magic and Religion," *Sociological Review*, January, 1909, pp. 20–35.

———, (19) "The Psychological Nature of Religion," *American Journal of Theology*, January, 1909, pp. 77–85.

———, (20) "Three Types of Behavior," *American Journal of Psychology*, XX (1909), 107–19.

———, (21) *The Psychological Origin and the Nature of Religion*, Archibald Constable & Co., London (1909), pp. 95.

———, (22) "La Religion conçue comme fonction biologique," *Report of the Sixth International Congress of Psychologists*, Geneva, 1909, pp. 118–25.

———, (23) "Les Relations de la religion avec la science et la philosophie," *ibid.*, pp. 125–37.

———, (24) *A Psychological Study of Religion: Its Origin, Function, and Future*, New York and London, Macmillan, 1912 (pp. xiv+371); put into French by L. Cons, under the title *La Psychologie de la Religion* (Bibliothèque de Philosophie contemporaine), Paris, Alcan, 1914.

———, (25) "La Religion comme type de conduite rationnelle," *Revue philosophique*, LXXIV (1912), 321–37.

———, (26) "Dynamism, the Primitive Nature Philosophy," *Journal of Religious Psychology*, V (1912), 305–16.

———, (27) "Sociology and Psychology," *American Journal of Sociology*, XIX (1913), 323–42.

———, (28) "Sociologie et Psychologie," *Revue philosophique*, LXXV (1913), 337–57.

Leuba, J. H., (29) "Can Science Speak the Decisive Word in Theology?" *Journal of Philosophy*, X (1913), 411–14.

————, (30) "An Answer to Professors Shotwell and Hocking," *ibid.*, X (1913), 634–37.

————, (31) "Sociology and Psychology," *Psychological Bulletin*, X (1913), 461–66.

————, (32) "The Task and the Method of Social Psychology," *ibid.*, XI (1914), 445–48.

————, (33) "Theologie und Psychologie," *Religion und Geisteskultur*, Göttingen, 1914, pp. 109–18.

————, (34) "William James and Immortality," *Journal of Philosophy*, XII (1915), 409–16.

————, (35) "The Task and the Method of Psychology in Theology," *Psychological Bulletin*, XII (1915), 462–70.

Reviews of Leuba have been published as follows: Ames, E. S., *American Journal of Theology*, January, 1913; Belot, *Revue philosophique*, 1914; Cooley, W. F., *Journal of Philosophy*, X, May 22, 1913; Leuba's rejoinder, *ibid.*, X, July 17, 1913; Shotwell and Hocking, *ibid.*, X, June 5, 1913; Leuba's rejoinder, *ibid.*, X, November 6, 1913; Talbert, E. L., *Philosophical Review*, July, 1913; Wobbermin, G., *Religion und Geisteskultur*, 1913, 282–91.

Lombard, E., *De la Glossolalie*, Paris, Fischbacker, 1911.

Lovejoy, A. O., "The Desires of the Self-Conscious," *Journal of Philosophy*, IV (1907), 29–39.

Marett, R. R., (1) *The Threshold of Religion*, London, 1909.

————, (2) "Magic," in *Encyclopedia of Religion and Ethics*.

————, (3) "Prayer," in *Encyclopaedia Britannica*.

————, (4) "Religion—Primitive," *ibid.*

————, (5) "Ritual," *ibid.*

————, (6) "Mana," in *Encyclopedia of Religion and Ethics*.

Marie et Vallon, "Des Psychoses religieuses," *Archives de Neurologie*, II, 429 ff.

Marshall, H. R., (1) *Instinct and Reason*, New York, 1898.

————, (2) "The Function of Religious Expression," *Mind*, VI (1897), 182–203.

————, (3) "Psychotherapy and Religion," *Hibbert Journal*, VII (1909), 295–313.

Marshall, H. R., (4) "Religion: A Triologue," *The Outlook*, CIX (March 10, 1915), 587–93.

————, (5) *War and the Ideal of Peace*, New York, 1915.

McComas, H. C., *The Psychology of Religious Sects*, New York, 1912.

McDougall, William, (1) *Introduction to Social Psychology*, Boston, 1909, chap. xiii, "The Instincts through Which Religious Conceptions Affect Social Life."

————, (2) *Body and Mind: A History and a Defense of Animism*, New York, 1913.

————, (3) "Suggestion," in *Encyclopaedia Britannica*.

Mead, G. H., (1) "The Definition of the Psychical," *Decennial Publications of the University of Chicago*, 1903.

————, (2) "Social Psychology a Counterpart to Physiological Psychology," *Psychological Bulletin*, VI (1909), 401 ff.

————, (3) "What Social Objects Must Psychology Presuppose?" *Journal of Philosophy*, VII (1910), 170–80.

————, (4) "Social Consciousness and the Consciousness of Meaning," *Psychological Bulletin*, VII (1910), 397 ff.

————, (5) "The Mechanism of Social Consciousness," *Journal of Philosophy*, IX (1912), 401–6.

————, (6) "The Social Self," *ibid.*, X (1913), 374–80.

Mercier, C. A., *Conduct and Its Disorders Biologically Considered*, London, 1911, especially chap. xxii.

Messer, A., "Zur Werthpsychologie," *Archiv für gesammte Psychologie*, XXXIV (1915), 157–88.

Miller, L. H., "The Religious Implicates of Bergson's Doctrine Regarding Intuition and the Primacy of Spirit," *Journal of Philosophy*, XII (1915), 617–32.

Mitchell, W. C., "Human Behavior and Economics: A Survey of Recent Literature," *Quarterly Journal of Economics*, November, 1914.

Moore, A. W., "Truth Value," *Journal of Philosophy*, V (1908), pp. 429 ff.

Moore, J. S., (1) "The System of Values," *ibid.*, VII (1910), 282–91.

————, (2) "The System of Transcendental Values," *ibid.*, XI (1914), 244–48.

Morrison, H. T., "A Big Revival Two and a Half Years After," *Christian Century*, Chicago, December 21, 1911.

Moses, Josiah, *Pathological Aspects of Religions*, Monograph Supplement, *American Journal of Religious Psychology and Education*, Vol. I (Worcester, Massachusetts), 1906.

Mosiman, E., *Das Zungenreden*, Tübingen, 1911.

Münsterberg, H., (1) *The Eternal Values*, Boston, 1909.

———, (2) *Psychotherapy*, New York, 1909.

Murisier, E., *Les Maladies du sentiment religieux*, Paris, 1909.

Nicholson, R. A., *The Mystics of Islam*, London, 1914.

Overstreet, H. A., "God as the Common Will," *Hibbert Journal*, XIII (1914), 155–74.

Pacheu, J., "Sur la méthode en psychologie religieuse," *Revue de Philosophie*, 1912, pp. 371–92.

Peabody, F. G., "Mysticism and Modern Life," *Harvard Theological Review*, VII (1914), 461–77.

Perry, R. B., (1) *The Approach to Philosophy*, New York, 1905, chap. iii, "The Religious Experience."

———, (2) "Truth and Imagination in Religion," *International Journal of Ethics*, XV (1904), 64–82.

———, (3) "The Religious Experience," *The Monist*, XIV, 752–66.

———, (4) "Religious Values," *American Journal of Theology*, XIX (1915), 1–16.

Pfister, O., *Die psychologische Enrätseling der religiösen Glossolalie*, etc., Leipzig, Deuticke, 1912.

Pierce, A. H., (1) "An Appeal from the Prevailing Doctrine of a Detached Subconscious," Garman Memorial Volume, *Studies in Philosophy and Psychology*, Boston, 1906.

———, (2) "Should We Still Retain the Expression 'Unconscious Cerebration' to Designate Certain Processes Connected with Mental Life?" *Journal of Philosophy*, III (1906), 626–30.

———, (3) Review of "Symposium on the Subconscious," *ibid.*, IV (1907), 523–28.

———, (4) "The Subconscious Again," *ibid.*, V (1908), 264–71.

Poulain, A., *The Graces of Interior Prayer*, London, 1912.

Pratt, J. B., (1) "Types of Religious Belief," *American Journal of Religious Psychology and Education*, March, 1906.

———, (2) *The Psychology of Religious Belief*, New York, 1907.

Pratt, J. B., (3) "The Psychology of Religion," *Harvard Theological Review*, I (1908), 435–54.

———, (4) "Religionspsychologie in den Vereinigten Staaten," *Zeitschrift für Religionspsychologie*, II (1909), 89–98.

———, (5) "An Empirical Study of Prayer," *American Journal of Religious Psychology and Education*, March, 1910.

———, (6) A Japanese translation of "The Psychology of Religion," 1911.

———, (7) "The Psychology of Religion," *Journal of Religious Psychology*, October, 1912.

———, (8) "The Subconscious and Religion," *Harvard Theological Review*, April, 1913.

Prince, M., (1) "The Psychology of Sudden Religious Conversion," *Journal of Abnormal Psychology*, I (1906), 42–54.

———, (2) "A Symposium on the Subconscious," *ibid.*, April–May, June–July, 1907, pp. 22–43 and 58–80. Participants: Münsterberg, Ribot, Jastrow, Janet, Prince.

———, (3) "Professor Pierce's Version of the Late Symposium on the Subconscious," *Journal of Philosophy*, V (1908), 69–75.

———, (4) *The Unconscious*, New York, 1914.

Pringle-Pattison, A. S., "Mysticism," in *Encyclopaedia Britannica*.

Rademacher, "Die Religionspsychologie, ihre Entstehungsgeschichte, Methode, und Bewertung," *Theologie und Glaube*, III (1911), 633–47.

Ranson, S. W., "Studies in the Psychology of Prayer," *American Journal of Religious Psychology and Education*, I (1904), 129–42.

Rhys-Davids, Mrs. C. A. F., *Buddhist Psychology: An Inquiry into the Analysis and Theory of Mind in Pali Literature*, London, Bell, 1914.

Ribot, Th., "De la Valeur des questionnaires en psychologie," *Journal de Psychologie normale et Pathologique*, January–February, 1904.

Riley, I. W., (1) *The Founder of Mormonism: A Psychological Study of Joseph Smith, Jr.*, New York, 1902.

———, (2) "Mental Healing in America," *American Journal of Insanity*, LXVI (1910), 351–63.

Rogers, A. K., (1) *The Religious Conception of the World*, New York, 1907.

——, (2) "Relation of the Science of Religion to the Truth of Religious Belief," *Journal of Philosophy*, I (1904), 113–18.

——, (3) "The Determination of Human Ends," *Philosophical Review*, XXIV (1915), 583–602.

Royce, J., (1) *Studies in Good and Evil*, New York, 1898.

——, (2) *The World and the Individual*, 2 vols., New York, 1900–1901, Vol. II, pp. xii ff. and Lecture VI, "The Human Self."

——, (3) *Outlines of Psychology*, New York, 1906.

——, (4) *The Sources of Religious Insight*, New York, 1912.

——, (5) *The Problem of Christianity*, 2 vols., New York, 1913.

——, (6) "George Fox as a Mystic," *Harvard Theological Review*, VI (1913), 31–50.

Ruckmich, C. A., "The Use of the Term Function in English Text-Books of Psychology," *American Journal of Psychology*, XXIV (1913).

Rumbull, E. A., "The Changing Content of Sin," *Open Court*, January, 1908.

Runze, G., *Die Psychologie des Unsterblichkeitsglaubens und der Unsterblichkeitsleugnung*, Berlin, 1894.

Russell, Bertrand, (1) "The Free Man's Worship," *Philosophical Essays*, 1910.

——, (2) "The Essence of Religion," *Hibbert Journal*, XI (1912), 46–62.

——, (3) "Mysticism and Logic," *ibid.*, XII (1914), 780–803. Cf. Pringle-Pattison, A. S., "The Free Man's Worship; Consideration of Mr. Bertrand Russell's Views on Religion," *ibid.*, XII (1913), 47–63.

Ruyssen, Th., "Le Problème de la personnalité dans la psychologie religieuse: A propos de quelques travaux récents," *Annales psychologiques*, XVIII (1912), 460–77.

Schiller, F. C. S., (1) *Humanism*, London, 1903, chap. xii, "The Desire for Immortality."

——, (2) *Studies in Humanism*, London, 1907, chap. xv, "Gods and Priests"; chap. xvi, "Faith, Reason, and Religion."

Schiller, F. C. S., (3) "Philosophy, Science, and Psychic Research," *Proceedings, Society for Psychical Research*, XXVII (1914), 191–220 (contains discussion of "soul").

Schlüter, J., "Religionspsychologische Biographienforschung," *Archiv für Religionspsychologie*, I (1914), 202–10.

Seashore, C. E., "The Play Impulse and Attitude in Religion," *American Journal of Theology*, October, 1910.

Segond, J., *La Prière: Essai de psychologie religieuse*, Paris, 1911.

Sharpe, A. B., *Mysticism; Its True Nature and Value*, London, Sands & Co.

Sidgwick, Mrs. Henry, "Spiritualism," *Encyclopaedia Britannica*.

Smith, H. P., "The Hebrew View of Sin," *American Journal of Theology*, October, 1911.

Smith, W. R., and others, "Priest," *Encyclopaedia Britannica*.

Stählin, W., (1) "Die Verwendung von Fragebogen in der Religionspsychologie," *Zeitschrift für Religionspsychologie*, V (1912), 394–408.

———, (2) "Der Almanach des Coenobium," *ibid.*, VI (1913), 145–54.

———, (3) "Experimentelle Untersuchungen über Sprachpsychologie und Religionspsychologie," *Archiv für Religionspsychologie*, I (1914), 117–94.

Starbuck, Edwin D., (1) *The Psychology of Religion*, London, 1899.

———, (2) "The Feelings and Their Place in Religion," *American Journal of Religious Psychology*, I (1904), 168–86.

———, (3) "The Foundations of Religion and Morality," *Proceedings of the Religious Education Association*, Boston, 1905, pp. 245–50.

———, (4) "Original Sin," *Homiletic Review*, December, 1906.

———, (5) "As a Man Thinketh in His Heart," *ibid.*, January, 1908.

———, (6) "Moral Education in the Schools," an essay in a volume published by Ginn & Co.

———, (7) *Religious Education in the New World-View*, Beacon Press, Boston (pamphlet).

———, (8) "The Child Mind and Child Religion," a series of articles in the *Biblical World*, beginning January, 1909.

Starbuck, Edwin D., (9) "The Play Instinct in Religion," *Homiletic Review*, October, 1909.

———, (10) "Unconscious Education," *Kindergarten Review*, November, 1910.

———, (11) Articles on "Backsliding," "Climate," "Double-mindedness," "Doubt," and "Female Principle," in Hastings' *Encyclopedia of Religion and Ethics*.

———, (12) "Development of the Psychology of Religion," *Religious Education*, VIII (1913), 426–29.

———, (13) "The Psychology of Conversion," *Expository Times*, February, 1914.

Reviews of Starbuck: Stählin, W., *Archiv für gesammte Psychologie*, XVIII (1910), 1–9; Faber, H., *Das Wesen der Religionspsychologie*, Tübingen, 1913, pp. 12–25; Leuba, J. H., *Psychological Review*, VII, 509 ff.; Coe, G. A., *Philosophical Review*, September, 1900.

Stratton, G. M., *Psychology of the Religious Life*, London, 1911. Reviews of Stratton: Galloway, G., *Mind*, 1913, pp. 131–34; Coe, G. A., *Philosophical Review*, November, 1912; Leuba, J. H., *International Journal of Ethics*, XXIII (1912–13), 88 ff.

Strong, A. L., (1) *The Psychology of Prayer*, The University of Chicago Press, 1909.

———, (2) "The Relation of the Subconscious to Prayer," *American Journal of Religious Psychology and Education*, I (1906), 129–42.

Tawney, G. A., (1) "The Period of Conversion," *Psychological Review*, XI, 210–16.

———, (2) "The Nature of Crowds," *Psychological Bulletin*, October 15, 1905.

Van Teslaar, J. G., "The Problem and the Present Status of Religious Psychology," *Journal of Religious Psychology*, VII (November, 1914), 214–36.

Thomas, N. W., "Sacrifice," in *Encyclopaedia Britannica*.

Thorndike, E. L., (1) *Educational Psychology*, New York, 1903, chap. xiv, "Broader Studies of Human Nature."

———, (2) *Educational Psychology*, Vol. I, "The Original Nature of Man," New York, 1913.

Trotter, W., *Instincts of the Herd in Peace and War*, New York, 1916.

Tufts, J. H., "Ethical Value," *Journal of Philosophy*, V (1908), 517–22.

Underhill, Evelyn, (1) *Mysticism: A Study in the Nature and Development of Man's Spiritual Consciousness*, 3d ed., London, 1912. Review by Taylor, A. E., *Mind*, XXII (1913), 122–30.

———, (2) *The Mystic Way: A Psychological Study in Christian Origins*, London, 1913.

———, (3) *Practical Mysticism: A Little Book for Normal People*, London, 1914.

Urban, W. M., *Valuation; Its Nature and Laws*, London, 1909.

Vorbrodt, G., (1) "Zur Religionspsychologie: Prinzipien und Pathologie," *Theologische Studien und Kritiken*, 1906, p. 237.

———, (2) *Zur theologischen Religionspsychologie*, Leipzig, Deichert, 1913.

Wallas, G., *The Great Society*, New York, 1914.

Watson, J. B., "Psychology as the Behaviorist Views It," *Psychological Review*, XX (1913), 158–77.

Whitehouse, O. C., and others, "Prophet," in *Encyclopaedia Britannica*.

Witmer, L., "Mental Healing and the Emmanuel Movement," *Psychological Clinic*, II, Nos. 7–9.

Wobbermin, G., (1) *Zum Streit um die Religionspsychologie*, Berlin, Schömberg, 1913.

———, (2) *Die religionspsychologische Methode in Religionswissenschaft und Theologie* (Systematische Theologie nach religionspsychologischer Methode), Bd. I, Leipzig, 1913. Review by Stählen, W., in *Archiv für Religionspsychologie*, I (1914), 279–98.

Woods, J. H., (1) *The Value of Religious Facts*, New York, 1899.

———, (2) *The Practice and Science of Religion*, New York, 1906.

Worcester and others, *Religion and Medicine*, New York, 1908.

Wright, W. K., (1) "A Psychological Definition of Religion," *American Journal of Theology*, XVI (1912), 385–409.

———, (2) "The Evolution of Values from Instincts," *Philosophical Review*, XXIV (1915), 165–83.

Wundt, W., (1) *Völkerpsychologie, 2. Band: Mythus und Religion,* Leipzig, 1906; revised edition in 3 vols., 1910–15. Reviewed by Gardiner, H. N., *Philosophical Review* (1908), pp. 316 ff.; Thieme, K., *Zeitschrift für Religionspsychologie,* IV (1910), 145–61; Mead, G. H., *Psychological Bulletin,* III, 399 ff.; Faber, H., *Das Wesen der Religionspsychologie,* Tübingen, 1913, pp. 33–55.

——, (2) *Probleme der Völkerpsychologie,* Leipzig, 1911.

——, (3) *Elemente der Völkerpsychologie,* Leipzig, 1913.

TOPICAL BIBLIOGRAPHY

[Numbers in parentheses refer back to the Alphabetical Bibliography.]

BIBLIOGRAPHIES

Lists of Current Psychological Publications

Psychological Bulletin (monthly), and
Psychological Index (annual), both published by the Psychological
  Review Co., Princeton, New Jersey.

Bibliographies of the Psychology of Religion

Berguer, G., *Psychologie religieuse; Revue et bibliographies générales*,
  Genève, Kündig, 1914.

Contains the only extended general bibliography of this
subject. It is preceded by brief analyses of problems and points
of view, with references to the writers who represent each point
of view.

Faber, H., *Das Wesen der Religionspsychologie*, Tübingen, 1913.

Gives a list of writings, chiefly German. This list will be found
especially useful by anyone who desires to work up the movement
among German theologians to secure a psychological basis for
systematic theology. To the titles listed by Faber should be
added works by Vorbrodt and Wobbermin published in 1913 (see
Alphabetical Bibliography).

Bibliographies of Primitive Religion

Marett, R. R., "Primitive Religion," *Encyclopaedia Britannica*,
  XXIII, 67.

King, I., *The Development of Religion*, New York, 1910, pp.
  355–61.

Note also sources and authorities given in cyclopedia articles
by Aston, Lang, Marett, Thomas, W. R. Smith, and Whitehouse
(see Alphabetical Bibliography).

Religious Autobiographies

Burr, A. R., *Religious Confessions and Confessants*, Boston, 1914. Gives a long list.

Bibliography of Social Psychology

Howard, G. E., *Social Psychology: A Syllabus and a Bibliography*, Lincoln, Nebraska, 1910.

Consult also Thomas, W. I., *Source Book for Social Origins*, Chicago, 1909.

Bibliography of Thirty Works on the Psychology of Religion by Catholic Writers

Lindworsky, J., "Religionspsychologische Arbeiten katholischer Autoren," *Archiv für Religionspsychologie*, I (1914), 228–56.

Bibliography of the Psychology and Metaphysics of Value

Dashiell, J. F., "An Introductory Bibliography of Value," *Journal of Philosophy*, X (1913), 472–76.

To this list should be added the following more recent publications:

Brown, H. C., "Value and Potentiality," *ibid.*, XI (1914), 29–37.

Kallen, H. M., "Value and Existence in Art and in Religion," *ibid.*, XI (1914), 264–76.

Moore, J. S., "The System of Transcendental Values," *ibid.*, XI (1914), 244–48.

Perry, R. B., "Definition of Value, *ibid.*, XI (1914), 141–62.

——, "Religious Values," *American Journal of Theology*, XIX (1915), 1–16.

Sheldon, W. H., "Empirical Definition of Value," *Journal of Philosophy*, XI (1914), 113–24.

Wright, W. K., "Evolution of Values from Instincts," *Philosophical Review*, XXIV (1915), 165–83.

See also Berguer, G., *La Notion de Valeur*, Genève, 1908.

MAGAZINES DEVOTED PRIMARILY TO THE PSYCHOLOGY OF RELIGION

American Journal of Religious Psychology and Education, founded in 1904 by G. Stanley Hall, succeeded 1912 by

Journal of Religious Psychology, Including its Anthropological and Sociological Aspects, Worcester, Massachusetts (Quarterly, $3.00 a year). Editor, G. Stanley Hall.

Zeitschrift für Religionspsychologie, Leipzig, Barth; founded 1908, discontinued after six years.

Archiv für Religionspsychologie, Tübingen, Mohr (12 marks a volume); founded 1914; only one volume issued thus far. Editor-in-chief, Dr. W. Stählin.

CYCLOPEDIAS ESPECIALLY VALUABLE FOR THE PSYCHOLOGY OF RELIGION

For definition of psychological terms, consult Baldwin's *Dictionary of Philosophy and Psychology*.

Two cyclopedias, the *Encyclopaedia Britannica* and Hastings' *Encyclopedia of Religion and Ethics*, are rich in anthropological material. The student is advised to consult, in addition to the bibliographies of primitive religion already mentioned, the Index of the *Britannica*. The last volume of Hastings published to the present date is Vol. VIII. The student should be on the lookout for the new volumes as they appear. This cyclopedia contains a vast aggregation of material by writers of many sorts. It is not organized on the basis of any scientific classification, but rather on that of popular terminology, as "Charms" and "Images and Idols." Many articles have subdivisions that follow the religious divisions of mankind. Thus, under "Magic," an introductory article of general character by Marett is followed by fifteen others by as many writers on magic in the different religions. See, for other examples, "Death and the Disposal of the Dead," "Human Sacrifice," and "Life and Death."

At many points the student will find valuable historical material in the various dictionaries of the Bible, the *Jewish Encyclopedia*, and the *Catholic Encyclopedia*.

GENERAL POINTS OF VIEW IN PSYCHOLOGY

For a critical exposition of the notion of functional psychology, see Angell.

On the history and use of "function" in psychology, see Dallenbach; Ruchmich.

On self-psychology, see Calkins (1, 3, 4, 5, 8).

On the voluntaristic, dynamic point of view, including relation of mind to evolution, see Judd (1, 2, 3).

On behaviorism, see Watson.

For a comparison of structuralism, functionalism, and behaviorism, see Creighton.

On the mind-body relation, see McDougall (2).

History of the Psychology of Religion

Ames (5, chap. i); Pratt (3, 4); Rademacher; Berguer; Faber; Wobbermin (2, chap. xv).

Methods and Principles in the Psychology of Religion

On the use of question circulars, see Thorndike (1); Ribot; Urban (in *Philosophical Review*, XIV, 652 ff.); Stählin (1, 2); Haynes; see also reviews of Starbuck.

On the analysis of religious biographies and autobiographies, see Burr; Schlüter.

On anthropology as psychology of religion, see Wundt (2), and his German critics, for whom consult Faber, Wobbermin (1, 2), and Aschkenasy.

On experimental methods in the psychology of religion, see May (*Journal of Philosophy*, XII [1915], 691); Stählin (3).

On conditions that must be met if psychology of religion is to be science, see Flournoy (2); Leuba (3, 9, 11); Höffding (3); King (4); Woods (1, 2); Billia.

On functionalism in the psychology of religion, see King (9, chap. i); Ames (5, chap. ii); Calkins (7).

General Works on the Psychology of Religion

No work even ,approximately covers the enormous field. Each author selects an area or a set of problems, though generally with the intention of securing insight into the general nature of religion. In addition to the characterization of recent works by Ames, Durkheim, Höffding, James, King, Leuba, Pratt, Starbuck, Stratton, and Wundt already given in chap. i, it will be sufficient to say that, for a systematic marshaling of many sorts of data, Ames (5) will be found most convenient; for a similar wide range of literary data of religion as inner life, Stratton will serve best. James (2) and Starbuck (1) offer valuable personal confessions in abundance. Cutten (1) has collected typical data on a wide range of topics, but his analysis is popular rather than critical. As to points of view, emphasis upon religion as affective life is represented by James (2), Pratt (2), and Starbuck (1 and 2); functionalism that connects religion with biological processes is represented by Ames (5) and King (9); Stratton emphasizes logical relations more than functions; Wundt is more interested in ideational structure and history than in the functions involved; Höffding (1) has produced the *locus classicus* on religion as valuation; Leuba's general works (21 and 24), which deal primarily with the establishment of a positivistic conception, and with the differentiation of religion from magic, are to be followed by one or more others that will deal in greater detail with the content of religion; Durkheim endeavors to derive the primitive religious ideas wholly from the organized life of primitive groups.

EFFORTS TO DETERMINE THE FUNDAMENTAL PSYCHOLOGICAL CHARACTERISTICS OF RELIGION

In addition to the general works on the psychology of religion, already listed, see Leuba (24), who gives on pp. 339–61 a classified list of definitions of religion; Starbuck (2); Wright (1); Colvin; Seashore; Marshall (1, 2, 4); McDougall (1); Calkins (2); Perry (1, 3, 4); Wundt (1, III, 509 ff.); Aschkenasy.

SOUL, SELF, PERSON

In general, and primarily, "soul" is a metaphysical conception, "self" a psychological conception, and "person" an ethical and legal conception. A further distinction has to be made between the primitive notions of body-soul (*Körperseele*), and separable soul or "spirit." On the rise and development of these notions, see Ames (5, chap. vi); Wundt (1, Vol. IV); Durkheim, and the bibliography of primitive religion.

On the present status of the doctrine of the soul, see McDougall (2).

The concept "soul" has largely disappeared from psychology. But "self" remains. (*a*) It refers to the individual uniqueness and unity of mental life. (b) Consciousness of self is commonly supposed to depend upon organic sensations, or upon kinesthetic sensations. (c) But the increasing prominence in psychology of the motor aspects of mind (desire, attitude, action, adjustment), tends toward a further determination of the self as a *dynamic* unity. See Judd (1, 2, 3), and James (3). (d) Further, analysis of the genesis and growth of self-consciousness shows that self-consciousness is itself social consciousness. See Royce (1, 2, 3); Mead (5, 6); Baldwin; Cooley.

A good idea of the place of the "self" in present psychology can be had by comparing the following with one another:

James, W., *Principles of Psychology*, Vol. I, chap. x.
Pillsbury, W. B., *Essentials of Psychology*, chap. xvi.
Stout, G. F., *Groundwork of Psychology*, chaps. xiv, xviii.
Angell, J. R., *Psychology*, chap. xxiii.
Judd, C. H., *Psychology*, chap. xii.
Calkins, M. W., *Introduction to Psychology*, chaps. i and xii.

In the article, "The Self in Scientific Psychology" (*American Journal of Psychology*, XXVI [1915], 495–524), Professor Calkins gives many footnote references to sources.

A "person" is primarily one who has rights or value that entitles him to a place in our ultimate regard. But the present tendency to think of the self as social and dynamic, and the growing prominence of the study of values, are reducing the distance between the concept of "self" and that of "person."

On the significance of "persons" for the Christian religion, see Buckham (1); Royce (4).

On the nature of our knowledge of persons, and of our fellowship with them, see Schiller (3); Coe (9); Bradley, chap. xiv.

On the problem of personality in the psychology of religion, see Ruyssen; Fite.

On personal immortality, see Schiller (1, 3); Howison; Hyslop (1, 2); Runze; Hall (2); Bergson (2); Bradley; Leuba (8, 34).

Values

For a general classified bibliography of value, see "Bibliographies."

Works on general psychology rarely contain anything specific on valuation. But discussions of feeling, sentiment, and volition touch upon the root ideas involved, as *e.g.*, Angell's *Psychology* (revised edition, New York, 1908), p. 320 and chap. xxi.

The only extensive general psychological discussion of values in English is that of Urban. It is fundamental and critical, but it suffers from a highly abstract method of presentation. The interest of Münsterberg (1) is that of philosophical construction rather than of psychological analysis.

On kinds and classifications of value, see Tufts; Moore, A. W.; Moore, J. S. (1 and 2); Coe (4); Perry (4); Messer.

On the relation of value to (*a*) validity as a whole, including belief in the external world; (*b*) social consciousness, and (*c*) the problem of teleology and of the existence of God, see Rogers (1, 3). Urban in chap. ii opens the question as to the senses in which valuation implies reality. His final conclusion (pp. 422 ff.) is that "worth experience in its entirety corresponds to a larger world of reality than the limited regions of existence and truth" (p. 427), and that "existence" and "truth" have meaning as predicates "only when they add to the intrinsic value or reality of an impression or idea" (p. 427). The relation of this to voluntarism and pragmatist tendencies may be gathered from p. 54: "In general, then, we may conclude that feeling of value is the feeling aspect of conative process, as distinguished from the feeling-tone of simple presentations."

RELIGION AS SOCIAL EXPERIENCE

For the bibliography of social psychology, see under "Bibliographies."

Concerning the instinctive bases of social satisfactions, see McDougall (1); Thorndike (2, chaps. vii and viii).

On the genesis and nature of the ego-social consciousness, see Mead (2, 3, 4, 5, 6); Baldwin; Cooley; Royce (1, 2, 3).

On the objects of social consciousness—what they are, and how they are known—see Ames (6); Coe (9); Boodin (1, 2).

On crowds and other assemblies, see Le Bon; Tawney; Wallis, chap. viii; Gardner; Trotter.

On the social functions of religion, see "Bibliographies of Primitive Religion"; Durkheim; Wundt (1); Royce (4); Adams;

Marshall (1, 2, 4, 5); Draghicesco; Ellwood; Haw; Overstreet; Fite; Rumbull; Coe (2, chap. xi).

THE PHENOMENA OF CONVERSION AND OF REVIVALS

For the earliest studies of the psychology of conversion, see references to Hall, Daniels, Leuba, Burnham, Lancaster, and Starbuck in the first footnote of chap. i. The most extended study is that of Starbuck (1), with which compare James (2, Lectures IX, X); Hall (1, Vol. II, chap. xiv); Coe (1, chaps. i–iii, and 5); Caldecott; Prince (1); Tawney (1); Fursac (1).

On counter-conversions, see Heidel; Burr.

On revivals, see Davenport; Dike; Morrison; Fryer; Bois; Fursac (2).

THE SUBCONSCIOUS

The subconscious makes its appearance in a great number of recent writings. Many psychologists have dealt with the general concept of mental life below the "threshold," as James Ward in his article "Psychology" in the *Britannica* (XXII, 559 f.), and Münsterberg, in *Grundzüge der Psychologie* (Leipzig, 1900), I, 215–31. On the other hand, popular writings on mental healing, self-control, telepathy, spiritism, and religion commonly assume as established a great deal that is not recognized by professional psychologists. There is comparatively little literature that deals critically with particular facts that are thoroughly ascertained. The student should bear in mind that subconscious processes and mechanisms are not open to observation. They should not be taken as facts, but as inferences. The question "Just what has been observed, and what has been inferred?" may well accompany the reading of instances. Much first-hand material in the way of instances will be found scattered through the *Proceedings of the Society for Psychical Research.* The interpretation of them in terms of a "subliminal self" comes chiefly from Myers, F. W. H., *Human Personality and Its Survival of Bodily Death* (London, 1903). Another theory of a sort of second self has appeared in many medical writings, particularly of the Freudian school. Morton Prince (4) distinguishes a "co-consciousness" and an "unconsciousness," both of which he regards as having psychical quality. Further points of view will be found in Prince (2, 3), and a criticism of the whole notion of a "detached subconsciousness" in Pierce (1, 2, 3, 4). Jastrow (1 and 2) gives the most extended discussion from the point of view of the professional psychologist.

On the subconscious in religious experience, see James (2, Index under "Subconscious"); Coe (7); Pratt (8); King (5); Strong (2).

On glossolalia (or "speaking in tongues"), see Henke (1); Hayes; Mosiman; Lombard; Le Baron; Pfister.

THE PSYCHOLOGY OF MYSTICISM

In the following list an effort is made to pick out from the enormous literature of mysticism a very short set of writings that will enable the beginner: (a) to recognize the mystical tradition in various religions; (b) to realize vividly how certain experiences seem to the mystic himself; (c) to become acquainted with the main types of religious interpretation of the present day, and (d) to distinguish from all these the specifically psychological analyses that have thus far been made.

On the mystical tradition in Catholicism, see Poulain; in Protestantism, Jones (1) and Inge (1); for an attempt to establish the unity of both, Underhill (2).

On the mystical tradition in other religions, see Abelson; Nicholson; Rhys-Davids; any exposition of Hinduism.

On how mystical experiences seem to the mystic himself, there is nothing more vivid or detailed than St. Teresa's descriptions of her own experiences in:

St. Teresa, an Autobiography, ed. by J. J. Burke, New York, 1911.
The Life of St. Teresa of Jesus, Written by Herself, ed. by D. Lewis.
The Interior Castle, London, 1904.
See also James (2, Lectures XVI, XVII); Hügel; Inge (2).

For the exposition, defense, and criticism of mysticism, see Underhill (1, 3); Hügel; Sharpe; Buckham (2); Fleming; Jones (3); Boutroux; Hocking, Part V; Ewer; Peabody; Russell (3).

For psychological analyses, see Leuba (6, 7, 12); Delacroix; Royce (1, 6); Coe (3, 6, 12); Ames (10).

THE PSYCHOLOGY OF PRAYER

A brief classified bibliography of history and forms of prayer will be found in Marett's article "Prayer," in the *Encyclopaedia Britannica*.

On the origins of prayer, see Farnell, Lecture IV, "The Evolution of Prayer from Lower to Higher Forms"; Marett (1, chap. ii: "From Spell to Prayer"), also (3); Ames (5, chap. viii); Wundt (1, last volume, pp. 449–59).

On prayer as a present-day problem of Christians, see Coe (2, chap. xi); Fosdick; Ames (9).

On the psychological structure and functions of prayer, see Strong (1, 2); Pratt (5); Calkins (6); Ranson; Beck; Hartshorne.

INDEX

[This Index covers all specific references to authors in the text and all descriptive matter in the Topical Bibliography. For a complete list of authors see the Alphabetical Bibliography.]

ADLER, F., 242 (note 1).

Adolescence, 79 f., 94, 111, 163 ff., 165 (note), 195.

Aesthetic experience, 40, 227, 249. *See also* Art; Beauty, Religion of.

ALLONNES, G. R. DE, 210 (note).

AMES, E. S., ix, 2 (note 3), 11, 21 (note 2), 28 (note), 30 (note 2), 56, 71 f., 325 (note), 350.

AMOS, 109 f., 182.

Anesthesia, 158 ff., 195, 267, 278.

ANGELL, J. R., 21 (note 2), 33, 35.

Animism, 83, 102, 231 (note). *See also* Spiritism, Ancient and Modern.

Anthropology, 51 ff., 76 ff.

Anthropomorphism, 91 f., 97, 100 f., 212, 227, 237, 249 f., 258, 303, 306.

ANTIN, M., 164 (note 1).

Architecture, 111 f.

Art, 110 ff., 251. *See also* Aesthetic experience; Beauty, Religion of.

Artistic inspirations, 199 ff.

Asceticism, 137, 147 ff.

Assurance. *See* Witness of the Spirit.

Astarte, 94.

Augury, 304.

AUGUSTINE, 3, 155.

Authority, xi, 126, 128, 130, 136, 146. *See also* Dogma; Freedom.

Autobiographies, Religious, 50, 347.

Automatisms, 177, 185, 187, 188 f., 190, 193 ff., 209, 264, 267, 268, 272, 278 f., 287 f., 298.

Babylonian religion, 108, 286.

BAKEWELL, C. M., 258 (note).

BALDWIN, J. M., 27 (note).

Baptism, 91, 114.

Baptist churches, 155.

Beauty, Religion of, 69.

BEECHER, H. W., 200.

Belief, Religion considered as, 59 f., 61. *See also* Dogma; Theology.

BENEDICT XIV, 9.

BERGSON, H., 291 (note 1).

Bible, 5, 115, 304.

BINET, A., 45 (note).

Biology, x, 22–25, 35 ff., 231 (note). *See also* Evolution.

Body and mind, 277 f. *See also* Animism.

BOODIN, J. E., 256 (note).

BRADLEY, F. H., 255 (note).

BREASTED, J. H., 90 (note), 98.

BROWNING, R., 206.

BRYANT, W. C., 200.

Buddhism, 60, 154, 162, 172 f., 188 f., 223, 239 f., 271, 281 f.

BURNHAM, W. H., 1 (note 1).

BURR, A. R., 50 (note).

BURROUGHS, J., 73.

CALKINS, M. W., 19 (note 2), 252 f.

CARVER, T. N., 243 (note 4).

Catholic church, 9, 263, 266, 273, 275, 280, 281, 306.

Catholic writers on psychology of religion, 347.

Celibacy, 150, 279.

Ceremonies and festivals, 79, 86, 88, 90, 97, 105, 108, 111, 114, 123, 125 f., 128, 139, 180, 182, 184, 236.

Childhood, 99, 195 (note 1), 198, 298. *See also* Adolescence.

Christ, The Living, 269, 273, 296.

Christian religion, The, xii f., 3 f., 5 f., 70, 93 f., 109–11, 114 f., 129, 151 (note), 154 f., 157, 184 ff., 226, 241, 259 f., 269 ff., 275, 276 f., 283, 287, 304, 309, 319. *See also* Catholic church; Protestantism.

Christian Science. *See* EDDY, MRS. M. B.

Churches. *See* Institutions, Religious; Priesthood; Catholic church; Protestantism; Christian religion.

Clairvoyance, 267.

COE, G. A., 1 (note 1), 41 (note 1), 48 (note), 160 (note 1), 208 (note), 278 (note 2).

COIT, S., 100, 243 (note 5).

Communion with God, Sense of, 267.

Confession, 316 f.

Conservation of value, 71, 296 f.

Contagion, Mental. *See* Suggestion.

Contemplation, 270, 302.

Conversion, 1, 10, 46 f., chap. x, 353.

COOLEY, W. F., xi (note).

Cosmic consciousness, 267.

Creeds, 114, 127, 128. *See also* Theology.

CREIGHTON, J. E., 32 (note).

Crowd action, 119 ff., 132, 134, 136, 144 (note).

Crusades, The, 119, 124.

Culture, Relation of religion to, 110 f., 232 f.

CUMONT, F., 154 (note).

Custom, 77, 112, 123, 143.

CUTTEN, G. B., 350.

Dance, Religious, 79, 166, 176, 194.

DANIELS, A. H., 1 (note 1).

DARWIN, C., 218.

Death, xiv, 83 f., 104, 241, 288. *See also* Spirits; Spiritism; Future life.

Definition, Nature of, 59, 62.

DELACROIX, M., 1 (note 2), 10, 49 (note 2), 139, 281 (note).

Deliberative groups, 131 ff.

Democracy and religion, 243, 319.

Depressive states. *See* Pleasure and pain in religion.

Desire, Nature of human, 66 ff., 172 f., 218 ff., 230, 300, 318, 320.

DEWEY, J., 25 (note).

DICKINSON, G. L., 296 (note).

DIKE, S. W., 156 (note).

Dissociation, Mental, 202 f., 204 ff.

Divided self, 280 f.

Dogma, xii, xv, 5 f., 125, 126, 180, 235, 244, 275. *See also* Theology; Authority.

Doubts, 46, 276, 281.

DOWIE, J. A., 130, 180, 224 (note 2).

Drama, The, 110.

Dreams, 183, 205 (note).

DUNLAP, K., 202 (note).

DURKHEIM, E., ix, 2 (note 1); 10, 350.

Duty, Religion of, 69, 242 f.

Ecclesiasticism. *See* Institutions, Religious; Priesthood.

Economic values and religion, 40 70 (notes 1 and 3), 108 f.

Ecstasy, 266 f.

EDDY, MRS. M. B., 130, 180, 224 (note 2), 281.

Education, 67, 68, 111 f., 126, 129, 135, 145, 150, 222 (note).

Ego and *alter. See* Self.

Egyptian religion, 90, 98, 108 f., 287, 302.

Einfühlung, 99, 104, 173, 287, 292, 297.

ELLIS, R. S., 296 (note).

EMERSON, R. W., 23, 200 f.

Emotion, 160, 195, 312. *See also* Feeling.

Emotional thinking, 99 ff. *See also Einfühlung.*

Epilepsy, 278.

ERIGENA, JOHANNES SCOTUS, 284.

Ethical value and religion, 40, 71 (note), 74, 114, 149 f., 154, 183 f., chap. xiii, 249, 277, 309 f., 317. *See also* Morals, Religion and.

Eucharist, The, 91, 114, 127, 267, 307.
Evangelical movement, The, 155.
Evil, 150. *See also* Sin.
Evolution, 52 f., 115, 176, 189, 190 f., 215 ff., 221 (note 2), 244, 268, 289, 293, 318, 325.

FABER, H., 56.
Faith, 134, 173, 242, 312, 318, 322.
Fatigue, 279.
Fear, 62 (note), 101, 126, 131, 138, 225.
Feeling, Religion as, 60.
Fetishism, 87.
FEUERBACH, L., 4.
FICHTE, 256 (note).
FISKE, J., 38.
FLETCHER, M. S., 3 (note 1).
FOSDICK, H. E., 318.
FRANCIS, ST., 155.
FRAZER, J. G., 64 (note), 89.
Freedom, 134, 138, 172, 242, 276. *See also* Authority.
FREUD, S., 217 (note), 316, 353.
Friends of God, 155.
Friendship, Religion as, 262.
Functions of religion: the concept of function, 22 ff., 299 f.; the functional view of religion as a whole, 62 ff., 65 ff.; functions of early religion, 87 f.; functional differentiation of religion, 117; functions of the religious crowd, 124 f., 143 f.; of the sacerdotal group, 129 ff., 144; of the deliberative group, 133 ff., 145 f.; functions of religion with respect to the individual, 137 ff., 143 ff.; functions of asceticism, 147 ff.; of conversion, 168 ff.; of the shaman, 177 ff.; of the priest, 180 ff.; of the prophet, 186 ff.; of religious leadership in general, 191 f.; the evolution of functions, 227 f.; functions of mysticism, 279–85; of the future in the life of the present, 289, 295; of prayer, 315–20. *See also* Psychology; Psychology of religion.

Future life, 181, 228, chap. xvii. *See also* Death; Spirits.

Geographic factor in religions, 108.
German views of American psychology of religion, 56 ff.
Ghost dance, 79.
Glossolalia, 185, 194, 211 (note 2).
God: ethical significance of, xiv; fluidity of god-ideas, 59 f.; Are gods mere means to human ends? 63 ff., 320; nationalistic ideas of God, 75 (note); *mana* the tap root of the god-idea, 88; theriomorphic and anthropomorphic gods, 91 f., 97, 101 f.; genesis of the idea of God, chap. vi; relation of god-ideas to social and political organization, 109 f.; god and priest, 126 f.; the idea of god in deliberative religion, 135; how repressive conceptions of the divine arise, 148; no dividing line between fellowship with men and with God, 173 f., 245, 248; the God of the prophets, 184, 223, 228; God as personal, 237 f.; the Christian God, 241, 260, 271, 283, 288 (*see also* Jesus); why the god-idea grows, 257–59; pantheism, 267, 272; divine response to prayer, 304–10; probable permanence of faith in God, 326. *See also Mana*.
GOETHE, 200, 282.
GÖRRES, J., 9 (note 1).
Greece, Religion of, 86, 286.
GRIGGS, E. H., 243 (note 2).
Group conduct, Religion as, chap. viii. *See also* Social aspects of religion.
Growth, Religious, 154 f.
Habit: habit formation, 129, 135, 168; habit as determining group action, 123 f.; habit and automatisms, 272 f.
HADLEY, S. H., 168 (note).
HALL, G. S., 1 (note 1).
Hallucinations, 205, 272, 287.
HAMILTON, W. R., 153, 204 (note 2).

HARRISON, J. E., 49 (note 4), 86 (note).
HARTSHORNE, H., 55 (note).
HAW, G., 242 (note 2).
Healing, Religious, 131, 187, 224 (note 2), 267, 312, 316.
Heaven and hell, 287, 289.
HEGEL, 4.
HEIDEL, W. A., 154 (note).
HENKE, F. G., 211 (note 2).
Hero-gods, 97.
History of religion, 4.
HOCKING, W. E., 111 (note), 256 (note).
HÖFFDING, H., ix, 11, 55, 71, 296, 350.
Holiness, 114, 150, 267.
HOLLINGWORTH, H. L., 38 (note 3), 39.
HOLMES, O. W., 201.
Holy Spirit, The, 309.
HOSEA, 109, 184.
Human nature. See Nature.
Humanity, The religion of, 243.
HUME, 4.
HUXLEY, T. H., 248.
Hypnosis. See Suggestion.
HYSLOP, J. H., 291, 292 (note).
Hysteria, 278.

Ideals, 134, 138, 242 f. See also Values.
Ideational factors in religion, 156 f., 164 f.
Ideo-motor action, 120 (note 2).
Idols, 258 f., 305.
Illumination. See Intuition.
Illusion of the finite, 272. See also Maya.
Immediacy, 173 f., chap. xv, 263, 275, 282 f., 285, 291.
Immortality, 295 f. See also Future life.
India, Religions of, 151 (note), 238 ff., 263, 266, 270 f., 273, 275 ff., 281, 283 f., 286 f., 302. See also Buddhism.
Individual, Religion as related to the, 76, 91, 115 ff., 132 f., 135, chap. ix, 138, 140, 141, 162, 174, 190, 197, 212, 236 f., 250, 283. See also Self, The.

Ineffability of mystical experience, 269 f.
Infancy, 142.
Inner life, Religion as, 144 f., 263, 309.
Insanity, 278.
Inspirations, Religious, 80, 167 (note), 184, 185, 194, 199 ff., 203, 209, 211, 265, 267, 273, 282. See also Literary inspirations.
Instability, Nervous. See Neurotic constitution.
Instinct: nature of, 24 f., 34, 41; the social instincts, 24 f., 141, 293; basal in religion, 78; in crowd action, 123 f.; in deliberative group action, 133; instinct and reason, 137 ff., 227; instinct and custom, 143; instinct and asceticism, 147 f.; sexual instinct, 150, 163 ff. (see also Sex); instinct in conversion, 156, 161 ff.; Are instincts good? 220 f.; Is there a religious instinct? 322 ff.
Institutions, Religious, 88, 109, 112 ff., 115, 193, 244. See also Social aspects of religion.
Intellect in religion, 145 f.
Introspection, 45 f., 252, 313.
Intuition, 263, 268, 273, 274–76, 322 f.
ISAIAH, 154, 182, 224 (note 1), 259.
Israel, Religion of, 76 (note), 82, 94, 103, 108 ff., 110, 129, 154, 182 ff., 223, 225 f., 258 f., 283, 286 f., 307.

JAMES, W., ix, 1 (notes 1 and 2), 11, 16, 49 (note 2), 50, 56, 57, 100, 138, 147 (note), 152, 158 (note), 173, 261, 268, 269, 271, 276 (note), 350.
JANET, P., 278 (note 1).
Jansenists, The, 194 (note 2).
JASTROW, J., 354.
JEREMIAH, 224 (note 1).
JESUS, 51, 110, 151, 184, 185, 186–88, 208 (note), 213, 223, 226, 260, 262, 269, 283, 296, 317.
JONES, H., 243 (note 5).
JONES, R. M., 155 (note 1).

JUDD, C. H., 26 (note).
Justice as a religious concept, 109 f., 237, 240 f., 243.

KIDD, B., 137 (note 1).
KING, I., ix, 2 (note 1), 10, 11, 29 (note 1), 30 (note 1), 56, 89 f., 350.
Kingdom of God, 187, 226, 228.
Knowledge of other minds, Our, 254–56, 291.

LADD, G. T., 160 (note 2).
LANCASTER, E. G., 1 (note 1).
Language, 143.
Laymen, 146.
Leaders, Religious, 115 f., chap. xi, 223 f.
LEUBA, J. H., ix, xi, 1 (notes 1 and 2), 2 (note 2), 10, 56, 63, 65 (note), 66, 69 (note), 71, 89, 255 (note), 350.
LINCOLN, A., 188.
Literary inspirations, 199 ff., 273, 282.
LLOYD, H. D., 243 (note 5).
Lot, Casting the, 304.
Love, 24 f., 109, 151, 154, 164 (note 1), 185 f., 188, 227, 253, 256 f., 259–62, 283 ff., 293, 295, 319. See also Parental instinct; Sex.
LOVEJOY, A. O., 41 (note 2), 67 (note 1), 220.
LUCRETIUS, 4, 154 (note).
LUTHER, 155.

Magic, 79, 82 f., 84, 89 ff., 97 (note 1), 105, 264.
Man. See Nature: human nature.
Mana, 59, 81, 88, 90, 96, 98, 104, 144, 237, 306.
MARIE, A., 194 (note 2).
MARSHALL, H. R., 137 (note 2), 139, 220, 256 (note).
MARY, THE VIRGIN, 151, 273.
Mass, The. See Eucharist.
MATHER, COTTON, 206 (note).
MAY, M. A., 54 (note 2).
Maya, 239.
McDOUGALL, W., 24 (note), 163 (note 1), 231 (note).

MEAD, G. H., 21 (note 2), 142.
Medicine man. See Shaman.
Mediumship, 267, 294.
Metempsychosis, 287.
Methodism, 145 (note).
Mind reading, 178, 206 (note).
MOHAMMED, and Mohammedanism, 129, 188, 190, 209, 223, 273, 277, 281, 302.
Moki snake dance, 79.
Monarchic conceptions of God, 109, 148.
MONOD, G., 210 (note).
Monotheism, 75 (note), 109.
MONTGERON, 194 (note 2).
MOORE, A. W., 40 (note 2).
MOORE, J. S., 35 (note).
Morals, Religion and, 110, 125, 128, 280. See also Ethical value and religion.
Morbidness, 155 (note 3).
Mormonism, 130, 180.
MÜNSTERBERG, H., 32 (note), 352.
Multiple personality, 210 f.
MURISIER, E., 245 (note).
Music, rhythm, etc., in religion, 110, 158, 166 f., 167 (note), 176.
MYERS, F. W. H., 353.
Mystery cult, 127, 154.
Mysticism, xiii, 2, 139, 155, chap. xvi, 302, 354.
Myth and mythology, 84 f., 110.

NASSAU, R. H., 87 (note), 100 (note).
National religions and nationalism in religion, 74 (note), 109, 126, 129, 181, 237, 242.
Nature: natural law, 170 (note), 214, 215, 221; nature-powers 97, 105; nature and man, 213 f.; human nature, 216 f., 221, 241, chap. xix.
Neo-Platonism, 284.
Neurotic constitution, 188, 190, 278, 281. See also Pathological states.
New Thought, 140 (note), 267.
Non-religious persons, 321.

Nutrition as a mental function, 36 f., 216.
OGDEN, R. M., 32 (note).
Omens, 307. *See also* Augury.
Oracles, 178, 267.
Oratorical inspiration, 200.
Originality, 192, 201, 282, 318. *See also* Evolution.
OVERSTREET, H. A., 260 (note).

Painting and sculpture, 111, 305 f.
Pantheism, 267, 284.
Parental instinct, 11 f., 24, 94, 162 f., 164 (note 1), 236 f., 293, 299 f.
PASCAL, 3.
Passivity, 271 f.
Pathological states, 175, 188.
PAUL, 2, 155, 184 ff., 188, 190, 225, 226, 277.
Peace of mind, 149, 310.
PEARSON, K., 256 (note).
Persian religion. *See* Zarathustra, and Zoroastrianism.
Persons, chap. ii, 30, 42, 67, 227 f., chap. iv; 233 ff., 239, 245, 267, 288, 292, 320, 350. *See also* Self, The.
Philosophy, 96, 110, 232, 251.
Philosophy of religion, 4.
PIERCE, A. H., 203, 354.
Play, 40.
Pleasure and pain in religion, 137 ff., 149, 269, 276.
PODMORE, F., 292 (note).
Political organizations and religion, 109.
Possession, 177, 184, 185, 208, 212 f., 263, 265 ff., 272.
"Power, The," 123, 194.
PRATT, J. B., ix, 1 (note 2), 2 (note 3), 10, 350.
Prayer, 90, 114, 127 f., 137, chap. xviii. *See also* Worship.
Premonitions, 267.
Presence of another, Experience of the, 197 f., 246, 267, 273 f.

Priesthood, 80, 112, 125 ff., 134, 144, 176, 180 ff., 184, 185, 187, 189, 308 f., 319.
Primitive man, 77 (note).

PRINCE, M., 207 (note 1), 217 (note), 353 f.
Prophets and prophetism, 176, 182 ff., 206, 223, 228, 238, 248 f., 250, 257–59, 265 f., 282, 283, 309.
Protestantism, 6, 9, 109, 115, 134 f., 145, 154, 275, 302.
PSEUDO-DIONYSIUS, 284.
Psychic research, 265, 289 ff., 294 (note).
Psychology: the psychologist's fallacy, xi, 170 (note); the newness of scientific psychology, 5; structural and functional points of view, chap. ii, 230 ff. (*see also* Functions of religion; Structure); psychology as analysis of states of consciousness, 15–17; as analysis of behavior, 17 f.; as analysis of the experience of being a personal self, 19 ff., 27, 31, 252 f.; the nature of mental functions, 32–42; abnormal psychology, 20; order-of-merit method, 38 (note 3), 54; genetic psychology, 141; evolution of mind, 215 ff., 299; modern psychology not intellectualistic, 230; psychology deals with experience as shared, 246 ff., 253; psychic research, 289 ff.; current psychological publications, 346.
Psychology of religion, The: is in its first stages, ix; early writers on, 1 f.; previous attempts to psychologize religion, 2 ff.; psychology covers all religious experiences, 7 ff.; problems of both structure and function are included, 10 ff., 57; question circulars as sources of data, 44 ff.; sacred literatures as a source 49 ff.; anthropology as a source, 51 ff.; experimental methods in the psychology of religion, 53 ff.; American work in, 56 ff.; Wundt's view as to method, 57 f.; psychology of religion essential to a history of mind, 233; bibliographies of the psy-

chology of religion, 346; magazines of, 347 f.; cyclopedias, 348; history of psychology of religion, 349; methods, 349; general works, 349.

Question circulars, 44 ff.

Racial traits in religion, 116 f.; 123.
Reality, Knowledge of, 229 ff.
Reason and religion, 137 ff.
Relaxation, Muscular, 140, 276, 282.
Religion: as an object of study, chap. i; on definitions of religion, 13 (note), 59; religion a complex function, 41; preliminary analysis of, chap. iv; defined as belief, 59, 61; as feeling, 60; as a whole reaction, 60 f.; conceived functionally, 62 (see also Functions of religion); as a social fact, 62 f., 143 (see also Social aspects of religion); related to both the ends and the means of life, 63 ff., 137 ff.; religion and values, 68 ff., chap. xiii (see also Values); beginnings of religion in the race, chap. v; earliest religion a group affair, 76 f.; a matter of custom, 77; not a department of life, 78; grows out of instincts, 78; main features of early religion, 79 ff.; mobility of religion, 98; differentiation of religion into religions, chap. vii; Is the religious reaction painful? 137 ff. (see also Pleasure and pain in religion); religion as inner life, 144 f., 263, 309; as individuation, 146; religion not co-extensive with conversion or with sense of sin, 154; ideational elements in, 156 f.; sensory elements in, 157 ff.; religion and adolescence, 166; religion as ethical communion, 184–86; as reverence for truth, 248 f.; religion and the subconscious, chap. xii; religion a discovery of persons

and of society, chap. xiv; religion as friendship, 262; bibliographies, 327–45, 346–55.
Revivals of religion, 119, 123, 125, 155 f., 157 (note), 161, 167, 267, 312, 353.
RHYS-DAVIDS, C. A. F., 271 (note).
Ritual, 112, 114, 126, 127, 128 (note), 134, 138, 139, 302. See also Ceremonies and festivals.
Roman religion, 98 (note), 110, 124, 154, 305.
ROYCE, J., 49 (note 2), 62 (note), 256 (note).

Sacerdotalism. See Priesthood.
Sacrament, 81, 126 f. See also Eucharist; Baptism.
Sacred and secular, 113, 236.
Sacrifice, 81 f., 126 f., 304, 306.
SALTER, W. M., 242 (note 1).
Salvation, 131, 147 f., 226.
Satan, 309.
SAUL, 182, 265.
Savage mind, The, 52, chap. v, 98 ff., 226 f., 264.
SCHILLER. F. C. S., 291 (note 1), 296 (note), 297.
SCHLEIERMACHER, 3, 60.
SCHROEDER, T., 94 (note).
Science and scientific method: each science selects its data, x, xi (note), 244 f.; dogmatism in science, xv, 244; the religion of science, 69, 248; influence of the sciences upon religion, 110 f.; the concept of nature (see Nature); the universality of scientific propositions, 172 (note), 231 (note), 239; science not the whole of discovery, 233, 243 f.; phenomenalism, 234 f.; scientific hypothesis, 247 f.; science and immediacy, 247–49, 251, 256 f.
Scriptures, Sacred, 126.
Self, The, 19 ff., 27, 41, 133, 138, 141 ff., 152 f., 160 f., 162, 164, 169, 171, 195 ff., 213, 252–54, 280 f., 318 f., 322 (note), 350 f. See also Individual, Religion as related to the; Persons.

Sensation a factor in religious experiences, 157 ff., 164, 278.

Sex and reproduction, 24 f., 37 f., 80, 86, 92 ff., 150, 163 ff., 165, 175, 216, 222 (note), 279, 281, 293.

Shamanism, 80, 176 ff., 182 f., 187, 190, 265 f., 270.

SHARPE, A. B., 9 (note 1).

SHELDON, W. L., 243 (note 1).

Sin, 46, 138, 149 ff., 154, 225 f., 228, 277, 310.

SMITH, JOSEPH, 130, 180.

Social aspects of religion: society as adjustment between selves, 27 f., 235 f.; as an ultimate mental category, 39; society as involved in individual consciousness, 67 f., 197, 250 ff. (see also Self, The); grades of society, 125, 228; the social instincts, 141; social values in religion, 69, 71 f., 87 f., 109 f., 119 ff., 162, 171 ff., 213; social organization of religion, chap. viii (see also Churches); religion as social control, 137, 140, 190, 191 f.; religion and the social movement of today, 115, 226, 233 f., 240 f., 242, 256 f.; the future life as a social problem, 294 f.; prayer as social sharing, 315–17; preeminence of social instincts, 324; bibliography of social psychology, 347; references on religion as social experience, 352.

Soul, The, 350 f. See also Animism; Spirits; Self.

SPENCER, H., 38.

SPILLER, G., 243 (note 5).

Spiritism, Ancient and Modern, 265, 267 f., 286, 289, 353. See also Animism.

Spirits, 83 f., 97, 102 ff., 257, 264, 265, 267.

STAEHLIN, W., 54 (note 1).

STANTON, H. C., 210 (note).

STARBUCK, E. D., ix, 1 (note 1), 10, 44, 47 (note), 56, 57, 152, 153 (note), 154, 162, 171, 350.

STONE, B. W., 194 (note 1).

STRATTON, G. M., ix, 2 (note 2), 10, 49 (note 3), 56, 256 (note), 350.

STRONG, A. L., 314.

Structure: structural and functional psychology, chap. ii, 221, 230 ff.; structural aspects of the idea of God, 97 f.; of the crowd, 120–24; of the sacerdotal group, 126–29; of the deliberative group, 131–33; of conversion, 156–58; evolution of man considered structurally, 215–19; structure of mystical experiences, 268–79; structure and function not exactly parallel, 298 f.; structure of prayer, 303–15.

Subconscious, The, xiv, 6 (note), 167, chap. xii, 270, 353.

Suggestion, 80, 120 f., 126 ff., 128 f., 132, 151, 166, 173, 177 f., 187, 211, 267, 274–78, 311 f., 317.

SUNDAY, BILLY, 123.

Supernatural, The, 9, 207 f., 263.

Symbolism, 114, 127, 134 f., 269, 306.

Taboo, 82, 113 f., 128, 144, 181, 288.

TAGORE, R., 12, 21, 164 (note 1).

Telepathy, 292, 353.

TERESA, ST., 354.

TERTULLIAN, 3.

Testimony, Religious, 170, 173.

Theology, 3 f., 87, 110, 115, 118, 208 (note), 218, 232.

Theosophy, 277.

Theriomorphism, 91, 97, 101 f.

THORNDIKE, E. L., 18 (note 2), 29 (note 2), 34 f., 67 (note 2), 120 (note 1), 148 (note 2), 163 (note 1), 220, 222 (note).

Todas, Religion of the, 108.

Tongues, Speaking in. See Glossolalia.

Totemism, 81, 101, 109, 114, 236, 241 f., 306.

Trance, 166, 176 f., 182, 185, 264, 274.

Transubstantiation. See Eucharist.

Tribal consciousness, 76 ff., 109, 237, 242.
Trinity, The, 269, 284.
Truth-value, 40, 227, 239, 248 f.
TUFTS, J. H., 40 (note 3).

UNDERHILL, E., 354.
Unio mystica, 274 f., 283.
URBAN, W. M., 35, 41 (note 3), 352.

Validity of religious experience, 174 f.
VALLON, C. H., 194 (note 2).
Values, 10 f., 20, 39, 61, 65 ff., 87 f., 106, 169, 171, chap. xiii, 227 ff., 245, 289, 302, 324, 347, 351.
Via negativa, 270 f., 275, 277, 283 f.
Visions, 183, 185, 190, 193, 199, 205, 265, 268, 269, 304. *See also* Hallucination; Shamanism.

WALLIS, W. D., 62 (note).
War, The European, 74 f., 129 f., 220, 248, 308.

WATSON, J. B., 18 (note 1).
WESLEY, J., 155.
WHITEFIELD, 155.
Witchcraft, 84, 119, 208.
Witness of the Spirit, xiv, 157, 193, 205, 266 f.
Wonder-working, 187. *See also* Shamanism.
WOODWORTH, R. S., 160 (note 2).
Worship, 55(note), 88, 134, 137, 144.
WRIGHT, W. K., 62 f., 71.
WUNDT, W., ix, 2 (note 1), 5, 10, 56, 57 f., 61 (note), 97, 103, 350.

XENOPHANES, 258.

Yoga, 267.

ZARATHUSTRA, and Zoroastrianism, 70 (note 3), 223, 287, 302, 309.
ZUEBLIN, C., 243 (note 3).